Everyday Law
for Actors

T0346422

Everyday Law for Actors

ROBERT WOODS

APPLAUSE
THEATRE & CINEMA BOOKS
Guilford, Connecticut

APPLAUSE
THEATRE & CINEMA BOOKS

An imprint of Globe Pequot, the trade division of
The Rowman & Littlefield Publishing Group, Inc.
4501 Forbes Blvd., Ste. 200
Lanham, MD 20706
ApplauseBooks.com

Distributed by NATIONAL BOOK NETWORK

British Library Cataloguing in Publication Information available

Library of Congress Cataloging-in-Publication Data

Names: Woods, Robert (Law teacher), author.
Title: Everyday law for actors / Robert Woods.
Description: Lanham, MD : Applause Theatre & Cinema Books, [2021] |
  Includes bibliographical references and index. | Identifiers: LCCN 2021003725
  (print) | LCCN 2021003726 (ebook) | ISBN 9781493059096 (paperback) | ISBN
  9781493059102 (ebook)
Subjects: LCSH: Actors—United States—Handbooks, manuals, etc. |
  Performing arts—Law and legislation—United States.
Classification: LCC KF390.A35 W66 2021 (print) | LCC KF390.A35 (ebook) |
  DDC 343.7309/94—dc23
LC record available at https://lccn.loc.gov/2021003725
LC ebook record available at https://lccn.loc.gov/2021003726

Contents

Acknowledgments   vii

Introduction: How to Use This Book   ix

PART 1: Contract Law for Actors

1 Offers and Acceptances, or Did You Make a Deal or Not?   3

2 Four Other Requirements for Valid Contracts and Three Reasons Why a Contract Is Invalid   11

PART 2: Negotiating Your Contract

3 An Introduction to Negotiating   25

4 Stage Productions   29

5 Film   37

6 Television, Commercials, and New Media   49

PART 3: Working with the Actors' Unions

7 An Introduction to Actors' Unions   57

8 Eligibility Rules and Requirements   61

PART 4: Working with Your Team

9 Agency Law for Actors   67

10 Managers and Management Contracts   75

11 Talent Agents and Talent Agency Contracts   85

12 Attorneys and Retainer Agreements   89

PART 5: **At Home and on the Job**

13 Landlord-Tenant Law: Types of Tenancies, Rent Control Laws,
    Obligations of the Landlord, and Assignments and Sublets   99

14 Employment Law for Actors: Discrimination in the Workplace,
    Sexual Harassment, Workplace Safety, and Immigration Laws   115

PART 6: **How to Produce and Protect Your Own Projects**

15 Business Organizations, or Why You Don't Want a
    Sole Proprietorship or Partnership   131

16 Business Organizations, or Why You Want a Corporation
    or Limited Liability Company   139

17 Copyright Law for Actors   153

18 Trademark Law for Actors   165

19 Don't Get Sued, or How to Avoid Committing Torts   173

20 Get It in Writing! Contracts You Will Need When Producing   185

21 Get It in Writing! Cast and Crew Contracts   193

22 Get It in Writing! Using Music in Your Project   197

Glossary   205

Notes   209

Index   221

Acknowledgments

First and foremost, I must thank wholeheartedly all of the actors, young and old, that I have had the good fortune and privilege to act with, direct, represent, advise, and get to know in the entertainment industry, both stage and film. This book is written for them in the hope that it will both help them in their careers and smooth their paths in life.

I would also like to thank Rena Cook, Clayton Guiltner, and Lee Wilson, who read an early draft of this book and provided valuable feedback and suggestions on content and revisions.

Finally, I would like to thank my mother, Jane Hall Rodkin, who introduced me to the theater as a young child, first taking me with her to rehearsals of the many plays and musicals in which she appeared and then getting me on stage as a child actor in my first plays. It is because of her that I have had a lifelong love affair with the theater, acting, and the entertainment business. I dedicate this book to her.

Introduction: How to Use This Book

This book is designed to be a resource and reference book for both professional working actors and those who aspire to be. It is intended for those just starting out, for those who have been making a living at it for a long time, and for every actor in between. If you are an actor, you can benefit from knowing more about the everyday law that affects your trade. Even if you are a well-established "star" with a full team of lawyers, agents, managers, and business managers working with you, you will still find this book useful because you can be more familiar with all that "legalese" and "business mumbo jumbo" that maybe you never fully understood.

Actors are artists. But actors must also be smart businesspeople. They don't call it "show business" for nothing. This is your career, and the more you can learn, know, and understand about the nuts and bolts of the business side of acting and the laws that affect that business, the better prepared you will be to move ahead with confidence and succeed.

However, unless you are a legal nerd (like me), you probably won't want to read this book from cover to cover in a single sitting. Instead, you should dip into a particular chapter as you need it. You just booked a new role in a movie and want to know more about contracts—check out chapters 1, 2, and 5. You are planning to join one or more of the actors' unions and want to know more about the unions, the costs, and the rules; that's in chapters 7 and 8. You're moving and need to sign a new lease or need to get out of your current lease;

chapter 13 is your source for landlord-tenant laws. Are you concerned about workplace discrimination, sexual harassment, or safety on the job? There is great information in chapter 14 on all of that. Do you like the idea of producing your own work? Then, now's the time to read chapters 15 to 22.

Every chapter is chockful of solid, useful information with specific details on the what, how, and why of the law and with plenty of examples and "war stories" to keep things entertaining and relevant.

Here's a road map for what you will find in each chapter:

Part 1. Contract Law for Actors

Chapter 1. Offers and Acceptances, or Did You Make a Deal or Not? This chapter explains the basics of making a legally valid contract—offers, counteroffers, and acceptances. This information illustrates exactly when a contract has been made and when it has not.

Chapter 2. Four Other Requirements for Valid Contracts and Three Reasons Why a Contract Is Invalid. This chapter delves deeper into the requirements for making a legally valid contract, covering consideration (the legal requirement of a mutual bargain), contractual capacity (both age and mental ability), mutuality of agreement, and legality, and it also covers three legal situations that will make a contract unenforceable—fraud, undue influence, and duress.

Part 2. Negotiating Your Contract

Chapter 3. An Introduction to Negotiating. This short chapter introduces the basic concepts, rules, and facts about negotiating actor contracts, regardless of the type of production or medium. This chapter provides an overview before chapters 4 through 6 explore more detail on negotiating stage, film, television, commercials, or new media contracts.

Chapter 4. Stage Productions. This chapters covers specific points that can be negotiated in an actor's contract for stage productions and how to negotiate to get the best deal.

Chapter 5. Film. This chapter continues the subject of negotiations, covering terms that can be negotiated in a film deal.

Chapter 6. Television, Commercials, and New Media. The discussions of negotiations and deal points are continued, focusing on contracts for roles in television shows. Contracts for commercials are also examined. Finally, the negotiation points for "new media," including Internet "webisodes" and similar productions, are discussed.

Part 3. Working with the Actors' Unions

Chapter 7. An Introduction to Actors' Unions. This short chapter introduces the major actors' unions, Actors' Equity and Screen Actors Guild-American Federation of Television and Radio Artists (SAG-AFTRA), and also provides information on the other unions for performers—American Guild of Variety Artists (AGVA) and American Guild of Musical Artists (AGMA).

Chapter 8. Eligibility Rules and Requirements. This chapter provides information on how to become eligible to join industry unions, how much it costs to be a member, and how joining a union or not has an impact on an actor's ability to work.

Part 4. Working with Your Team

Chapter 9. Agency Law for Actors. Actors often have multiple representatives—talent agents, talent managers, lawyers, publicists, and business managers. This chapter provides information about the general law of agency and how that law shapes and affects the relationships between actors and their representatives.

Chapter 10. Managers and Management Contracts. This chapter details working with talent managers, including the basic terms of management contracts and how to negotiate them.

Chapter 11. Talent Agents and Talent Agency Contracts. The analysis of agent relationships and contracts continues in this chapter, focusing on talent agents.

Chapter 12. Attorneys and Retainer Agreements. This chapter covers working with lawyers, the terms of lawyers' retainer agreements, and the rules of ethics and client confidentiality that lawyers must follow.

Part 5. At Home and on the Job

Chapter 13. Landlord-Tenant Law: Types of Tenancies, Rent Control Laws, Obligations of the Landlord, and Assignments and Sublets. This chapter describes the law covering the landlord-tenant relationship, including such important and useful information as different types of tenancies, rent control laws and how they work, obligations of the landlord to provide habitable and safe premises, and the rules on assigning or subletting your rented space.

Chapter 14. Employment Law for Actors: Discrimination in the Workplace, Sexual Harassment, Workplace Safety, and Immigration Laws. It is an unfortunate reality that discrimination still exists in hiring and working relationships. This chapter covers what needs to be known to guard against employment discrimination, sexual harassment, and unsafe working conditions. Work visa requirements for foreign actors working in the United States are also described.

Part 6. How to Produce and Protect Your Own Projects

Chapter 15. Business Organizations, or Why You Don't Want a Sole Proprietorship or Partnership. This chapter focuses on actors as producers, starting with the two types of business organizations that are common for general businesses but are inappropriate for producing projects—sole proprietorships and partnerships.

Chapter 16. Business Organizations, or Why You Want a Corporation or Limited Liability Company. This chapter details corporations and limited liability companies, which are best for producing projects and explains why they should be chosen as the vehicle for a production, the differences between them, and the advantages and disadvantages of each.

Chapter 17. Copyright Law for Actors. In this chapter, the laws protecting copyrights and copyrightable works are introduced and explained.

Chapter 18. Trademark Law for Actors. Branding is extremely important in today's marketplace, and trademarks are the legal protection for brands. This chapter explains the law of trademarks and their application in the entertainment business.

Chapter 19. Don't Get Sued, or How to Avoid Committing Torts. Many actors have heard of slander, libel, and rights of privacy but do not understand those rights or how they might be violated. This chapter covers those important torts and explains how to avoid committing them in productions and protecting against lawsuits for them.

Chapter 20. Get It in Writing! Contracts You Will Need When Producing. For those who want to produce their own projects, this chapter covers how to get the rights to the source material—plays, screenplays, books, and life stories—to produce each and provides information on how to negotiate typical contract terms for acquiring those rights.

Chapter 21. Get It in Writing! Cast and Crew Contracts. Those producing their own projects must make sure to get contracts with everyone working on the project. This chapter covers typical contracts and terms for various cast and crew deals.

Chapter 22. Get It in Writing! Using Music in Your Project. This final chapter details using music in projects, including how to properly license music for stage, film, and other projects, and even how to make money by becoming the "owner" of music that is composed for projects.

With the information provided in this book, you will be well armed for the show business side of the acting business. So let's get started.

Part 1

CONTRACT LAW FOR ACTORS

1

Offers and Acceptances, or Did You Make a Deal or Not?

You have just been offered a new role, and the producer of the project has handed you a contract. Before you sign it, you need to know some basics about contract law. Importantly, you need to know exactly at what point you have made the deal and when you have not. This is all governed by the contract law concepts of *offer* and *acceptance*.

WHAT IS A CONTRACT?

It is a common misconception that a contract must be in writing, and that without a written document, there is no contract. In fact, most contracts are not required to be in writing. Contracts for personal services—such as for acting services—are only required to be in writing if they cannot be completed within one year. An oral contract is just as enforceable in court as a written contract as long as the specifics of the parties' agreement can be proven. (Lawyers use the term *oral contract* rather than *verbal contract* because *oral* actually means "spoken," and *verbal* simply means "in the form of words," which could mean either written or spoken.) Proof is the primary reason for putting most contracts in writing. Suppose a producer and an actor make an oral agreement for the actor to appear in a film, and they agree on all important terms—the role to be played, the amount of pay, the dates of shooting, and on-screen credit. But later they have a disagreement about the amount of pay, and the actor wants to file a lawsuit to enforce their agreement. If the actor has no witnesses to the agreement, it may be the actor's word against the producer's, and the actor may not be able to prove the case. That's why it is always better to have a written contract; so that if disagreements do arise, the content of the agreement is written out, and there is no need to rely on the parties' memories or truthfulness in describing the agreement.

When is a contract "made"? A contract is formed when one party makes an offer, and the other party accepts that offer. This seems pretty straight-forward, right? It is, sort of. But the law has a way of taking simple things and complicating them with rules and exceptions to the rules. Let's take a closer look.

The Offer

An *offer* is the first proposal to make an agreement or enter into a con-tract. Every contractual relationship begins with an offer extended by one person to another. For example, suppose Tanya is producing a low-budget horror film, and she would like John to play a small role in it. She might make him an offer that would go something like this: "John, I'd like you to play the role of 'Tex.' The pay is $300 for one day of shooting." Tanya is the *offeror* (the person making the offer). John is the *offeree* (the person receiving the offer). He can decide if he is interested in her offer and wants to make a contract. If so, he can give an *acceptance* of the offer. On the other hand, he might make a counteroffer.

The Acceptance

Once an offer has been given, the offeree can make the contract by accept-ing the offer. An *acceptance* is simply the expression of agreement to the pro-posal. If John is willing to play the role of Tex for $300, he can accept Tanya's offer simply by saying, "yes, I will do that" or even just saying "OK." However, in the real world, it is common that an offeree does not agree to the precise terms of the offer. In many situations, bargaining occurs before agreement is reached. This back-and-forth bargaining is actually a series of counteroffers.

The Counteroffer

If an offeree chooses not to accept the exact offer that has been presented by the offeror (the person who made the offer), the offeree may make a differ-ent proposal back to the offeror. The offeree's proposal is a *counteroffer*. Remember, an offer is the *first* proposal to enter into a contract. Any subsequent proposal by either party is a counteroffer. If the offeree who has received the first offer changes the terms of that offer in any way, two things happen: the original offer is rejected, and a counteroffer is proposed. Now the opportunity to make the contract rests with the original offeror, who can choose to accept the counteroffer as is, reject it and make a second counteroffer, or reject it and end the negotiations.

For example, Tanya made her offer for John to play the role of Tex for $300. John wants to play the role, but he knows that the minimum compensation for one day's work under the SAG-AFTRA contract for low-budget films (theatrical films with a budget between $700,000 and $2.5 million) is $630,[1] and he knows that the budget for Tanya's film is $2.3 million. Even if John is not yet a member of SAG-AFTRA, he can still use the union rate as a benchmark for the negotiations. John says to Tanya, "I'd love to play the part, but I need at least SAG-AFTRA scale." (In the entertainment industry, *scale* means the minimum compensation allowed under union contracts.) John has now made a counteroffer by changing Tanya's proposal on the amount of compensation. Tanya might then respond that she cannot pay John union rates because the film is a nonunion film and not a SAG-AFTRA union film. She might make a further counteroffer to pay John $400. John might come back with one more counteroffer of $500. If that amount is acceptable to Tanya, she can accept John's counteroffer.

In this example, the roles of offeror and offeree change back and forth several times, as each counteroffer is rejected and a new counteroffer is made. Only when Tanya expresses agreement with John's last counteroffer is a contract made.

There are several things to consider when looking at offers, counteroffers, and acceptances to determine whether a contract has been made and, if so, at what point it was.

Offers Limited by Time or Manner of Acceptance

An offer can be limited by time or by manner of acceptance. Such an offer can be accepted and a contract made, only if the limitation is met.

When a producer makes an offer to an actor to play a role in a film, TV show, commercial, play, or other project, it is quite common for the offer to be limited by time. The producer always has a deadline, such as a shooting start date or the first day of rehearsals. The producer cannot wait indefinitely for the actor to decide whether to accept the offer, so the producer may set a deadline for the actor's response. For example, Tanya's offer to John might be phrased this way: "John, I'd like you to play the role of 'Tex.' I need an answer no later than one week from today." Tanya's offer is limited by time, and at the end of one week, her offer will expire. Once an offer expires, it can no longer be accepted. If John wants the job, he must accept the offer within that one week. If he waits longer than one week, then the offer expires and John cannot accept the offer, no matter how much he may want to.

How long does an offer remain valid if no specific time for acceptance is given? If there is no stated time for the offer, it remains valid and available to be accepted for a "reasonable" period of time. There is no fixed definition of *reasonable*. If the parties cannot agree on that point, it may be left to a judge or jury to eventually decide what period of time was reasonable in the particular situation. If Tanya makes her offer to John on June 1, and the first day of principal photography for the film is June 30, a reasonable time for John to accept the offer might be two weeks at most. If John does not accept the role, Tanya will need time to offer the part to another actor before the film begins shooting.

An offer can also be limited in the method of acceptance. If so, the offer can only be accepted by the required method, and any other method of acceptance will be legally ineffective to accept the offer and make the contract. Suppose Tanya calls John to make the offer, but she only reaches his voice mail. She leaves a message. "Hi John, I'd love for you to play the role of 'Tex.' The part shoots for one day. The pay is $500. If you want to accept, please send me an email, confirming. Thanks." Tanya has specified the method of acceptance—an email—because she wants his acceptance clearly stated in writing, so there is no confusion about it. What if John returns Tanya's call and leaves her a voice mail, saying, "Hi Tanya, I'd love to play the part of 'Tex.' Count me in!"? John did not accept the offer in the required manner of an email; hence, no contract is made. Of course, Tanya can always choose to waive the required method and accept John's voice mail message as his acceptance of the offer, despite her request for an email acceptance. But if she wants to be a stickler, she can insist on the email. If John fails to send the email, Tanya can legally offer the part to another actor. John cannot raise a complaint and has no legal recourse because he did not accept according to the requirements of the offer.

In the case of a producer directly offering a small role to an actor, such a legally strict requirement of an email acceptance might be unlikely. But this type of situation may well occur when the producer does not communicate directly with the actor and instead makes the offer through the actor's agent or manager. In that case, a producer might be much more insistent on receiving a written acceptance because it may be the only proof that the actor is actually bound by a contract. Suppose the agent calls the producer and leaves a voice mail saying, "Yes, Anne Actor accepts your offer and would love to play the part," but the producer does not receive any email or other written confirmation. A problem can develop if Anne Actor later changes her mind and wants to drop out of the project. If she has not yet signed a formal contract, and the producer has no written evidence that she accepted in the first place, the producer may have no way to enforce the contract.

Although many actors will want to take any role they are offered, circumstances do change, and an actor may need to get out of a project. Suppose you are offered a small part in a short film. The producer asks you to email your acceptance to him, and you do so. But before the film begins shooting, you are offered a guest starring part in a TV series. Unfortunately, the shooting schedules conflict, and you cannot do both. The TV series will be a much more visible platform for your talents, and the pay is much greater than the short film, so you want to accept the TV series role. Perhaps you never signed a formal contract for the film, so you think you can get out of it. But you did send an email accepting the part. That email is an acceptance of the short film producer's offer and legally constitutes a written contract, so if the producer wants to, he can hold you to it. If you drop out of the film anyway, and the producer suffers some damage as a result, he can sue you for breach of contract.

Would any reasonable producer in the real world refuse to accommodate an actor's opportunity for a big role just because shooting schedules conflict? And would any producer really sue an actor for breach of contract if the actor drops out of a film? The answer to both questions is "yes."

A famous example of scheduling conflicts is the 1985 film, *Back to the Future*. The producers wanted to cast Michael J. Fox in the lead role of Marty

McFly, but Fox was signed to the TV series, *Family Ties*. The schedules of the film and the TV series conflicted, and the TV series producers would not let Fox out to do the film. The producers then cast Eric Stoltz as McFly. However, after the first few weeks of shooting, the producers could see that Stoltz was just not right for the part. He was released, and the producers went back to Fox. A compromise was reached: Fox shot the TV series during the day and the film at night. That was a brutal schedule for him, of course, but because Fox was under contract for the TV series, it was the only way he could do the movie at all.[2] As it turned out, the film was a huge success, spawning two sequels and launching Fox's feature film career. But this success story was only possible because the film's producers were willing to concede to the requirements of the TV series producers on shooting schedules.

An example of breaching a contract and dropping out of a film had a less happy ending for the actor involved, Kim Basinger. The film was *Boxing Helena* and was produced by Main Line Pictures. It was announced in the trade papers that Basinger had agreed to star in the film, but she later dropped out of the project over disagreements with the director about the script. Another actor (Sherilyn Fenn) was cast, but the movie flopped. The producers sued Basinger for breach of contract. Basinger disputed that any contract had actually been reached, claiming that she only made an unenforceable oral agreement to star in the film.[3] Basinger made the mistake of thinking that an oral contract was not a "real" contract. The producers not only insisted the oral contract was enforceable, but they were also able to prove their claim in court. Basinger lost the case, and she was ordered to pay $8.1 million in damages to Main Line Pictures. That drove Basinger into bankruptcy.[4] The court judgment was later reversed on appeal, but Basinger reportedly still paid about $3.8 million to finally settle the case.[5]

Terminating Offers

Offers can be withdrawn or terminated by the offeror. An offer can only be accepted and a contract made, if the acceptance is given while the offer is still "live." Once an offer has been withdrawn or terminated, it is "dead" and cannot be accepted.

Just as a producer may limit the time for acceptance of an offer by an actor, the producer may choose to cancel the offer completely. Sometimes, the project itself is canceled. Other times, the actor takes too long to respond to the offer, and the producer has to move on to another actor because a start date for the project is looming. In both cases, the offer to the actor may be withdrawn.

The actor Bill Murray famously has no agent, manager, or publicist. The only way to reach him is to call an 800-number and leave a voice mail.[6] Sometimes, this has led to producers offering Murray a role, but giving up when they don't hear back from him. In *The Big Bad Book of Bill Murray*, Robert Schnakenberg tells the story of director Terry Zwigoff offering Murray the film *Bad Santa*. According to Schnakenberg, Murray said he would do the film, but when the time came to sign his contract, he could not be found. Zwigoff is quoted as saying, "I left several messages on his answering machine, but after a few weeks of hearing nothing, we eventually moved on."[7] Zwigoff had no choice but to terminate the offer by withdrawing it; he ended up casting Billy Bob Thornton, and the film was a box office success. What if Murray had eventually returned Zwigoff's calls, but only after Thornton had been cast? Murray could not legally have accepted the offer because the offer had been withdrawn. It was no longer available to be accepted.

Offers Must Be Definite and Certain

For an offer to be capable of being accepted, it must be clear and definite. If a contract is to be formed, the parties must know exactly what they have agreed to do. If the offer is unclear or indefinite, the agreement may be too uncertain to be enforced. The reason for this is simple.

Although the parties may think they know what their agreement is, there could be a dispute later on. If one of the parties files a lawsuit to enforce the agreement, the judge in the case must be able to fully understand it. If the offer was not clear and definite, it might be impossible for the judge to know what was actually agreed on, so an order enforcing the agreement could not be made.

In *Indecent Proposal*, a billionaire (played by Robert Redford) offers David Murphy (Woody Harrelson) $1 million for "one night" with David's wife, Diana (Demi Moore). The billionaire does not specify what will happen during that one night. Does the billionaire mean dinner, a movie, and moonlit walk on the beach? Or does he have something more intimate in mind? Although this made for a riveting and controversial hit movie, as a legal offer, it would have been a flop because the offer was too indefinite and accepting it would not have formed a legally binding contract.

The problem with indefinite offers arises regularly in the entertainment industry. It is quite common for actors to be approached about playing a part in a film or stage production that is still in development. The producer may make an offer that is indefinite in many respects because the project has no start date, the budget is not yet fixed, or financing is not yet in place. For example, suppose you have a friend who is an aspiring film producer. You have read the screenplay, which is good, and your friend would like you to play the lead role. However, she is still working on raising the money to shoot the film. She sends you the following email:

> I would love for you to play the lead role of "Stephanie" in my film, *A Long Afternoon*, assuming, of course, that you are available when the film is ready to begin production. As you know, I'm still working on financing, so I can't yet commit to the amount of your compensation or the shooting dates, but we can talk about that later. I think this part is perfect for you! Please let me know what you think.

This is not a definite and certain offer. Such basic terms as compensation and working dates are not yet specified. Even if you send an email back to the producer and accept the role, neither party is actually bound to it because no legally enforceable contract has been formed. The producer is not legally obligated to give you the part because it was not a valid offer. The producer can freely offer the part to another actor, and you will have no legal cause to complain. On the other hand, if you change your mind about doing the role, if and when the film is actually financed, you can also back out with no legal liability.

As you can see, it is important to recognize when a contract has been legally made, but it is equally important to know when no contract has been made. A legally binding contract has been formed only when there is a definite and certain offer that is accepted exactly according to its terms, on time, and in the manner required before the offer is withdrawn or terminated. If all of those conditions are met, you have a deal.

2

Four Other Requirements for Valid Contracts and Three Reasons Why a Contract Is Invalid

Chapter 1 explained that when an offer is accepted, a contract is made. This is generally true. But there are four additional requirements to make sure the contract is legally valid, and those will be discussed in this chapter. There are also three defenses that will invalidate a contract, even after it was made.

CONSIDERATION

An important requirement for an enforceable contract is *consideration*— something of value that is given in exchange for a promise. Consideration is what makes a promise enforceable as a contract. If a promise is made, but nothing of value is received in exchange for the promise, the promise can be broken with no legal consequences (although there may be moral or social consequences). The promise is not a contract and is not legally enforceable. But if the person making the promise receives something in return, then the promise becomes a contract because there is consideration for the promise. Consideration may be something of value actually given in the present time, but it can also be a promise by the other party to provide something valuable in the future.

Another way of understanding consideration is to think of it as an exchange of benefits and burdens. In the usual contract, both parties receive something of benefit. Likewise, both parties typically have a burden or, in other words, an obligation to do something. This is known as *mutuality of obligation.* Let's go back to the example of the contract between Tanya and John for the small role in Tanya's film. We must ask two questions about what the consideration is for that contract: Do both parties have a benefit? Do both parties have a burden? The answer is "yes" to both questions. Tanya receives a benefit—she gets the part of Tex played in the film, and John receives a benefit—Tanya pays him $500. But John has a burden; he must show up on set at the required time and perform the role. Tanya also has a burden; she must pay John the $500. Because the parties have exchanged benefits and both have burdens, there is consideration for the contract.

Adequacy of Consideration

Sometimes a party argues that the consideration for the contract is inadequate. If the party believes that the benefit is too little or the burden is too great, it may be asserted that the contract lacks consideration and is not legally enforceable. But courts typically will not examine whether the consideration for a contract is adequate or fair. Courts leave it to the parties to make their own deal. In our system of a "free market," the parties are given the freedom to agree on their own exchanges and fix their own values. If the parties have freely bargained for the exchange, the value of the benefits received by each party will not be questioned. If one party makes a bad deal, unfairness or inadequate consideration cannot be claimed and that party is bound to the contract. The value of the transaction does not even have to be significant. Some legal commentators have said that a "peppercorn," so long as it is bargained for, is enough consideration for a legal contract.

How might this issue of inadequate consideration come up for actors? Consider the case of Keanu Reeves and the movie, *The Watcher. The Matrix* was released in 1999, and Reeves became a superstar. One year later, *The Watcher* was released by Universal Pictures, but Reeves gave no interviews about the movie, and he was basically absent from all publicity for it. He didn't even have top billing, instead being billed behind James Spader and Marisa Tomei. According to various news sources, Reeves claimed that he had made an oral agreement with the film's director, Joe Charbanic, to play a small role in the film—"Griffin"—to help Charbanic raise financing, but that he never agreed to play a large role in the film. After Reeves agreed to appear in the film, Charbanic was able to greatly enlarge the budget (to a reported $30 million), and he rewrote the script to make the role of Griffin a major character. Reeves then wanted to drop out of the project, but his attorneys advised against it, apparently afraid it might lead to a similar situation as the judgment against Kim Basinger for dropping out of *Boxing Helena*[1] (see chapter 1). Reeves made the movie, but refused to provide any publicity when it was released. In an interview Reeves gave to the *Calgary Sun* newspaper in 2001, he was quoted as saying, "I never found the script interesting, but a friend of mine forged my signature on the agreement. I couldn't prove he did and I didn't want to get sued, so I had no other choice but to do the film."[2] Whether Reeves's signature was forged or whether that was merely his story a year after the film was released to terrible reviews is unclear. It was also reported that Reeves was outraged that his costars Spader and Tomei were each paid $1 million for the film, while he worked for SAG scale (about $2,000 per week in 1999), despite his status as an A-list superstar. Reeves probably could not have argued that there was inadequate consideration in his contract. Although SAG scale was absurdly low pay for Reeves at that time, it appears that he freely bargained with Charbanic and agreed to do the part for SAG scale. Courts leave it to the parties to make their own deal and will not question the value of the benefits received by each party. Reeves seems to have made a bad deal, but he was bound by the contract and could not claim unfairness or inadequate consideration.[3]

There are other possible arguments that Reeves might have employed to get out of his commitment to *The Watcher*. Several legal defenses that can be used to break a contract or to prove that a contract was never legally made in the first place do exist. We will examine those in this chapter, but first, let's look at contractual competence.

COMPETENCE OF THE PARTIES

Both parties to a contract have to be legally competent to enter into a contract. Various things can interfere with or prevent legal competence.

Language

If the parties speak different languages, there may be an inability to communicate and an inability to agree. If a contract is written, but one party cannot read the language, it is not legally possible to make the contract because there cannot be a meeting of the minds. The party who cannot read that language cannot really know what the agreement is intended to be. For actors, this problem may occur in international productions of either film or stage. US actors are frequently hired to act in films produced by foreign production companies, to perform in international touring companies of stage plays and musicals, or to make TV commercials that will be broadcast only in foreign countries. The contract for international work might be in the language of the hiring country. If actors cannot read that language, they are not actually competent to enter into the contract, and the contract is void.

> Jamard Brown is a triple threat actor/singer/dancer. He auditions for a new production of *Chicago* in Hamburg, Germany, and is cast! The contract arrives, but it's in German. Jamard can recognize the name of the show, his role, and the amount of pay in Euros, but otherwise he cannot read a word of the contract. He signs it anyway and returns it to the producer.

Jamard does not have a legal, valid contract because he is unable to understand the meaning of the contract and, therefore, lacks contractual capacity. He might go ahead and do the job, but if he arrives in Hamburg and discovers that his housing arrangements are poor, or he is not being reimbursed for his airplane ticket, he will have a problem.

To ensure a legal contract, the actor (or producer) must make sure there is an English-language translation of the foreign language contract. Actors should not take the producer's word for what the contract says. They should get a contract they can read. The producer might not have even read the contract if it was drafted by the producer's lawyer, or the producer might be less than honest about its content. A contract should never be signed unless an actor, his or her agent, and/or his or her lawyer can read it.

Mental Ability

If one party lacks the mental capacity to understand the agreement, no contract can be formed because of lack of competence. Mental inability can be caused by alcohol, drugs, or mental illness. The legal test is whether a person is able to understand the nature and effect of entering into a contract or, put another way, can comprehend the contract's nature, purpose, and consequences. If the person's mind is clouded by alcohol or drugs (which can be legal medications and illegal substances such as cocaine or heroin), the contract is not validly made. In the entertainment business, as in other businesses, it is fairly common for deals to be discussed over drinks at the local industry watering hole, at cocktail parties, or during meals in which alcoholic beverages are served. Having a drink or two may not prevent a legal agreement from being reached, but if the parties consume so much alcohol that they cannot understand the nature, purpose, or consequences of their agreement, the agreement is void. A good rule of thumb is to go ahead and enjoy the social activities but wait until the next day when all parties are sober before agreeing to a proposed contract.

Contractual Age

In every country, there is an age at which people become legal adults and are able to do such things as vote, drink alcohol, and enter into contracts. This is referred to as the *age of majority*. In most US states, this is 18 years old (or 21 for drinking alcohol). Minors, persons younger than the age of majority, are not legally competent to make a contract. If a minor enters into a contract, the minor can *disaffirm* (reject or cancel) the contract any time until the becoming of legal age (and in many states even for a reasonable amount of time after the legal age is reached). If the minor disaffirms the contract, the other party to the contract may be required to give back any money that the minor has paid or return any property to the minor. Looked at from the point of view of the adult party to the contract, this rule may seem unfair. But the rule is designed to protect children from their own lack of experience and to prevent adults from taking advantage of them. The policy of the law discourages adults from making contracts with minors. The safest course would be simply to refuse to do business with a minor. However, that is often not possible when it comes to actors. If a role calls for a child, then a child must play the part, and that means the child must have a contract. Parents often think they can sign the contract on behalf of their child, and then the contract will be valid. However, this may not be true. If the child is performing the acting services, it is the child's contract and not the parents' contract. The child may still have the legal right to disaffirm the contract.

The normal law concerning minors' contracts has been changed in states where the entertainment industry is prominent. In California, contracts with minors who provide artistic or creative services can be approved by a judge, and then the minor is bound—the contract can no longer be disaffirmed, even though the minor is still younger than the legal age. New York has a similar law, but it applies only if the minor either resides in the state of New York or the creative services are performed in the state. Other laws may simply eliminate a minor's right to disaffirm with respect to certain types of creative services, such as modeling.

One well-known case of this last type of law involved the actress Brooke Shields. When Shields was only 10 years old, she was working as a model. One of her jobs for a magazine required her to pose nude in a bathtub. Garry Gross was the photographer. Shields's mother signed the contract on her daughter's behalf. When Shields was 15 years old, she wanted to stop Gross from using the photographs, and she attempted to disaffirm the contract. But a law in New York allows parents to give a written consent to the use of photographs of their minor children. Because Shields's mother had signed the contract, the court held that the contract was valid, even though Shields was a minor at the time the contract was made.[4]

THERE MUST BE A MEETING OF THE MINDS

It seems obvious and no need to say it, but the most fundamental rule for making a contract is that the parties must actually agree with each other. The making of a contract must be *mutual*, freely made by each of the parties. To put it another way, there must be *mutuality of agreement* between the two parties. However, human communication is imperfect. Sometimes it seems as if each person understands what the other person is saying, when actually they are talking about completely different things. One party is thinking about one set of facts, but the other party is thinking about a different set of facts. Neither party realizes the confusion is occurring. The law sometimes says, there is no "meeting of the minds"—the parties' minds have not really communicated. There is no mutuality of agreement. When this happens, no contract is formed because there is no actual agreement.

Take the hit Broadway musical, *The Lion King*, as an example. After 20 years on stage and following 25 separate international productions, Disney announced the first international tour of *The Lion King* in 2018. The tour commenced in March 2018 and included stops in the Philippines, Singapore, Korea, Taiwan, and South Africa.[5]

Elizabeth is new to New York, a fresh graduate from the musical theater program at her university. She sees an audition for *The Lion King*. Thinking it is for replacements for the Broadway production, she eagerly attends the audition—

and much to her surprise, she is offered a role! She accepts, thrilled to land her first Broadway show. Only when she receives the written contract does she see that she has not been offered a role in the Broadway production but, instead, in the international touring production. Elizabeth has only just arrived in New York and doesn't want to immediately leave to go on tour. Is she stuck—bound by her oral acceptance of the role?

Legally, no. This is a classic example of a lack of meeting of the minds. Elizabeth thought she was auditioning for the Broadway production. The producer thought Elizabeth understood that she was auditioning for the international tour. The parties did not have a meeting of the minds. There was a mutual mistake about a critical fact—which production was it? As a result, the contract was not actually formed because there was a failure of basic communication. The parties' minds did not meet, so there was no mutuality of agreement.

LEGALITY
The final requirement for a valid contract is legality. The subject of the contract must be something that is legal to do. This is rarely a problem. However, laws can change, and what was legal at the time the agreement was made by the parties can become illegal later. A contract to perform in a production of *Hamlet* for a summer "Shakespeare-in-the-park" group could be affected if the laws change, and live events are no longer permitted to be performed in the park. In that event, all contracts with actors in the show would become void because of illegality.

THREE DEFENSES TO CONTRACTS
Even after a contract is made, there are three defenses that will enable a party to get out of the contract.

Fraud
Fraud occurs when a party to a contract intentionally makes a false statement of fact. In other words, the party lies about the fact, knowing that it is a lie and knowing what the truth is. Fraud can be used as a defense if the fact is important to the contract, and if the lie is told for the purpose of convincing the other party to make the deal. In this situation, the party who has been told the lie can rescind the contract.

Returning to the case of Reeves's contract to act the role of Griffin in *The Watcher*, could Reeves have argued fraud as a way to rescind the contract? He claimed that he signed on to do a small role only. Charbanic, the director, later acknowledged that he rewrote the screenplay after Reeves signed on. Charbanic was quoted in news reports as saying, "The script did change. It got bigger than [Reeves] wanted. He wanted it to be a little boutique film."[6] Was Reeves defrauded? It depends on what, if anything, Charbanic said to Reeves about the role of Griffin. Imagine a scenario in which Charbanic told Reeves that Griffin was only a small role to get Reeves to agree to play it, and imagine that at the time he had that conversation with Reeves, Charbanic secretly planned to rewrite the screenplay and enlarge the role once Reeves had signed on. Under this scenario, fraud could be found. Charbanic would have made a false statement about the size of the role, knowing the fact was false and making the statement to convince Reeves to enter into the contract. Of course, this scenario is entirely imaginary. The details of the conversation between Reeves and Charbanic about the role of Griffin were never made public and are known only to the two men themselves.

Undue Influence

Undue influence happens when a person is persuaded to enter into an agreement that is not really desired. The person who exercises the undue influence usually puts a great deal of pressure on the other party and works on that party's mental, emotional, or moral weakness. The pressure is so great that it overcomes the weak person's will. The weak person may still recognize that the agreement is not desirable but has lost the power to resist. When the stronger person is able to impose his or her will on the weaker person and take unfair advantage of that weakness to obtain agreement to a contract, there is undue influence. This often occurs in contracts with the elderly or sick—people whose minds have been weakened by age or illness. But it also happens to actors.

> Lindsay has been struggling along in small roles in the film industry for three years since graduating from college. Then she gets a call from her agent. "Lindsay, good news! I've booked you into a featured role in a major film. There's only one little catch. You need to do a full frontal nude and sex scene with the leading actor. I know you don't want to do nudity, but this is your big break!

You have to say yes to this one. If you turn it down, I don't think you'll ever have an opportunity again. And if you say no, maybe we won't be able to work together any longer."

Lindsay is being put under heavy pressure by her agent here. She doesn't want to perform this kind of role, but she doesn't want to lose her chance, and her agent's thinly veiled threat to drop her as a client only adds to her stress. She knows she should refuse, but she gives in. Lindsay is the victim of undue influence.

Undue influence can also occur when contracts are discussed at inappropriate times or inappropriate places. Actors may face intense contract discussions during social events, for example. Time can also be a factor. An agent, manager, or producer may insist there is no time to think about the contract or to seek advice from others, perhaps because a production start date is looming. Be wary of these types of situations in contract negotiations, and do not succumb to the pressure.

Duress

Legal duress is when someone is compelled to do something by the threat of force, the actual use of force, or unfair intimidation, pressure, or bullying. If the person is compelled to agree to a contract, the duress prevents the agreement from being genuine, and the contract can be canceled. Because the party suffering the duress had no choice but to make the agreement, the duress prevents the exercise of free will that is essential to a valid contract.

There are two kinds of duress: physical duress and economic duress. Physical duress involves the actual use of force or an immediate threat that force will be used if the person does not agree to the contract. Physical duress in contracts rarely occurs. Economic duress occurs when one party is under severe economic pressure, and the other party takes advantage of that to force agreement to a contract. It often appears in situations that one party is badly in need of certain goods or services, and the other party refuses to provide them unless more money is paid or something else is given up.

Duress is legally a bad thing. But in the television business, economic duress employed by actors against producers of a hit TV series occurs on a regular basis and is treated as a normal business practice!

When actors are cast in lead roles for a new TV series, they are typically required to sign multiyear contracts, ranging from five to seven years in length. The producer of the series wants the actors tied to it in case the series is a hit and runs for several years.[7] The contracts will provide for salary increases each year but in limited amounts, typically about 4–6%. Initial compensation is usually quite good, ranging from mid-five figures per episode for regular actors to six figures per episode for established stars.[8] But it is also typical that if a series becomes a hit, the actors begin to chafe at their perceived low salaries after a few seasons. They want to renegotiate. The producer has no incentive to renegotiate because the actors are already under contract for up to seven years. However, the actors have some leverage. All of a given season's episodes for a TV series usually complete filming by late spring. The actors are then on *hiatus* (industry term for a break in continuous broadcasting of a series) until summer, when filming resumes for episodes of the new season that will begin broadcasting in late September or early October. Sometimes, actors refuse to return to work unless the producer agrees to increase their compensation. This creates a situation of economic duress for the TV series producer. How? It's all about the economics of television.

Television shows make money by selling advertising. A half-hour episode of a comedy series will actually consist of (on average) 22 or 23 minutes of show content and 7 or 8 minutes of advertising. Likewise, a one-hour episode of a drama series will have about 44–46 minutes of content and 14–16 minutes of advertising. The cost of advertising on a TV show is based on the number of people watching the show, so a hit show which draws more viewers can charge more money for each 10-, 15-, or 30-second advertisement. The average cost of a 30-second commercial in a primetime TV show on network television is in the range of at least $75,000, and a hit series is much higher.[9] In 2019–2020, the cost per 30-second commercial on *Modern Family* (a hit comedy series) was about $148,000.[10] Multiply that by 16 (the number of 30-second commercials in a half-hour episode), and ABC network's income per episode for *Modern Family* in 2019–2020 was in the $2.3 million range.

The other aspect of TV advertising practices is the so-called "upfront" market weeks in New York, which occur during late May to early July. The television networks put on big shows for advertisers, with TV stars and flashy presentations. The advertisers are then given the chance to buy commercial time up front (in other words, months before the new fall TV season) at negotiated prices. As much as 80% of all available advertising time for the upcoming TV season is sold during the upfront weeks.[11] This is a big financial bonanza for the networks, but it is also a big commitment by the networks to their advertisers. If there is any delay in a TV show coming back on the air in the fall season, the networks must compensate the upfront advertisers accordingly. Television show producers are therefore under pressure to make sure that the new season of their show is ready to broadcast according to the network's schedule. Any balking by the actors in a series when it is time to return to filming in the summer thus presents a significant problem for a producer. But in fact, that happens frequently.

For example, on July 24, 2012, the six lead actors for the series *Modern Family* filed a lawsuit in the Los Angeles County Superior court, asking the court to declare their contracts to be void. The actors wanted the show producer, Twentieth Century Fox Television, to increase their salary from the roughly $65,000 per episode for Sofia Vergara, Jesse Tyler Ferguson, Eric Stonestreet, Julie Bowen, and Ty Burrell (and about $100,000 per episode for series star Ed O'Neill) that they had received in the third season (the series premiered in 2009).[12] Twentieth Century Fox Television was put in a bind because it had a contractual commitment to ABC Television to deliver new episodes of *Modern Family* for the fall. This pressure resulted in the producer agreeing to a new contract only two days later, on July 26, 2012. The salaries for the actors were reportedly raised to about $170,000 per episode for season four, increasing to about $350,000 per episode by season eight, and the actors also received a small percentage of the show's back-end profits (money made by the producer when the series is sold to US cable networks, independent television stations, and international networks for reruns).[13] The salary renegotiation was repeated in 2017 after the eighth season, when the actors' salaries were increased again to about $500,000 per episode for its final two seasons.[14]

This sort of high-pressure negotiating tactic can occur with any hit series. *Modern Family* is only one example of many. Other high-profile negotiations have included *Friends*, *The Simpsons*, *The West Wing*, and *The Big Bang Theory*, as well as the much-publicized negotiations by Ellen Pompeo, star of *Grey's Anatomy*, which resulted in her receiving a $20 million annual salary, making her the highest-paid actress on television.[15]

Economic duress is a defense to a contract and can result in a judge holding that the contract is void. But that never occurs in the television business when actors put producers under economic duress. There is simply too much money being made by everyone, so these sorts of pressure negotiations are accepted as normal business for a hit TV series.

The basics of contract law discussed in this chapter should help inform actions when a contract is offered. But beyond knowing when a contract has been made or not, or when to legally get out of a contract, actors need to know how to negotiate their best deal. Chapters 4 through 6 cover contract negotiations for actors in various media.

Part 2

NEGOTIATING YOUR CONTRACT

An Introduction to Negotiating

In chapters 4–6, we will talk about the specific terms of an actor's contract and what can and cannot be negotiated. Those terms vary depending on what type of project it is. A stage play has certain points to be negotiated, and a film or television show has different points. A television commercial has its own specific terms, and an Internet web series will have points that differ from all of these others.

Actor contracts can be quite simple and entirely standard in their terms. SAG-AFTRA has simple form contracts on its website, and Actors' Equity Association has a document library with rule books for various regional theaters. Sample actor contracts are readily available on the Internet via Google search.

The extent to which a contract can be negotiated depends on the flexibility of the employer offering it and the clout of the actor. Form contracts should be read thoroughly before signing them. This is not the time to sign first and ask questions later. Once signed, all the terms of the contract are binding, whether read or not.

When an actor is offered a union job, the employer might provide the applicable union contract to the actor or, for larger roles might present a tailored contract. If the job is nonunion, either party can prepare the contract. Typically, the producer will present the actor with a proposed contract, but there is no rule that prevents the actor from writing up a draft contract and presenting it to the producer. Regardless of which party drafts the contract, it should contain at least the five basic terms, which can be remembered as the "five W's"—who, what, when, where, and why.

1. *Who* are the parties? The actor is one party, and the producer, production company, film company, theater, or other employer is the other party.
2. *What* is the job? The contract must identify the title of the play, film, television show, or other project, and the role to be played by the actor.
3. *When* will the job take place? This covers the dates of rehearsal, production, principal photography, commercial filming, postproduction, tour, or other applicable dates.
4. *Where* will the job take place? The contract should provide the name and location of the theater or describe the extent of a tour; state whether a film will be shot locally, at a film studio, or on location; or identify the studio or production lot where a commercial or TV show will be filmed.
5. *Why* is the actor doing the job? The "why" means the contract's consideration (see chapter 2 for a discussion of consideration). Will the actor be paid, and if so how much? If no pay, is the actor doing the job for résumé credit, a copy of the footage for the actor's demo reel, as a showcase, or some other consideration?

A simple agreement can be written up on paper or can be written in an exchange of emails, text messages, or other written communications between the two parties. Whatever method is used, be sure to get the contract signed. If electronic communication is the method, a typed name will typically serve as a signature.

Actor contracts can be considerably more detailed than these five basics, of course. The terms that can and should be negotiated are discussed in the following chapters.

Many people are not comfortable negotiating for themselves at all, and that is why it is best to have a talent agent or lawyer who can negotiate on your behalf. They can be more objective and ask for things you deserve but that you might be reticent to press for. So if you have an agent or lawyer, tell them what you want and then let them do the work for you. (See chapters 11 and 12 for information on working with talent agents and attorneys.)

But whether your representative negotiates your deals, or you do it yourself, remember this: It is a basic truth of negotiations (especially in the entertainment industry) that you don't get what you *deserve*; you get what you *ask for*. So don't be afraid to ask. Remember, the producer wants to hire you, or you would not be negotiating a contract in the first place. You are not going to lose the job by asking for reasonable terms in the contract. If you ask for outrageous things, of course, the producer may become frustrated, but as long as you don't stray beyond the bounds of normal, reasonable requests, you should not be afraid to negotiate.

4

Stage Productions

In this chapter, the basic points to negotiate in a contract for a role in a stage production are covered. In negotiations, you should not hesitate to ask for any reasonable terms. You may not get everything you ask for, but if you don't ask for something, you certainly won't get it. What should you ask for in a stage deal? Let's start with the money.

SALARY

The amount of salary you can get may depend on whether the production is under the Actors' Equity union jurisdiction and whether you are a member of Actors' Equity. There are many nonunion theaters, and the amount of pay in those theaters may range from a mere token payment for "travel expenses" to something close to Equity union minimum. Community theater will be strictly volunteer, as will most "membership" theaters where the acting troupe consists of regular members. But larger theaters may pay their actors. Each theater is different.

It is important to recognize that once you are a member of Equity, you are no longer allowed to work in a nonunion production—with a couple of exceptions. You may be able to work on an Equity "guest artist" contract, even though most other actors are nonunion. You may also be able to work if the theater has a special Equity contract that allows union members to work there without pay or with limited pay under certain conditions.

For example, Los Angeles has four special Equity contracts: (i) the Hollywood Area Theatre contract, for theaters with 599 seats or fewer, in which the amount of pay is based on the number of seats and other factors, (ii) the "99-seat" contract (theaters seating 99 or fewer persons), in which salaries are based on minimum wage, (iii) the 50-Seat Showcase that permits Equity members to work without pay in theaters of 50 seats or fewer to present plays and/or scenes in limited performances, and (iv) the Self-Produced Project that permits members to perform without pay in member-produced theatrical productions in theaters of 99 seats or fewer, as long as the members working on the project are part of a collaborating group and are not employed by any producing entity.[1] There may be good reasons why you might want to work for little or no pay. For example, two Equity actors worked in a 50-seat theater in Hollywood because the play, *Behind the Lie*, was the US premiere of a two-character play by a prominent Chinese playwright, so it was not only an opportunity to sink their teeth into meaty roles never before performed by US actors but was also a good showcase.

Another example is the Chicago Area Theatre contract used in theaters with a capacity of 900 seats or fewer within 35 miles from the Chicago city limits, covering both commercial and not-for-profit theaters. It is a tiered contract with amount of pay depending on seating capacity and number of performances per week. There are also special contracts for the San Francisco Bay Area, Orlando Area Theatres, New England Area Theatres, New York Showcases, and New Orleans. In addition, Equity provides separate contracts for many different types of theaters, including cabaret, casino, dinner theater, Disney World, outdoor drama, and university theaters, to mention just a few.

If the theater is an Equity union house, the performers under Equity contracts cannot be paid less than the established minimum salary, unless a special contract (such as those mentioned) applies. Most Equity contracts provide for a minimum salary during the rehearsal period and a contractual salary during all performance weeks. Others, such as theaters under the League of Resident Theatres (LORT) contract, provide for a contractual salary from the first day of rehearsal.

But even in Equity theaters, the producer may not be required to only cast Equity members in their productions. The theater may be allowed to use a mix of union and nonunion talent. The Equity contract will not necessarily protect the nonunion actors, so they need to negotiate their own contracts. Of course, if the theater is not a union house at all, actors need to negotiate their own agreements. In such negotiations, the Equity minimum compensation for that market may be a good benchmark for the amount of salary.

Additional Duties Pay

All Equity contracts include provisions for overtime pay for work extending beyond specified hours. The contracts also provide pay for additional work assignments, such as dance captain, accepting an extra role or understudy assignment, doing a chorus part in a musical, a six months' rider for an extended tour, a featured bit, or extraordinary risk. If the theater is non-Equity, you can still negotiate for additional pay for duties such as these. What is "extraordinary risk"? If you are being "flown" in a production of *Peter Pan*, you are engulfed in pyrotechnics and smoke as the Wicked Witch in *The Wizard of Oz*, or you are playing D'Artagnan in *The Three Musketeers* and have multiple swordfights, that qualifies.

There are a number of points other than money that you should consider negotiating.

BILLING

As you move up from ensemble to larger roles, you want to make sure to negotiate your billing. For a starring role, you should ask for billing "above the title," which means that your name will appear on the marquee, advertising, and the printed program before the title of the show. If you cannot get above-the-title billing, or you are playing a supporting role, negotiate for billing below the title in a particular position. For example, if you negotiate third billing, your name will appear third in the list of actors. You can also negotiate for "no less than" a certain position, so that your name may appear higher but will appear no lower than, say, sixth billing. You may even negotiate for your name to appear last, with additional words such as *and starring*, *with*, or even *and*. Finally, you could negotiate for your name to appear inside a box, so that it is set off from all other actor names.

Wendy has been offered the part of Masha in a nonunion production of *Vanya and Sonia and Masha and Spike* with a 4-week rehearsal period and 4-week run. She negotiates rehearsal pay of $300 per week and performance pay of $500 per week. Because Wendy is well-known to area audiences, she is able to negotiate her billing to appear at the end of the list of actors in a box, so that her credit appears as:

```
          and
     Wendy Westwood
       as "Masha"
```

MORE REMUNERATIVE EMPLOYMENT

You should ask for a more remunerative employment (MRE) clause if you are signing on for a long run of a show, a long tour, or even a short run if you have auditioned for other, larger projects and are still waiting to hear from them. The MRE clause allows you to leave the show for a short period of time (or entirely, if the run is short) if you are offered MRE, such as a high-paying commercial or film.

OUT CLAUSE

If you are agreeing to a tour or to join a long running show, you want to negotiate for an "out"—the right to terminate your contract completely after giving appropriate notice. Four weeks' notice is a reasonable time.

In Wendy's contract to play "Masha," she does not ask for an "out clause" because it is a relatively short run, but she does negotiate an MRE clause. One week after rehearsals have begun, Wendy lands a featured role in *Mad Max Meets the Guardians of the Galaxy*, which pays $50,000 and begins principal photography one month later—during the run of the play. Wendy tells the play's producer that she needs to exercise her MRE clause, and the producer graciously agrees and releases her from the contract, congratulating her on the big break. (Wendy's understudy is also pleased because she now will play "Masha.")

AUDIO AND VIDEO RECORDING AND PUBLICITY PHOTOS

It is increasingly common for theaters to record rehearsals or performances and then to post such recordings to social media, such as YouTube or Facebook, for promotion and marketing. You should ask about this during negotiations, and if recording is to take place, you can negotiate for additional pay for the use of such recordings. In a similar vein, you should carefully negotiate the theater's use of your headshot or other publicity photos. These should be restricted to use in the program for the play or publicity and advertising for the performances but not for general theater use or other uses. One actor who was playing the title role in *Macbeth* for a small theater was later dismayed to find that one of the publicity photos of himself in character had been used by the director as the cover art for the director's new book on Shakespeare's plays—without, of course, paying the actor any money for the use of that photo. The actor sued the theater, director, and publisher for misappropriation of his rights of publicity and privacy.[2]

WORKING HOURS AND CONDITIONS

Equity contracts limit the number of hours of work per day and per week, as well as mandate when rest breaks must occur. For example, an Equity Guest Artist can work no more than 42 hours per week before the first performance and 32 hours per week after the first performance, depending on the theater's tier level. If you are working in a non-Equity theater, you need to negotiate your working hours for yourself. Also negotiate the number of performances per week, the days off, and any time required for publicity, such as newspaper, radio, or TV interviews or appearances. If you are working in a university theater, be sure to negotiate whether you will have any teaching requirements. If you are touring, negotiate whether you have any duties for packing up or moving sets or loading into a theater or packing out of one. And don't forget to negotiate tech rehearsal requirements, especially for a touring show.

DRESSING ROOMS

The negotiation of dressing rooms will vary, depending on the size of the role you are playing (i.e., star part or chorus member), the number of dressing rooms available at the theater, and the location of those dressing rooms vis-à-vis the stage. You won't be able to negotiate this point if you are just in the ensemble, but if you have a large role, you should definitely bring this up. Besides the size of your dressing room and whether you share it (and with how many others), you might need to negotiate its location. If your role requires you to change costumes multiple times during the play, you should negotiate for a dressing room close to the stage and, ideally, on the same floor to reduce the distance or amount of stairs you will have to climb going to and from the stage to the dressing room. If dressing rooms are far away, you should negotiate for a private quick-change booth and a dresser to be located in the wings.

Lydia Lark is playing the title role in *Victor/Victoria*. She changes costumes numerous times during the show. Because the theater's dressing rooms are in the basement, downstairs from the stage, she negotiates for a quick-change booth in the wings. She also specifies that it have a portable clothes rack 7 feet high, because Lydia is 5'11" and she doesn't want her full-length gowns dragging on the stage floor.

If you are performing in an outdoor venue, negotiate for an indoor dressing room, and make sure it has adequate heat or air conditioning. You don't want to be performing Juliet in a summer, outdoor production of *Romeo and Juliet* in Phoenix and changing costumes outside in 105°F heat.

HOUSING AND TRANSPORTATION

If you are being hired to work in a city other than where you live, you need to negotiate for housing, *round-trip* transportation from your home city to the theater location (make sure you have that round-trip ticket because you don't want to be stuck in Boise or somewhere in Europe or Asia when the show closes), and local ground transportation on location (rental car, taxi or Uber, subway fare, etc.). For housing, you should negotiate for "first-class" accommodations if you can or, in any event, for "clean, sanitary, and safe" accommodations. Negotiate as well for nonsmoking rooms as necessary. Negotiate for what will be included in the housing—is there cable TV and Wi-Fi for Internet access? Are linens and towels provided? You should also negotiate for "per diem"—a fixed amount paid to you per day (usually in cash) to cover meals and miscellaneous expenses. A typical amount might be between $20 and $50 per day, depending on the cost of living in the city where the theater is located.

WORKERS' COMPENSATION INSURANCE

All Equity contracts require the theater to have workers' compensation insurance coverage. This insurance protects all "employees" (including actors) for any injuries or illnesses suffered as a result of work. However, non-Equity theaters may attempt to avoid carrying this insurance on the theory that actors are volunteers who are not paid or are otherwise not employees of the theater. This can present a problem if an actor is injured during a rehearsal or performance. A young actor performed for a well-known New York theater that specializes in Shakespearean works. He suffered a groin injury during rehearsals of a staged combat scene. Only then did he discover that the theater carried no workers' compensation insurance. He had no personal medical insurance, so he was unable to afford effective treatment, and the injury lingered on for many months. Avoid this problem; ask if the theater provides such insurance, and if it does not, negotiate to have the theater add you as an additional insured person on its general liability insurance policy or negotiate for health insurance coverage.

SUBSEQUENT PRODUCTIONS

You can and should negotiate for the right to be part of the cast if there is a subsequent larger production—for example, the show moves to a larger theater or a bigger city or goes on tour. One actor discovered the disadvantage of not getting this point in writing. He appeared in a major role in the showcase production of a new musical play. The producers promised him that he would be part of the show if it went to Broadway but didn't put that in his contract. The showcase was successful, and the show did later transfer to Broadway and became a hit. But the producers recast all the parts for the Broadway production, and the actor was not included. He had no recourse because he failed to get the producers' promise included in his contract.

MOST FAVORED NATIONS

This is a clause that gives you equal rights with other actors if they are getting a better deal. Producers often say that everyone is getting the same salary, when in fact they are not. A "most favored nations" clause guarantees that if someone else is getting more (and you find out about it), you will get that same, higher salary. A most favored nations clause actually can apply to any conditions of employment and not just salary. The dressing room, transportation, housing, and per diem are common subjects for most favored nations that you should consider negotiating.

MISCELLANEOUS

Depending on the play and its requirements, you may want to negotiate other perks or special conditions. For example, if the producer wants you to change your hairstyle or hair color, you can negotiate that the theater will pay for it and pay to maintain it. If you are in a dance-heavy show, you may want to negotiate for new shoes to be provided on a regular basis. In one dinner theater production, an actor negotiated massages. Stars can negotiate anything from bottled water and snacks in the dressing room to matinees off. Negotiate whatever is appropriate for the size of the role you are playing. Again, remember not to overreach or you risk irritating the producer. You might even alienate other cast members if you successfully negotiate for something that is wildly out of the normal range for your size role. So ask for what you want, but keep realistic expectations in mind. Salary, working conditions, and housing and transportation should always be negotiated. Other points, such as dressing rooms and MRE and most favored nations clauses might only be within your reach if your role is large or starring. On the other hand, it never hurts to put in a reasonable "ask." The worst that can happen is the producer says "no." But if you don't ask at all, it's definitely a no.

5

Film

Many of the contract points discussed in chapter 4 for stage productions will also apply to actor contracts in films, so it might be best to review those before tackling this chapter. But there are many other points that are specific to film deals.

COMPENSATION

Film compensation can have multiple parts to it: salary, per diem, profit participation, box-office bonuses, and overage pay.

The basic compensation is the salary. Whether you are a member of the union (SAG-AFTRA) is important. Although there are many nonunion films made, most films other than very low budget will be covered by the SAG-AFTRA contract. There are different SAG-AFTRA contracts for different types of films depending on budget, so the amount of salary differs, but each contract has its own minimum compensation. We will use the basic contract as our example. Even if you are not a member of the union, you can use the union minimums as the measuring stick for your negotiations.

The two basic types of SAG-AFTRA theatrical film contracts are for day performers, and for weekly performers. If you will work only one or two days, you will probably be offered a day contract. But if you will work four or more days, you will probably be offered a weekly contract. If you are playing a small role in the film and you are not already an established film actor, you may not be able to negotiate above the minimum rate. But if you already have some film credits, or if the part you are playing is a featured or supporting role, you can negotiate for above minimum. Perhaps you can negotiate for twice or three times the minimum amount. When a client of mine produced a half-hour show for a cable network, most of the actors were not "names" and were paid the minimum for a weekly contract. One actor was well-known from a regular part in a long-running television show, and he negotiated for twice the minimum. The star negotiated for even more, plus a small percentage of profits.

If your part is a lead role, you might ask for much more than scale, but you have to keep the budget in mind. If you are playing the lead role in a film with a modest $5 million budget, you can ask for a salary of five figures even if you are not a well-known actor. If you are a name actor, you can negotiate for higher amounts. Of course, if you have achieved the status of being a name actor, you will likely have an agent who will advise you on the amount of compensation to ask for.

As part of the basic salary, you should negotiate an overage amount. If the shooting extends beyond the anticipated schedule, you should be paid additional salary for additional days, prorated for each additional day that you work. You should also negotiate any free days of services, either before shooting begins or during postproduction. It is worth noting here that a film's schedule is divided into three parts: preproduction (all the time before the cameras roll), principal photography (the actual filming), and postproduction (editing the film, creating special effects, and sound mixing). As an actor, you may be needed during preproduction for makeup tests, building of prosthetics or masks, wardrobe fittings, rehearsals, and travel time to shooting locations. You may be required during postproduction for automatic dialogue replacement (ADR) in case the recording of your dialogue during filming was of poor quality for some reason or alternate versions of dialogue are needed for censorship purposes, such as television use of the film in certain foreign countries. All of this is "working" time, of course, and you can negotiate for pay for such times. But if you are already receiving above-scale compensation, the producer may ask you to provide a certain number of preproduction and postproduction days for free—in other words, for no additional pay.

Brent has always worried that his 5'2" height would limit his opportunities as an actor, but now his height is paying off. He has been cast as the small but powerful Prime Leader from the planet Zontax in the sci-fi movie, *Interstellar Highway*. His character has horns, a tail, and furry wings, so he is needed in preproduction for building of those pieces. The film will shoot in Malta, so he will also need two days to travel to the location from his home in Los Angeles, and two days to travel back when principal photography concludes. Because he is a newcomer and his role is featured but not starring, his agent negotiates a salary of three times the minimum SAG-AFTRA compensation. The producer wants him to provide four days in preproduction and the two travel days for no additional pay.

For an actor in Brent's situation and receiving his salary level, it would probably be appropriate to agree to two free days of preproduction services, but the producer wants four days. Brent could reasonably ask to be paid for the additional two days of preproduction and the two days of travel time. (Under the 2017 SAG-AFTRA contract, a travel allowance of $500 per day must be paid if the actor is not otherwise paid for the day.) As a negotiating chip, Brent could offer to provide two free days of postproduction services for ADR, if needed. This would be a fair counteroffer to the producer's request.

If your role is starring, large, or important to the project, you can negotiate for a pay-or-play provision. This protects you against being suddenly fired from the project, without a good reason and not getting paid. Pay-or-play means that you still get paid, even if you don't play. This type of provision will not be available to most actors on a film, but if the role merits it or you are already an established film actor or have a name, this protection can be asked for.

Also if you are playing a substantial role or you are an established film actor or have a name, you can negotiate for some type of profit participation. There are two basic types: a percentage of net or gross profits and box-office bonuses. Net profit participation is the normal type of profit participation for most actors. Only established stars are able to negotiate for gross profit participation. (It was reported that Arnold Schwarzenegger received 20% of "adjusted gross receipts" for *Terminator 3*, but even then he received nothing until the film reached the break-even point.[1])

A typical amount of net profit participation that you could ask for would be in the range of 1–5%. That would be worded in the contract in a manner such as, "Actor shall be entitled to receive an amount equal to three percent (3%) of one hundred percent (100%) of 'Net Profits'." This means that if the film's revenues put it into net profits, you will receive 3% of all of those net profits. This is also sometimes referred to as *points*—one point is 1% of net profits.

What exactly is meant by "net profits"? The calculation of motion picture profits is extremely complicated. But in a nutshell, a film enjoys net profits after it has earned enough money from all sources to pay off the cost of production, the cost of advertising and prints (making multiple copies of the film for display in theaters), and the costs of distributing the film. In the convoluted world of motion picture accounting, it is quite common for films to earn hundreds of millions of dollars at the box office, plus millions more from other sources such as DVD sales, online streaming, and pay TV and other TV sales and still show a loss on paper. In 2003, *Terminator 3* earned $428 million from worldwide box office and just barely reached the break-even point. *Harry Potter and the Order of the Phoenix* brought in more than $600 million, but accounting documents in 2009, two years after its release, still showed a loss of $167 million.[2] Because of this method of accounting, it is rare that any net profits are actually paid out to net profit participants.

Why bother to negotiate for net profits if they are so unlikely? Well, it is possible for a film to reach net profits, and if it does, you can get a nice payday. And even if that particular film does not get into profits, you can establish your entitlement to receive a profit participation, which you can then use when you negotiate for your compensation in later film projects.

An alternative to net profit participation is box-office bonuses. The payment of these is more certain if the film is a success and reaches certain levels at the box office. For example, you might negotiate that if the film reports box office sales of $100 million, you will receive a bonus payment of $25,000. If the film then hits $150 million, you will get another bonus payment of $25,000. And you will continue to get additional bonuses for each additional $50 million of reported box office. A particular source of box office figures will be agreed on for the purpose of such bonuses, such as an industry standard publication like *Variety* or *The Hollywood Reporter*. If you are able to negotiate box-office bonuses like this in a smash hit movie, this can provide a big payday.

Imagine that John Slattery had negotiated these exact box-office bonuses for his fairly small role as "Howard Stark" in *Avengers: Endgame*. (This is an imagined example for clarification purposes only and may bear absolutely no relationship to John Slattery's actual compensation for the film.) IMDb.com reports that the movie earned more than $2.7 billion at the worldwide box office. That would mean that Slattery would have earned $1.35 million in box-office bonuses. Of course, this is an extreme example, but it shows that this type of bonus should be negotiated whenever possible.

For all points of compensation, it is a good idea to negotiate for a most favored nations provision. If another actor with a similar size role as yours gets a better deal, your deal should be likewise upgraded.

CREDIT

There are multiple facets of a credits negotiation.

First, you want to negotiate placement of your name on screen or, in other words, in the film as it plays on the screen in a theater or later on a television or computer screen. If you are playing only a small role as a day player, you will likely receive credit only in the final roll of credits at the end of the film, along with all other actors appearing in the film. If you are playing a larger role or a starring role, or you are a "name" actor, you can negotiate for more visible placement of your name on screen. If you are the star of the film, you can seek above-the-title credit, which means that your name appears on screen before the title of the film appears. If you are not the star or, you are, but you cannot get the producer to agree to above-the-title credit, you should negotiate your placement below the title. This means that after the title of the film appears on screen, your name will appear in a particular order with other actors, such as first position (the first name of an actor after the title) or third position (the third name of an actor after the title).

You also need to negotiate whether your name will appear on a single card or a shared card. This means whether your name appears all by itself on screen or appears with other actors' names at the same time. Of course, single card is better than a shared card. If your name appears on a shared card, then you need to negotiate placement on that card. If your name shares the screen with one other name, you can negotiate for your name to be either on the top or the bottom of the two names or on the left or right side of the screen. If there are three or more names on the shared card, you can similarly negotiate for where your name appears.

Brent's agent calls him up and tells him that his credit has been negotiated for his role of Zontax Prime Leader in *Interstellar Highway*. He will receive below-the-title credit, in tenth position following the film's costars, on a shared card with another actor who is also playing a featured role. But the good news is, the agent has negotiated for Brent's name to appear on the left side of the shared card. Brent is pleased.

Second, once you have negotiated your on-screen credit, you also need to negotiate that same placement for paid advertising. This includes not only actual advertising for the film (such as billboards, newspaper ads, TV commercials, or ads on the Internet) but also the credits that appear on the DVD box. If you are the star or costar of the film, you can also negotiate for your name and your picture to appear in the artwork in advertisements, on posters, and on the DVD box cover art.

WORKING CONDITIONS

If the film is covered by SAG-AFTRA, you do not need to negotiate working conditions because those are extensively covered in the union contract. But if you are working in a nonunion film, there are some points you should negotiate. First, you want to negotiate the number of hours for turnaround, which is the time between when you leave the film set on one day and are required to return to the set the next day. SAG-AFTRA generally guarantees actors a 12-hour turnaround, which allows for enough rest between shooting days. You should negotiate for a similar period of time. Second, you want to negotiate meal breaks. SAG-AFTRA requires a meal break every six hours. Strive for the same. You want to negotiate insurance coverage. You want to make sure that the producer has obtained production insurance, covering you in the event that you are injured during the production. Finally, you want to negotiate the right to refuse to do anything that makes you uncomfortable, is dangerous, or otherwise could get you in trouble. Particularly on lower-budget films, directors sometimes cut corners. They ask actors to perform stunts that the actors are not trained to do, they fail to get permits to film in certain locations, or they wait until just before a scene is ready to shoot before informing the actor that it requires nudity or partial nudity. You want the right to say "no" without putting yourself at risk of being in breach of contract.

APPROVALS

The producer of the film will require you to agree that your name and likeness can be used for all purposes in connection with the marketing and distribution of the film. But you can negotiate for approval of which likenesses can be used. "Likeness" includes both photographs and artist drawings of your image. Ask for approval of both. You will probably be able to obtain the right to approve a certain percentage of photographs, such as 50 or 75%, and then only the ones you approve can be used by the producer. You can probably also obtain the right to request changes to any artist drawing.

If you are playing a major role in the film, you can also negotiate for script approval, so that if the script is rewritten in a substantial way, you can approve or disapprove of those changes. It would have been a good idea for Keanu Reeves to negotiate for script approval for his role of Griffin in *The Watcher* (see chapter 2). If you are the star of the film, you may even be able to negotiate approval of your fellow actors or even the director, although that is rarely granted to anyone except major star actors.

TRAVEL EXPENSES

Often, you may find yourself filming at a location far from home. You are entitled to travel expenses—roundtrip airfare, ground transportation to and from the airport, local ground transportation on location, hotel accommodations on location, and per diem. You get to enjoy the good life when you are working under a SAG-AFTRA contract. If you are flying more than 1,000 miles (with some exceptions), you will travel business class (or even first-class, if business class is not available) because that is mandated by the SAG-AFTRA contract. Even for nonstop flights of 1,000 miles or less, you can travel in "elevated" coach class. More good news is that you are entitled to per diem—an amount of money paid to you in cash to cover meals on location. SAG-AFTRA requires a certain minimum amount to be provided to actors to cover the costs of breakfast, lunch, and dinner if meals are not provided by the producer (such as meals provided on set). This is in the range of $60 per day. But you can usually negotiate for a higher per diem, ranging from $75 per day to $150 per day or more, depending on the size of your role or your stature as an actor. Any money you don't spend you can just pocket. Of course, as with all other terms, if you are working nonunion, you can use the union minimums as a basis for negotiations. Here again, try to get a most favored nations provision covering travel expenses, accommodations, and per diem.

Let's return to Brent and his role as Zontax Prime Leader. The film shoots in Malta. Because it's a big-budget sci-fi film and it's SAG-AFTRA, Brent will be provided with roundtrip business-class airfare to Malta, a hotel, and a shuttle to and from the hotel to the set. Brent's agent also negotiates for Brent to receive $80 per diem, even though Malta's prices are much lower than other parts of Europe. If Brent is frugal and buys bread, cheese, fruit, and cereal to keep in his hotel room for breakfast, eats lunch on set, and doesn't spend too much on dinner, he can save quite a bit of his per diem. Per diem is a nice little addition to an actor's compensation.

DRESSING FACILITY

Your dressing room on a film set will most likely be a trailer or motorhome and not a room inside a building. There are different types of motion picture dressing room trailers, which are described by the number of rooms in the trailer. The best is a private trailer, but that usually goes only to the stars. There are trailers divided into two rooms, three rooms, and four rooms. These trailers will have separate rooms with (typically) a sofa, desk and chair, and a private bathroom. There are also honey wagons that have five or more separate rooms for resting, each with a sofa and sink but no private bathroom. Obviously, the fewer rooms in the trailer, the better and more comfortable the space will be. If your role is large enough to merit a more private trailer space, you could then also negotiate for gadgets to be included in the trailer, such as a TV, a DVD or Blu-ray player, radio, CD, iPod or other music player hookups, a refrigerator, and even drinks and snacks of your choosing. You will spend many hours on set in your dressing room, so spend some time negotiating for those items that will make you most comfortable. Your deal on the dressing facility is another excellent subject for a most favored nations agreement. You don't want to find yourself stuck in a honey wagon if your costar has a better trailer.

VIDEO FOOTAGE AND DVD

One of the most valuable things you can get as an actor is video footage that you can then edit into your acting demo reel. Negotiate for the raw footage of your scenes if you can or at least the edited footage. You should also negotiate for a free DVD or Blu-ray copy of the film when it is commercially released. Yes, you could buy one at the store, but producers will generally agree to just give you a free one.

DUBBING AND DOUBLING

The film producer will have the right to dub your voice in other languages, so that the film can be easily distributed internationally. You don't have to negotiate about this, but if you speak more than one language fluently, you certainly can ask for the first opportunity to perform dubbing services in your other language(s). The producer will also have the right to "double" your body during filming. This may be needed for stunts that are too dangerous for you to perform or for scenes involving nudity or simulated sexual content that you are unwilling to perform yourself. Again, depending on the requirements of the script, you can negotiate what producers can double for you and what they cannot.

PROMOTIONAL REQUIREMENTS

It is generally in your best interest to participate in promotional appearances and other marketing activities. You want the film to succeed, and promotional appearances raise your profile as an actor. However, some producers can be too free to commit your time and energy to many such promotions, so you may want to limit the amount of appearances, interviews, or other activities. You may also want to negotiate for additional pay for these promotions or at least for transportation and housing expenses if you must travel for them.

EXCLUSIVITY

The producer may want to limit your right to take other employment during the contract term or, even afterward, such as during promotion and marketing of the film. Watch out for this. Many film producers also make "product placement" deals—agreements to use certain brands of cars (the Mini Cooper was key to the plot in *The Italian Job*) or certain products (Nike's Air Jordan shoes were worn by Jamie Foxx playing the President in *White House Down*). The film producer may want to exclude you from doing commercials for such products or for competing brands before the film is released or while it is playing in theaters. You should take note of any exclusivity clause in the contract and try to eliminate it or at least limit its effect.

MERCHANDISING

Depending on the type of film and your role in it, there may be merchandising potential, including t-shirts, posters, action figures, books, toys, or other items. You should negotiate for a percentage of merchandising proceeds if your image is going to be used on any product. A common provision given to an actor would be a 5% share of any merchandising revenues earned from using the actor's likeness. Along with this, you may find a producer seeking the right to make commercial tie-in deals. These are advertising deals that simultaneously advertise a product and a film (such as the promotion of the *Man of Steel* movie, in which Superman, played by Henry Cavill, appeared in Carl's Jr. TV commercials). Be sure to negotiate for additional compensation for any such commercial tie-in.

WARDROBE

You should negotiate for your wardrobe on two points: Who is responsible for providing it—you or the producer; and if the producer provides it, can you keep it after the production is complete? It's a small point, but depending on the quality of the wardrobe, could have a value of hundreds or thousands of dollars.

PREMIERES AND FILM FESTIVALS

It can be tremendously exciting and fun to attend the premiere of a new movie or a film festival where your movie is screened. There are film festivals all over the country and the globe. Premieres might occur in your hometown if you live in Los Angeles or New York, might be in the city where the movie was filmed, or might even be at a major film festival such as the Cannes Film Festival. Screenings at these events may be followed by question-and-answer sessions with the audience, actors, director, writer, and/or producer, and these can be quite stimulating and fun. There are two points you should negotiate here. First, you want to make sure that you are invited to attend, so you want to negotiate for free tickets for yourself and one guest. Second, you want to negotiate for travel expenses to all premieres and film festivals that are located further than some reasonable distance (perhaps 100 miles) from your home. The first point is usually easy to get a producer to agree to. The second may be harder, depending on the size of your role or your stature as an actor. If the producer will not agree to pay for your travel to premieres and festivals or perhaps does not have the budget for that, a fallback position is to ask that producers use their "reasonable best efforts" to get the film's distributor to pay for your travel.

RIGHT TO TERMINATE/STOP DATE

Last, give yourself an out. What if principal photography is delayed or postponed, and in the meantime, you book another job? Negotiate for the right to rescind the contract in such an event so that you don't find yourself tied to a project that just keeps being put off to some indefinite date in the future or that has a new schedule that conflicts with another job. What if you already have another job that will begin soon after this film ends, and then the film is postponed? One way to handle this situation is to negotiate a stop date, which is a firm date on which your services to this film will terminate. Producers do not like to agree to stop dates because they want the flexibility to reschedule, postpone, or extend principal photography, but if you already have other commitments, you have a valid reason for requesting a stop date.

Television, Commercials, and New Media

Compensation that is specific to television, the issue of restrictions for TV series actors, and negotiation points for commercials and for new media contracts will be covered in this chapter.

TELEVISION

Most of the points discussed in chapter 5 for negotiating a contract for film productions will also apply to work in television productions, so read chapter 5 before beginning this one.

Compensation

The basic idea of compensation for acting in a television production is the same as for acting in a film production. You are entitled to basic compensation, with the amount depending on how much you work. Just as with film, SAG-AFTRA sets minimum compensation rates for day performers and weekly performers. However, for television, the SAG-AFTRA basic contract also covers a third category—three-day performers, for contracts that guarantee the actor at least three days of work. All of these contracts—day, weekly, and three-day—are for work in a single picture. If you work on only one episode of a television series, you work in a special production that has only one episode, or work in a made-for-television movie (such as a Hallmark Channel movie), you are working on a single picture.

But because most television programs are ongoing, there are additional categories of contracts: weekly contracts for multiple pictures (meaning multiple episodes per week, such as a soap opera); series contracts in which the actor is guaranteed employment in at least 7 but less than 13 guaranteed episodes; series contracts for at least 13 episodes; and series contracts for more than 13 guaranteed episodes.

The SAG-AFTRA basic contract also defines a major role performer, for which special compensation rules apply. This is a performer who negotiates credit at the front of the show, credit on a separate card (or its equivalent in the roll) at the back of the show, or receives credit as "Guest Star," "Special Guest Star," "Starring," or "Special Appearance By."

> Kate Wang books a role in one episode of a comedy series, *Windy City News*. Her agent negotiates a Guest Star credit for her, so Kate is a major role performer. She is entitled to be paid for at least five days of employment because the series is a half-hour show. Kate's compensation must be at least the daily minimum rate, increased by 10%, multiplied by the actual number of days of employment.

For a one-hour series, the major role performer is entitled to be paid for at least eight days of employment. This special rate does not apply to actors employed under a contract for a day performer.

In film, there can be additional compensation, such as a percentage of net profits or box-office bonuses. Generally, these do not apply to TV. However, if you are fortunate enough to become a series regular on a long-running hit show, you may eventually be able to negotiate a small percentage of profits. Remember the contract negotiations for *Modern Family* that were discussed in chapter 2? During the negotiations for the fourth season, the six actors together were able to obtain a small percentage of profits. Although that amount was not disclosed in press reports, the percentage of profits for the three lead actors on *The Big Bang Theory* (i.e., Jim Parsons, Johnny Galecki, and Kaley Cuoco) was reported when they renegotiated their contracts at the end of the seventh season—1.25% each.[1] Of course, that was for the lead actors on one of the top shows on television, so view this as a special case and not the usual deal for series regular actors.

One other thing to be aware of for television productions is residuals! When a TV program is rerun, either on network or in syndication (broadcast on networks other than the original broadcast network or streamed on Internet channels such Hulu or Netflix), you get paid a percentage of your compensation again. The percentage declines with each additional rerun, but it never goes away completely. There is an exception. For programs made for basic cable (networks such as USA Network, TBS, Freeform, or Syfy), you can agree on an up-front buyout of all reruns on basic cable. The amount must be paid separately from your basic compensation, and it must be at least 200% of the SAG-AFTRA minimum compensation for your role.

> Kate had a great time performing in the episode of *Windy City News*. The episode was broadcast during the series' sixth season. The series is also streamed on the Hulu network and syndicated on the cable networks Freeform and Up. Kate is pleased to see residual checks arriving in her mailbox when her episode is broadcast on the cable networks and streams on Hulu.

Restrictions

One other point specific to television is worth noting. Because TV series are ongoing, actors who are regular or recurring characters on a series may be subject to certain restrictions that would not apply in a single film contract. For example, actors may have to agree not to change their personal appearance, such as changing hair color, growing (or shaving) a beard, or getting a visible tattoo. Actors may also be restricted from certain activities that might be considered dangerous, such as skiing, bungee jumping, auto or motorcycle racing, or flying in noncommercial airplanes, hot-air balloons, hang gliders, wingsuits, or parasails.

COMMERCIALS

Many commercials will be subject to SAG-AFTRA union rules, but there are also many nonunion commercials made. For union commercials, the compensation for filming will most likely be union scale. For nonunion, the amount is negotiable. Depending on how long the commercial runs, a higher payment for future use may be negotiated.

SAG-AFTRA has standard commercials contracts for both national commercials (a commercial that airs in the entire nation, such as during an episode of a network series) and regional commercials (that play in only one region of the country).

Exclusivity

Exclusivity can be important in commercials. You can agree not to perform in commercials for competing products, but if you do, SAG-AFTRA requires that you be paid additional money. If you become a spokesperson for a product, you can also agree to be exclusive to that product but only if your contract covers a particular period of time and guarantees you a certain amount of pay. Because most actors in commercials work for union scale, the purpose of SAG-AFTRA's exclusivity rule is to make sure that advertisers can only demand exclusivity for competing products and not for a wide range of products. Otherwise, advertisers might demand exclusivity for all products, the same way they do for spokespersons, which would be economically harmful to the ability of actors to work.

You will probably not have to be concerned about exclusivity, though. In practice, advertisers filter out actors with conflicts before the auditions. The audition notice will list all product conflicts, and actors who already have commercials running for a conflicting product will not be allowed to audition. The contract signed by the actor who books the commercial will then contain an exclusivity clause, prohibiting that actor from doing commercials for the listed conflicting products.

> Lee gets an audition for a Pepsi commercial, and she books it! She shoots the commercial, and it begins airing regionally after a few weeks. Later, Lee gets an audition for Coca-Cola. But the audition notice states that other soft drinks are conflicting products. Lee's commercial for Pepsi is still running, so she is not permitted to audition for the Coca-Cola commercial.

What happens if you agree to exclusivity in a commercial contract and then you actually do make a commercial for a competitor?

> Jason shoots a commercial for Mazda. He agrees to exclusivity. Six months later, he shoots a commercial for Ford. Then he gets a letter from Mazda's lawyer. Uh-oh, now what?

Shooting the commercial for Ford was a breach of Jason's contract. The producer of the Mazda commercial can sue him for damages, including canceling all additional pay he might otherwise receive for the running of the commercial. So be careful about exclusivity agreements.

Nondisclosure Agreements

On some audition notices, actors are advised that they will be required to sign a nondisclosure agreement before they audition. This is an agreement that the actors will not discuss the product, its marketing, or anything else they learn in the audition process without written permission.

Length of the Run

Union commercials are contracted for cycles of 13 weeks (so there are 4 cycles per year). Actors are paid a fixed amount for shooting the commercial and depending on how the commercial is used may be paid additional amounts each time the commercial runs. If the commercial is renewed for additional 13-week cycles, actors are entitled to more payment and may also be able to renegotiate and obtain higher pay for later cycles.

If you are shooting a nonunion commercial, you need to negotiate the length of use. You should limit the use of the commercial to a definite period of time and as short a period as possible. If the producer wants to continue using the commercial after that period expires, you can negotiate for more compensation.

Permissible Media

You should also negotiate where a nonunion commercial can be used. Is this a commercial for television or will it also be used on the Internet? If it will be used in more than one medium, negotiate for a higher rate of compensation. For example, the 2019 SAG-AFTRA Commercials Contract provides that if the commercial is used on YouTube, the actor is entitled to an additional fee of 15% of the session fee for each 30-day period of use on YouTube. The actor may be entitled to additional pay if the commercial also appears on the advertiser's or the ad agency's website.

You can use all of these union requirements when negotiating a nonunion commercial. Let's look at an example.

Courtney books a nonunion commercial for her local car dealership. The dealership wants to use the commercial on local TV and also will put it on the dealership's website and Facebook pages. Courtney asks for a "session" or "shooting fee," which will cover use of the commercial for one 13-week cycle. She asks for an additional fee of 10% of the session fee for use on the dealership's website and social media page. The contract specifies that at the end of the 13-week cycle, the dealership will stop using the commercial on TV and will remove it from its website and Facebook pages. Before shooting of the commercial, the dealership tells Courtney that it also wants to put the commercial on YouTube. She negotiates another 30% of the session fee for the YouTube use. Finally, the dealership wants Courtney to agree not to do commercials for any other car dealership. Courtney asks for, and receives, "exclusivity" pay of 50% more than the session fee. All in all, Courtney has negotiated excellent compensation for this nonunion, local commercial!

NEW MEDIA

SAG-AFTRA has two separate new media[2] contracts, depending on whether the budget is less than or more than $50,000. The primary difference between the two contracts is the amount of compensation, which of course is higher for higher-budget programs. The contract also has different rules for use on consumer-pay platforms (Internet channels that require the consumer to pay a subscription or other fee to view the content, such as Netflix) and free-to-consumer platforms (channels that do not require consumers to pay for access to the program or that have advertising within the program).

The union contract specifies that programs originally created for use on new media can be used on consumer-pay platforms for 26 weeks without further payment. If they will be used for additional periods of time, additional payment is due. The program can be used indefinitely on free-to-consumer platforms without additional compensation.

If you are negotiating a new media contract that is nonunion, you will need to negotiate your compensation and the length of time that the content can be used. In addition, you need to negotiate where the content can be used. You want to restrict the use to the Internet. If the producer wants to later use the content on traditional media (television, film, or DVD), you should negotiate for additional compensation.

You also need to negotiate your credit. Many new media programs have "click-through" credits, so that more information is provided if the consumer clicks on your name. You will want to negotiate what additional information is provided in that case.

Part 3

WORKING WITH THE ACTORS' UNIONS

7

An Introduction to Actors' Unions

Most actors begin their careers working in nonunion productions, but eventually they will want to join one or more of the actors' unions.

THE ACTORS' UNIONS

SAG-AFTRA

SAG-AFTRA used to be two separate unions. The Screen Actors Guild (SAG) represented actors in feature films and television productions that were shot on film. The American Federation of Television and Radio Artists (AFTRA) represented actors in radio and television productions that were broadcast live or recorded on videotape. AFTRA also represented other talent in radio and television, such as news and weather persons, announcers, singers and recording artists, promotion and voice-over announcers and other performers in commercials, stunt persons, and specialty acts. The two unions merged in 2012.

Actors' Equity (Equity)

Equity is the oldest of the actors' unions and was first formed in 1919. The union represents actors and stage managers in stage productions.

American Guild of Variety Artists (AGVA)

AGVA was founded in 1939 to represent performing artists and stage managers for live performances in the variety field. Today, it continues to represent its members in a variety of performance venues, including singers and dancers in touring shows and in theatrical revues,[1] performers in theme parks such as Disneyland, Universal Studios, and Six Flags Magic Mountain, skaters, circus performers, comedians and stand-up comics, cabaret and club artists, lecturers, poets, monologists and spokespersons, and variety performers working at private parties and special events. AGVA jurisdiction also includes the famous Rockettes at Radio City Music Hall and in Radio City Spectaculars.

American Guild of Musical Artists (AGMA)

This union represents opera and concert singers, production personnel, and dancers in principal opera, concert, and dance companies.

PROS AND CONS OF JOINING A UNION

Joining a union is a capital investment. The initiation fee for Equity is currently $1,700 (going up to $1,800 in 2022), and the initiation fee for SAG-AFTRA is currently $3,000. The initiation fee for AGVA is $750. The initiation fee for AGMA is $1,000. Once you are a member of a union, you must also pay annual dues, which are generally based on the amount of money earned working in jobs under that union's jurisdiction. Here are the current annual dues for the unions.

SAG-AFTRA

A minimum amount of $214.32 annually, *plus* 1.575% of earnings under a SAG-AFTRA contract. The maximum earnings subject to working dues are $500,000 per year.

Equity

A minimum amount of $176 annually in 2021, *plus* 2.5% of gross earnings under an Equity contract. The maximum Equity earnings subject to working dues are $300,000 per year. Gross earnings do not include the minimum portion of out-of-town per diem money.

AGVA

A minimum amount of $72 annually, *increasing* for earnings under an AGVA contract as follows: $5,000—$9,999, $96 annually; $10,000—$14,999,

$132 annually; $15,000—$24,999, $234 annually; $25,000—$34,000, $540 annually; and $35,000 or more, $795 annually.

AGMA

A minimum amount of $100 annually. Working dues are 2% of earnings under an AGMA contract but up to a maximum of only $2,000 a year.

So why should you incur these costs? Union membership pays off in access to union-only auditions, higher compensation, greater protection from abusive working conditions, and assistance in the event of breach of contract by producers (e.g., failure to pay your compensation or running a commercial beyond its agreed end date).

However, for an actor just starting a career or an actor living in a smaller market, joining a union may be unnecessary or even detrimental because once an actor joins the union, the actor is prohibited from working any nonunion jobs. In smaller markets, most of the jobs may be nonunion, including many nonunion commercials, which can be an excellent source of income and provide good footage for a demo reel. That said, most professional actors do live in the major markets, such as New York and Los Angeles, and so joining the union will be desirable.

How do union rules apply in right-to-work states? In those states, laws have been passed that say membership in a union is not required to work a job. In other words, you can be hired for a role in a union production without having to join the union. Currently, 28 states (and the territory of Guam) are right-to-work states. They are: Alabama, Arizona, Arkansas, Florida, Georgia, Idaho, Indiana, Iowa, Kansas, Kentucky, Louisiana, Michigan, Mississippi, Missouri, Nebraska, Nevada, North Carolina, North Dakota, Oklahoma, South Carolina, South Dakota, Tennessee, Texas, Utah, Virginia, Wisconsin, West Virginia, and Wyoming. You should note that New York, California, and Illinois are *not* right-to-work states, and those three states will encompass many of the work opportunities for actors. Also, be aware that living or working in a right-to-work state does not change the rules if you are already a member of an actors' union. The unions have strict prohibitions against union members working in nonunion jobs. If you do work in a nonunion production, you can be fined by your union or even expelled from membership.

Eligibility Rules and Requirements

How do you become eligible to join one or more of the actors' unions? Let us count the ways (and find the shortcuts and loopholes).

AGMA

Joining AGMA is as simple as signing up and paying the initiation and annual dues. No proof of work is required.

AGVA

To join AGVA, you must be offered an AGVA contract of employment.

ACTORS' EQUITY

The Equity website contains a page on "How to Join," which lists three methods for becoming eligible.[1]

Equity Employment

If you obtain employment under an Equity contract, you are eligible to join the union.

Sister Union Membership

Equity's sister unions are SAG-AFTRA, AGMA, and AGVA. The Guild of Italian-American Actors (GIAA) is also a sister union. However, GIAA is quite tiny, with only a handful of members and no apparent active productions, so for all practical purposes, it does not apply to this discussion.

When you have been a member of a sister union for one year *and* (i) worked under that union's jurisdiction as a principal, or (ii) worked an "under-five" contract (a contract for a role in a TV show where the actor has less than five lines of dialogue), or (iii) worked for at least three days of work as an extra (also known as "background" in film and TV), then you are also eligible to join Equity.

Equity Membership Candidate Program

Working in the Equity Membership Candidate Program (EMCP) at a participating theater is the third method of becoming eligible to join Equity. The EMCP permits actors and stage managers-in-training to credit theatrical work in an Equity theater toward membership. If you obtain a position at a participating theater, you can register as a candidate. There is a $200 registration fee, but that is credited against the initiation fee when you become eligible for membership. To be eligible, you must work a minimum of 25 weeks at one or more participating theaters. Once you complete 25 weeks, you can register for Phase 2 of the EMCP by paying an additional $200 within six months of completing Phase 1. Phase 2 allows you to work an additional 25 weeks. At any point during Phase 2 you can join Equity, as long as you do not have non-Equity work lined up in the future.

What this basic information does not reveal is the relative ease or difficulty of meeting any of those three eligibility criteria. Naturally, the most direct route is simply to attend the open auditions given for a union job and get the part. There are dozens of Equity theaters around the country. A list can easily be obtained by a Google search.

The sister union method of joining Equity has a neat loophole. You can join AGMA without proof of employment in an AGMA production—you can just join. You pay your $1,000 initiation fee and your $100 annual dues, and you are in. Then if you can obtain at least three days of work as an extra in an AGMA opera or ballet production, you are qualified to join Equity after one year of membership in AGMA. Most opera and ballet companies are always in need of supernumeraries (extras) to fill out crowd scenes. There are dozens of AGMA-signatory opera and ballet companies all around the United States. A list can be found on AGMA's website.[2] Check with your local opera or ballet company about their application requirements to be a supernumerary. Don't worry if you are not a singer or dancer because most supernumeraries have no singing or dancing experience. In fact, even in some of the major companies, such as the Metropolitan Opera in New York, the San Francisco Opera, and the Los Angeles Opera, supernumeraries might be dentists, housewives, or anyone else who just wants the thrill of being onstage.

SAG-AFTRA

There are four methods of joining SAG-AFTRA. Those methods are *not* clearly explained on the union's website, which only lists two methods of joining.[3] Here is information on those two methods and two other alternatives as well.[4]

Get a "Taft-Hartley" Certificate

This is a term often heard by actors but not well understood. The federal Taft-Hartley Act was enacted in 1948, affecting union jobs. For SAG-AFTRA, it allows a producer to hire a nonunion actor when the producer cannot find an available union actor who possesses the quality or skill essential to the role. Once the nonunion actor is cast, the producer fills out the Taft-Hartley paperwork, and the actor is then eligible to join SAG-AFTRA. The actor can work for up to 30 days without joining, and that 30 days can be on the project in which the actor is first hired or on subsequent union projects. But for any work beyond that 30-day point, the actor becomes a "must-join," meaning that the actor has no choice but to join the union to continue doing work that falls under the SAG-AFTRA jurisdiction.

Vouchers

If you earn three vouchers while working as an extra or background on a union film or TV show, you are eligible to join. This may not be that easy. Giving a voucher is in the discretion of the project's assistant director, and normally those background roles will go to actors who are already members of the union.

Sister Union

The third method is to be a member of a sister union for one year and work under that union's jurisdiction in a principal role. Notice that the sister union method for joining SAG-AFTRA is not as easy as for joining Equity because for SAG-AFTRA you must work under a principal role contract in the sister union. Working as an extra does not qualify you to join SAG-AFTRA. The sister unions for SAG-AFTRA are Equity, ACTRA (the Canadian union for film, TV, radio, and digital media performers), AGMA, and AGVA. Of course, if you have joined Equity by working as an extra under an AGMA contract, and you have landed any Equity principal role, you are eligible to also join SAG-AFTRA after one year of membership in Equity.

Taft-Hartley Yourself

The fourth method is relatively new and is acknowledged by many young actors to be an excellent way in. That method is to work in a SAG-AFTRA New Media Project. *New media* means "original and derivative entertainment productions made for initial release on new media platforms."[5] This includes web series and videos. In today's tech-friendly world, a web series can be produced pretty easily and inexpensively. Even if it has only one episode, all principal performers will become eligible for SAG-AFTRA. Because the production must sign a contract with SAG-AFTRA, recognizing the project as a "signatory" production, there must be at least one actor who is already a SAG-AFTRA member on board the production. That usually does not prove to be a stumbling block. The new media project's producers can simply cast one union actor and then cast all other roles with nonunion actors (including themselves). All of the nonunion actors will earn a Taft-Hartley certificate. How can you find new media projects? One young actor searched Craigslist for acting roles, found a producer doing a web series and looking for actors, and joined up with him for the one episode they produced, and all the actors became eligible through self-producing that series. Another actor produced his own web series after he moved to Los Angeles and thereby obtained union eligibility. A third acted in a multiepisode web series produced by her friends in their college town, and so became eligible for SAG-AFTRA before moving to her major market city.

If you decide to use this last method to become eligible to join SAG-AFTRA, you will need to be familiar with the various laws for producing projects to comply with the law and protect yourself from liability if something goes wrong. You can find that information in chapters 15–22.

Part 4

WORKING WITH YOUR TEAM

9

Agency Law for Actors

Most professional actors will have a talent agent who represents them. Many actors will also have a talent manager. The talent agent's job is to find work for the actor. The talent manager's job is overall career guidance. Many actors also want someone to advise them on contracts and other legal matters, especially if they are producing their own projects. That's the job of an entertainment lawyer. There are some star actors who have neither an agent nor a manager. Instead, they only have a relationship with a lawyer, who negotiates all of their contracts. However, this is usually feasible only for actors who are well-known enough that producers regularly come to them with offers of work.

To fully understand how to work with agents, managers, and lawyers, it is necessary for you to know a bit about the general law of agency. This is because talent agents, talent managers, and lawyers are all your *agents*—a person who represents someone else in business or personal matters—and you are the *principal*—the person who is represented.

An agency is a *fiduciary* relationship. This is a relationship involving the highest duties of trust and loyalty. Each party owes the other the highest standard of care. The fiduciary duty arises because the principal and agent must have confidence in one another and also because the agent is in a position to exert influence and dominance over the principal. This is particularly true for agents who represent actors.

CREATING THE CONTRACT AND SPECIFYING THE AGENT'S AUTHORITY

The agency relationship is created by a contract. The two parties reach an agreement that gives the agent authority to represent the principal. There are two basic types of agents: general agents, who have broad authority and are entrusted with general authority to act for the principal in all business matters, and special agents, who are authorized to act only in a particular transaction, under specific instructions, and with specific limits on the scope of the agent's authority. The agency contract usually states the rights and duties of the principal and the agent, the duration of the agency, and any other agreements made between the parties. In chapters 10–12, we will examine specific provisions of talent manager, talent agent, and lawyer retainer contracts.

The authority granted to the agent includes not only the specific authority stated in the contract (the *express* authority) but also includes the *implied* authority. The agent has the implied power to do whatever is reasonably necessary to carry out the express authority. A talent agent contract will not set forth the details of exactly how the agent will go about obtaining employment for an actor, and a talent manager contract will not spell out exactly how the manager will do the work of guiding the actor's career. The specifics are left to the agents and managers, who will do the things that agents and managers customarily do in the entertainment industry. The test of whether an agent has implied authority to do a particular thing is whether the agent reasonably believed he or she had authority to do that act.

> Roberta is a talent agent in a small agency. She represents thirty actors, including ingenue Hannah Harrington. Roberta checks the film and TV casting notices early each morning, identifies which of her clients appear to be right for the open roles, and then submits their headshots and résumés to the casting directors. Roberta often makes personal follow-up calls to casting directors to push a particular actor that she feels is really perfect for the part. Roberta sees a casting notice for an ingenue in *Midnight in Minneapolis*, a new romantic comedy. She submits Harrington for an audition and follows up the submission with a phone call to the casting director. Roberta persuades the casting director to call Hannah in for the audition. Hannah wows the producer and director at the audition and is offered the role. Roberta then negotiates the terms of Hannah's contract.

All of the work done by Roberta in this example is typical of talent agents, but likely none of that work is specifically spelled out in the talent agency contract between Roberta and Hannah. Roberta has the implied power to do those things because they are reasonably necessary to carry out her express authority—finding acting work for Hannah.

Besides express authority and implied authority, the law also recognizes something called *apparent authority*. This legal doctrine is designed to protect third persons who conduct business with an agent, reasonably believing that the agent has authority, which, in fact, the agent lacks. Apparent authority cannot be created by the words or conduct of the agent alone. Rather, apparent authority is based on what the principal causes a third party to believe about the agent's authority. If the principal, by either word or act, causes a third party to reasonably believe that the agent has authority to act for the principal in a certain way, then the agent will be clothed with the apparent authority to so act. The principal will be barred from later denying that the agent had that authority. In other words, the principal will be bound to whatever deal the agent made with the third person, if the agent had apparent authority to make that deal.

> After Hannah Harrington lands the role in *Midnight in Minneapolis*, she is suddenly hot. She is deluged with calls from CAA, Endeavor, and UTA, wanting to represent her. After meeting with them, she decides to sign with UTA. However, she has forgotten that Roberta submitted her for her last audition, for a small "art" film, and Hannah fails to tell the producer of that film that she has changed agents. Naturally, now that Hannah is a hot commodity, the producer of the art film wants her in the role. He contacts Roberta and negotiates a contract. Hannah is shocked when Roberta calls to tell her that the deal has been made.

Can Hannah get out of the art film? Probably not. By failing to tell the producer that Roberta was no longer her agent, Hannah caused the producer to believe that Roberta still had the authority to negotiate the deal. Roberta had apparent authority. Hannah will be bound to perform in the art film.

How could Hannah have avoided this problem? Of course, she should have called the producer of the art film and told him she had switched agents. But what about others in the industry who might still think Roberta is her agent? Hannah must notify all persons who previously dealt with Roberta and let them know that the agency relationship has ended. Once notified, those persons will know that Roberta no longer has any authority, so they cannot possibly claim that they reasonably believed the agent had any apparent authority. Because Hannah has just signed with UTA, a major talent agency, and is getting press buzz for *Midnight in Minneapolis*, the easiest way to notify the industry is to get a short article published in the trade papers, announcing her new agency affiliation. But to be really safe, Hannah should directly notify all persons who were dealing with Roberta.

DUTIES AND OBLIGATIONS
Now let's look at the duties and obligations that agents owe to their principals, and vice versa.

Agent's Duties to the Principal
Duty of Performance

The agent must use reasonable diligence and skill. If the agent fails to exercise reasonable diligence or lacks reasonable skill and as a result makes mistakes, and if these mistakes cost the principal some money or other benefits, the agent can be liable for breach of contract. For actors, it is important to make sure that they only agree to be represented by agents who are actually experienced in the entertainment industry. Your best friend may offer to represent you as a manager or act as your lawyer, but unless your friend is an entertainment professional, you should decline. There are many nuances in the entertainment business, particularly when it comes to employment contracts and union rules and obligations, and it would be easy for someone who is not experienced in these matters to make errors—errors that could cost you dearly.

Notification

The agent must keep the principal fully advised of all matters concerning the subject matter of the agency. Do not let your agent keep you in the dark. An agent, manager, or lawyer who fails to return phone calls or fails to respond to emails or text messages is not properly representing you.

Loyalty

A fundamental duty of an agent is to be loyal to the principal's interests. This means agents are forbidden from having any conflicts of interest or putting their interests ahead of yours.

Obedience

The agent must follow the principal's directions and not exceed the agent's authority.

Accounting

If the agent will handle money or other property for the principal, the agent has a duty to regularly account for and pay over to the principal all funds and property received on behalf of the principal. For actors, this duty is important because compensation checks for jobs are usually sent to the actor's agent or manager, who then deducts the commission and pays the balance over to the actor.

> Hannah Harrington works for three weeks on *Midnight in Minneapolis*. Each week, the producer writes her a paycheck for that week's compensation. The producer sends the check to Roberta, Hannah's agent. Roberta deposits the check in the talent agency's bank account and transfers 10% of the amount to herself. Roberta then writes a check to Hannah for the remaining 90%.

Principal's Duties to the Agent

Compensation

The agency contract will specify how the agent is to be paid. The principal must pay the agent as agreed. Many problems can arise if actors attempt to avoid paying their agent. Not only will the actor's relationship with the agent sour, but the agent might sue the actor for breach of contract. If the agent wins, the judgment will include not only the compensation that is owed to the agent but perhaps also interest accruing on that judgment until it is paid, plus court costs (which can easily run to thousands of dollars) and the agent's attorney's fees (again, many thousands of dollars).

Reimbursement

If the agent incurs out-of-pocket expenses while representing the principal, the agent is entitled to be reimbursed for those expenses. After all, it is the principal's business that is being conducted and not the agent's. As an actor, you are the one receiving the benefits of employment or other deals negotiated by your agent, so you must also bear the costs of obtaining those deals. This does not mean that you have to reimburse agents every time they take a producer out to lunch or pay for the agent's office expenses. You only need to reimburse expenses made directly on your behalf (if any).

Cooperation

The principal must cooperate with the agent. Simply put, this means the principal cannot interfere with agents in the performance of their duties. Let the agent do the job. That's why you engaged the agent in the first place.

TERMINATING AN AGENCY RELATIONSHIP

We have looked at how agency relationships are created, what the agent's authority is, and what the duties between the agent and principal are. Now we will look at the different ways that agency relationships are terminated.

Lapse of Time

The agency contract usually specifies that it will last for a certain length of time. When that time expires, the agency ends.

Purpose Achieved

A special agent may be engaged for only a particular transaction or job. When that job is completed, the agency is also completed and ends.

Occurrence of a Specific Event

The agency contract may specify certain events that will result in termination of the agency. These can include death or disability of either the agent or the principal, a change of living or working circumstances (e.g., the agent or principal moves to another state or country), or either party files bankruptcy.

Mutual Agreement

The principal and agent can always mutually agree to end their relationship.

Termination by One Party

The agency can be terminated unilaterally by either of the parties. The principal cannot force the agent to go on representing the principal against the agent's will, and the agent cannot force the principal to continue to allow the agent to act on his or her behalf. However, be aware that although a unilateral termination will end the relationship, it will not end the principal's obligation to compensate the agent for work that the agent has already performed.

When Hannah Harrington signs her new agency contract with UTA, it effects a unilateral termination of her agency relationship with Roberta. Roberta cannot stop Hannah from changing agents. But Roberta is still entitled to be paid her commission on all jobs that Hannah worked and all deals that were made while Roberta was her agent.

SOME BASIC DIFFERENCES BETWEEN AGENTS AND MANAGERS

Before we turn to specific terms of management and talent agency contracts (see chapters 10 and 11), let's look at some basic differences between talent managers and talent agents.

First, there is a difference in the amount of personal attention you should expect to receive. Talent agents represent dozens, even hundreds, of actors. It is the talent agent's job to get auditions for the talent represented and, then when an actor books a job, to help negotiate the terms of that contract. It is not a talent agent's job to groom the talent. That is the talent manager's job. A manager will represent far fewer people and will give each client much more personal attention. A good manager will guide your career, give you advice on which headshots to use, which audition songs to sing if you are a musical performer, where to take dance or singing lessons, and how to maximize your personal appearance. The manager should advise you about which jobs you should take and which jobs you should decline. A good manager will also introduce you to directors, producers, and others who may provide work opportunities in the future. Finally, and perhaps most importantly, managers will have relationships with talent agents and can introduce you to agents who will represent you. Many actors find that it is easier to get a manager first and then let the manager assist them in getting a talent agent.

Second, in California, it is actually illegal for a talent manager to directly seek employment for the clients. This is because talent agents are licensed in California and, therefore, regulated by the state, but talent managers are not licensed and not regulated. The purpose of the regulation is to protect artists from unscrupulous agents, who might overcharge their clients, mishandle their money, or otherwise cause them financial damage. The California statute defines a "talent agent" as "a person or corporation who engages in the occupation of procuring, offering, promising, or attempting to procure employment or engagements for an artist."[1] Only licensed talent agents are allowed to "procure" employment for actors. Talent managers, not being licensed, are prohibited from procuring employment for their clients. Instead, managers are supposed to merely guide the actor's career. The manager should work with the actor's talent agent, but it is the agent who should seek jobs for the actor. If a manager actually does obtain employment for an actor (or even attempt to obtain employment for the actor), not only is the statute violated and the law broken but the manager is also not allowed to obtain a commission from that employment.

A third difference is amount of compensation. Both managers and agents work on a commission basis. That means that their compensation is a percentage of the income actors earn from jobs in the entertainment industry. The standard commission for talent agents is 10% of an actor's compensation. The agent's commission comes "off the top," meaning the agent takes 10% of an actor's *gross* compensation, before any withholding of taxes or other deductions. A manager's commission ranges between 15% and 20% of an actor's gross compensation. Managers justify taking a higher commission because they represent fewer clients and so need to earn more from each client to make a living and also because they give more personal attention than an agent.

Notice that if you have both an agent and a manager, each one will take a commission. That means that you could be paying 25%–30% of your gross compensation to your representatives.

Although managers generally represent all types of talent, there are different kinds of talent agents. Some agents specialize in "theatrical work." (In the film and television industry, *theatrical* refers to work in film and TV and not to acting on stage in theaters. The latter is referred to as "legitimate stage" work—so called because in the early twentieth century, acting in stage plays was considered legitimate acting but performing in vaudeville or burlesque houses was not.) Other talent agents represent actors only for commercials. Others focus on modeling jobs. Still others represent only child actors or only legitimate stage actors. You may want to consider the type of work you do and choose different agents for different work. Alternatively, you might sign with a large, multifunction agency that can give you representation across the board.

When you are ready to engage either an agent or a manager, you will need to sign a contract. In chapters 10 and 11, we dig into specific contract terms for managers and agents.

10

Managers and Management Contracts

Cody Cotton has been building his résumé in Los Angeles, doing showcases, small roles in plays, bit parts in low-budget films, and an Internet series. Now he has been introduced to Marty Manager, a talent manager who wants to represent Cody.

Before Cody signs on the dotted line, let's take a look at specific terms of Marty Manager's management contract.

TERM OF THE CONTRACT

When you first sign with a manager, it will likely be for a one-year term. The manager does not want too long a commitment, in case the relationship does not work out, the manager finds that you do not get very much work, or your personalities just clash. You don't want too long a commitment either for the same reasons. However, most management contracts provide for options to extend the length for additional one-year terms. The tricky thing to know about these options is that the contract may give the choice only to the manager and not to the actor. For example, Marty Manager's contract may say:

Manager shall have the option to extend the term hereof for two (2) further, successive, one (1) year periods. Each of Manager's options shall be deemed *automatically exercised* unless Manager shall advise Artist in writing at least fifteen (15) days prior to the end of the initial one (1) year term that Manager elects not to extend the term.

As you can see by the italicized portions, the choice to extend is entirely Marty Manager's. Also, the extension is automatic unless Marty says otherwise. Marty wants to have the sole choice because if Cody Cotton's career takes off, Marty wants to continue to commission Cody's earnings. But if Cody's career does not advance as Marty desires, Marty wants the choice to terminate the relationship. However, this is a contract point that Cody (and you) should negotiate. Whether to extend the representation should be the actor's choice as well. You do not want to be locked into a manager who is not working out for you.

Exactly that situation happened to the well-known television host, Kelly Ripa. When she was still a teenager, she signed with Cathy Parker Management. Although the actual contract that Ripa signed may be different from the standard management contract that Cathy Parker Management used in 2012, that 2012 agreement was most definitely written strongly in favor of the manager and contrary to the interests of the artist.[1] That contract provided for an initial term of *three* years. It also provided that Cathy Parker Management could extend the term for *an additional three years* if any of three conditions were satisfied: (1) the artist earned at least $20,000 during the first three years (in other words an average of $6,666 per year), or (2) the artist was cast in *any* part in a TV show, or *any* part in a film, or was cast in *any* role in a Broadway show, or performed in a national commercial, or (3) the artist signed with a talent agent. This meant that if, during the first three years, the artist booked even one national commercial, or one small role in one episode of a TV series, or got a chorus job in a Broadway show, the actor could be tied to Cathy Parker Management for a total of six years. The same result occurred even if the artist got no work at all but did sign up with a talent agent during the first three years. The contract also was favorable to Cathy Parker Management on the subject of commissions. The manager received 20% of the artist's gross employment compensation, which is already on the high end of commission rates, but the really bad point was that commissions did not stop when the contract ended and the manager no longer represented the artist. Rather, Cathy Parker Management was entitled to the same 20% commission on all work the artist obtained for three years *after* the contract ended, if that work came from someone who the artist had "met and/ or become acquainted with" through Cathy Parker Management. In other words, if the artist was introduced, even casually, to someone by the manager and later obtained employment from that person, the artist was obligated to pay a commission to Cathy Parker Management for three years after the manager had stopped representing the artist.

In Ripa's case, as she matured as an artist, she became dissatisfied with her management contract with Cathy Parker Management and sought to end it. Eventually, she was forced to sue Cathy Parker Management and ask for the court's assistance in terminating the contract and recovering excess commissions she had paid.[2] Ripa won that lawsuit, but of course, as with any lawsuit, it was expensive and time-consuming.[3]

The lesson to be learned here is to be careful when signing up with a manager. Negotiate for a shorter initial term, and make sure you have equal rights with the manager to extend the term or not. Also make sure that you are not tied into unfair commissions. Once the management contract ends, the commissions should also end. The exception to this is that the manager is properly entitled to commissions for work that you obtained during the management contract term which continues on beyond the end of the contract.

> Cody is cast in a TV series while Marty Manager is representing him. The series continues after the management contract has ended. Marty is still entitled to commission Cody's earnings from that TV series.

Note that a manager should *not* be entitled to commission future work that the actor obtains after the contract ends, even if the actor had been introduced to the employer by the manager. That is part of the manager's job—to introduce actors to people. The manager is compensated for that work by commissions earned during the contract term, and that is quite sufficient and fair.

GRANT OF AUTHORITY TO THE MANAGER

The management contract will contain a clause granting the manager the right to conduct certain business on behalf of the actor. This often includes the rights to:

1. authorize publicity for the actor;
2. authorize the use of the actor's name and image (both photographs and drawn likenesses) and the actor's voice for commercials;
3. sign contracts on the actor's behalf;

4. hire and fire talent agents, business agents, and publicity agents for the actor;
5. collect money on behalf of the actor, endorse the actor's name on checks payable to the actor for the actor's services, and deduct the manager's commission from such money.

These are pretty broad powers. Managers will insist that they need these powers to properly represent actors and handle their affairs. However, these powers should not be given to the manager to exercise alone. The contract should be negotiated to provide that the manager must consult with the actor before doing these things.

COMPENSATION

Marty Manager is compensated by receiving a commission from all of Cody Cotton's artistic employment earnings during the contract term. Cody must pay Marty's commission even on jobs that Cody obtains for himself, completely independently of the work of either Marty or Cody's talent agent. Why should Marty Manager get a commission on work in which he was not involved? The answer is because Marty is providing overall services in guiding, shaping, and developing Cody's career, and so Marty is entitled to be compensated on any of Cody's artistic earnings.

The management contract usually also provides that the manager continues to be entitled to commissions on extensions and renewals of an employment contract. This applies even to contract extensions and renewals that occur after the management contract itself has ended and the manager no longer represents the actor.

Cody books a national commercial for Audi. Cody is paid the fixed SAG-AFTRA scale compensation for shooting the commercial. He is also paid for "program" use (when the commercial airs during a particular television program) each time the commercial runs during the initial 13-week cycle. Marty receives his commission on the money paid for those program use runs. The Audi commercial also runs as "wild spot" (the commercial is used independently of any program or is used on local programs). Cody's fixed shooting payment covers all wild spot runs of the commercial during the first 13-week cycle. During the first 13-week cycle, Cody's contract with Marty expires. Audi then renews the commercial for an additional 13-week cycle. Cody is entitled to more payment. Because Cody's Audi contract was renewed, Marty is also entitled to his commission on the renewal payment, even though the management contract expired during the first 13-week cycle.

Don't forget that Cody's talent agent may be able to renegotiate and obtain a higher compensation for a second 13-week cycle or later cycles (see discussion of commercials contracts in chapter 6). If so, Marty's commission (and the talent agent's commission) is a percentage of the higher negotiated amount.

There is a way to stop the bleeding and end the payment of commissions to a manager who no longer represents the artist. Cody should negotiate a "sunset" clause as part of the compensation clause. A sunset clause reduces the percentage of commissions payable over time, until they end altogether. A typical clause will read this way:

> After the termination of this agreement, compensation payable to manager for any engagement, employment or contract covered by this agreement shall be reduced to:
>
> Within 6 months after termination—10%
> More than 6 months but less than 1 year after termination—7.5%
> More than 1 year but less than 2 years after termination—5%
> More than 2 years but less than 3 years after termination—2.5%
> More than 3 years after termination—0%

Of course, this is just an example. The particular time periods and percentages are subject to negotiation between Cody and Marty Manager.

EXPENSES

A manager may incur certain expenses in representing an actor, such as international telephone charges, Federal Express charges for overnight shipment of documents to or from the actor, producers, or others, and travel expenses if the actor requests the manager to travel to some location where the actor is working. The manager is entitled to be reimbursed for those expenses. But this is another point to be negotiated. The actor should make sure that expenses above a certain amount, say $100, must be preapproved by the actor.

PACKAGING

An important point to be considered and, perhaps, negotiated is the manager's compensation on projects that the manager "packages." A project is packaged when the manager is involved as a producer or executive producer on a project but then also arranges for an actor who the manager represents to be cast in that same project. Packaging can also occur if the manager assists in any capacity in development of a project or distribution of the finished project. In these situations, the manager is typically compensated separately for work as a producer. Should the manager also be entitled to commission the compensation of the actor who is involved in the project, who is represented by the manager? Is the manager double-dipping by receiving compensation as a producer and also receiving compensation from an actor in the project? That is the issue, and it is certainly arguable that the manager should be restricted to one type of compensation per project. Some management agreements will address this issue directly and provide that if the manager receives compensation as a producer, he or she will not also commission the actor's compensation. It is a good idea to look for such a provision in the management contract and, if it is not there, to negotiate for including it.

INDEPENDENT CONTRACTOR PROVISION

A common "legalese" type of clause in a management contract will state that the relationship between the manager and the actor is not in the nature of a partnership but, rather, that the manager is an independent contractor. This has important legal ramifications. In a partnership, all partners have fiduciary duties to each other. That is, they owe each other the highest duty of trust and loyalty. Among other things, this means that partners cannot operate businesses that compete with the partnership's business. That would be a conflict of interest. But as independent contractors, managers owe no fiduciary responsibility to the actors they represent. Their only duties are those specified in the contract and those covered by the general law of agency. Of course, agency law provides that agents are in a fiduciary relationship with the "principal" (the person who the agent represents), so an "independent contractor" clause in a management contract cannot completely eliminate this responsibility. What it can do is eliminate the potential conflict of interest between the manager's representation of one actor, and the representation of all other actors on his or her roster. A typical management contract will specify:

> Manager's services are not exclusive. Manager shall be free to perform the same or similar services for others, as well as to engage in any and all other business activities. Nothing in this agreement shall limit Manager's right to represent

other persons whose talents may be similar to or who may be in competition with Artist, or to have and pursue business interests which may be similar to or may compete with those of Artist.

This kind of a clause is necessary because a manager represents many actors, and some of them will necessarily be the same type as others, setting up potential conflicts of interest. This clause takes away any legal liability of the manager for that.

ARBITRATION

One of the most common clauses in all business contracts today is an arbitration clause. Arbitration is a private method of resolving disputes. Rather than the parties going to court and having a public hearing before a judge and jury, an arbitration takes the dispute into a private conference room, where the dispute is resolved and the case decided by a hired arbitrator. An arbitrator can be a lawyer or a retired judge but can also be simply a person who is experienced in the field of work in which the dispute arose.

The biggest difference between an arbitration and a court case is that in a regular court case, the losing party has the option of appealing the decision to a higher court. But an arbitration decision is typically binding on the parties, with no right of appeal.

Another difference between court cases and arbitrations may be a contractual restriction on the types of money damages that can be awarded. For example, in a court case against a manager who has committed fraud, an actor could win money for compensation plus additional *punitive damages*—money awarded to punish the manager for committing the fraud. But an arbitration clause might eliminate the possibility of punitive damages being awarded.

The important thing to understand about arbitrations is that the parties must agree to this type of dispute resolution. Neither party can be forced to arbitrate the dispute without an agreement. But many management contracts now include arbitration clauses that say that the parties do agree to arbitrate all disputes. If there is a dispute later on, the required agreement to arbitrate is already in place.

ARTIST'S WARRANTIES AND REPRESENTATIONS

A *warranty* is a promise, and a *representation* is a statement of something asserted to be true. Most management contracts will have a clause containing warranties and representations given by the actor. Cody Cotton's contract with Marty Manager contains this clause:

> Cody warrants and represents that he has no restrictions or conflicts that would prevent him from entering into this contract. Cody warrants and represents that if he uses a "professional name" (not his true name), he has the right to do so and no other artist uses the same name. Cody warrants and represents that he is experienced in the entertainment industry.

Cody has made these promises to Marty. If those promises turn out to be untrue, Cody will be in breach of contract.

There are usually no warranties or representations made by the manager to the actor, but it would be a good idea to negotiate for some. Cody should request that Marty warrant that he is experienced in the entertainment industry and represent that he will fully and faithfully perform the terms of the agreement.

INDEMNITY

An indemnity clause guarantees that if the manager is sued by a third party as a result of the manager's representation of the actor, the actor will pay any money damages award that is assessed against the manager and will also cover the manager's attorney's fees in that lawsuit. There are a couple of points to negotiate here. First, the actor should add the crucial word *reasonable* to any promise to pay the manager's attorney's fees, so that the clause reads,

> Artist agrees to indemnify and hold Manager harmless from any and all loss, expenses, cost or damage, including *reasonable* attorney's fees and costs, arising out of or in connection with any claim by a third party arising from the representation of Artist.

Second, the actor should seek a reciprocal indemnity clause, so that if the actor is sued as a result of some misconduct by the manager, the manager must cover the actor's reasonable attorney's fees and pay any damages awarded against the actor.

INJUNCTIVE RELIEF

Generally when a contract is breached, the only remedy the court will award is money damages. However, if money damages are inadequate to solve the problem caused by the breach, the court may grant an injunction. An injunction is a court order that the defendant must stop doing some act or engaging in some conduct. In rare cases, an injunction may order a party to perform some particular act that the party has previously refused to perform. Injunctions are considered extraordinary remedies and will only be granted when the situation clearly requires it. But in many management contracts, there will be a clause stating that the manager can obtain injunctive relief against the actor to prevent a breach of the contract. Cody's contract with Marty has this clause:

> Artist acknowledges and agrees that Manager's right to represent Artist exclusively, and Artist's promise to engage Manager as Artist's exclusive representative, are unique, irreplaceable and extraordinary rights and obligations. Artist therefore agrees that any breach or threatened breach of this agreement shall be deemed to be material and shall cause Manager immediate, unavoidable and irreparable harm and damage which cannot be adequately compensated for in monetary damages in an action at law. Accordingly, Artist agrees that Manager shall be entitled to seek and obtain injunctive and other equitable relief to prevent Artist from breaching this agreement.

This might look scary to Cody, but he can breathe easy. This kind of clause is likely unenforceable in court. For most breaches of the contract by an actor, money damages are an adequate remedy. For example, if Cody fails to pay Marty's commission for a particular job, the court can award money damages equal to the amount of the commission owed. Even if Cody tries to terminate the contract early or retains another manager to represent him and fires Marty, that again just presents a case for money damages because the only injury suffered by Marty is the loss of commissions on Cody's earnings for the remainder of the contract term.

Because money damages will usually suffice, a court is unlikely to grant any injunction against an actor. Further, actors cannot be compelled to continue to work with managers. This would violate the principles of the Thirteenth Amendment of the Constitution, which forbids slavery and involuntary servitude. Managers may refuse to negotiate an injunctive relief clause out of the contract, but the clause probably will never be enforced by any court.

Now that we have considered these clauses of a management contract, in chapter 11 we will turn to the provisions found in a typical talent agency contract. Many of the clauses are the same, so we will limit our analysis to those that are new or different.

Talent Agents and Talent Agency Contracts

In the previous chapter, we looked at Cody Cotton's contract with his talent manager, Marty Manager. Marty guides Cody's career, but because of the law in California that prohibits talent managers from procuring employment for artists, Marty cannot get jobs for Cody. To get work, Cody has a talent agent, Audrey Agent. In this chapter, we will look at the provisions found in a typical talent agency contract. Many of the clauses are the same as those in a talent management contract, so we will limit our analysis to those that are new or different.

SCOPE OF REPRESENTATION

Many talent agencies will seek to represent an actor in as many different areas of the entertainment industry as possible to maximize the agent's potential commissions. A typical clause might read:

> Artist engages Agent as Artist's sole and exclusive agent and representative with respect to Artist's services, activity and participation in all branches of the entertainment, publication, and related fields throughout the world, including but not limited to merchandising, testimonials and commercial tie-ups, whether or not using Artist's name, voice or likeness.

This clause would cover not only acting services of all types (film, TV, commercials, stage, and Internet) but would also cover the actor's work in publishing. If the actor writes books (fiction or nonfiction), the agent would be entitled to represent the actor for publishing contracts on those books—and take a commission on the actor's book royalties. This clause also covers the actor's work in any field that is related to entertainment. That would include personal appearance engagements (such as at conventions like Comic-Con), concert tours and recording contracts if the actor is also a musician, and even art gallery showings if the actor is also a painter or sculptor. The contract also covers merchandising, product endorsements, and commercials of all kinds, so if the actor sells any products or lends his or her name to any products or services, the agent can commission the actor's earnings from those sales.

This is a clause you should seriously negotiate to limit the representation to only those aspects of your professional life that you want your agent to be involved in. Unless you are a star with a huge agency, it may be better to get specialists in each field. You need to strike out the excess categories.

> Cody is focusing his career on film and television work but also wants to do commercials because they are a good source of income. Cody also has a side gig as bass player in a rock band, which plays small clubs. His band is consistently engaged and does not need an agent to help get gigs. Cody needs the income from his band work to support himself, and he cannot afford to give away any percentage of that to his agent. Cody negotiates with Audrey Agent to represent him only for theatrical film and TV work. Cody signs with a different agent for commercials work. Audrey rewrites the contract to read, "Artist engages Agent as Artist's sole and exclusive agent and representative with respect to Artist's services, activity and participation in film and television engagements only."

TERM OF THE CONTRACT

Like a management contract, a talent agency contract will be for a specified period of time. Usually, the first contract with an agent will be for one year, and subsequent contracts will be for longer, perhaps two or three years. The agency contract may provide for automatic extensions of the term. If it does, make sure to negotiate for a mutual agreement on any extension.

In California, a law requires talent agencies to put a clause in their contracts that gives the actor the right to terminate the contract if there has been no bona fide offer of work for four consecutive months.[1] This gives you an "out" if your agent is not getting you any auditions. In states other than California, you can try to negotiate a similar right to terminate.

As with management contracts, be aware that termination of the contract does not terminate the actor's obligation to pay commissions for jobs obtained during the contract term. But also, as with management contracts, you should try to negotiate for a sunset clause, to end the commission payments over a period of time.

COMPENSATION

The standard commission for talent agents is 10% of the actor's *gross* compensation (before any withholding for taxes or other deductions). Talent agents who abide by SAG-AFTRA mandated provisions will limit their commission to that rate. However, it is common for talent agencies to set their own rates unless some state law limits the amount of compensation, and those rates are usually not negotiable. The base rate may be 10%, but it may increase for different types of work. For example, one General Services Agreement used by a Los Angeles talent agency sets the commission rates as follows:

> Artist agrees to pay Agency, and Agency agrees to accept, as and for its compensation, a sum equal to 10% of the gross compensation paid and/or payable, during or after the term hereof, under or by reason of every engagement, employment or contract covered by this agreement, now in existence or made or negotiated during the term hereof, and whether procured by Artist, Agency or any third party. *In lieu however of said 10%, Agency's compensation shall be with respect to*: (i) concerts, readings, recitals, and any other engagements presented in places where concerts, readings and recitals are given, and tours constituting or similar to any of the foregoing: *15%*; (ii) merchandising, testimonial and commercial tie-up rights and licensing of such rights: *20%*; and (iii) lectures and/or appearances of a similar nature: *20%*.

If the agency is permitted to represent the actor in concerts, personal appearances, or lecture tours, the commission can go up to 15–20%. The commission on merchandising and endorsement deals can also be 20%. Be aware of these potential increases in commission rates. You may not be able to negotiate them, unless you have become quite famous and achieved substantial negotiating power, but at least you will not be surprised when the agent deducts more than 10% from your paycheck.

RIGHT TO CURE A BREACH

You may find a clause in a talent agency contract (or a management contract) that gives the representative a right to "cure" a breach of the contract. For example, suppose your agent receives payment from a production company on your behalf for acting services you have performed. The agent deducts 10% commission but then fails to send the 90% balance to you. This would be a breach of the contract, as well as a breach of the agent's fiduciary duty to account. But if there is a cure clause, you cannot immediately sue. You must first give the agent notice of the breach, and the agent will have a certain number of days (commonly ranging between 5 to 30 days) to cure the breach by sending you the money. If the agent does so, there is effectively no breach of the contract.

> Cody has booked a role in one episode of *Made Men*, a TV series. He finishes shooting and is expecting payment shortly. Two months go by, but Cody has still not received any check from Audrey Agent. Cody calls the producer of the series, who says that the check for Cody's compensation was sent to Audrey Agent six weeks earlier. Cody then sends his agent a letter by registered mail: "Dear Audrey, I believe you are in breach of the contract between us because I have still not received any payment for my work on *Made Men*, even though the producer says you were sent the check. If there is some problem, please let me know." Audrey Agent mails the check to Cody 4 days later, which cures her breach of the contract.

The cure clause works in conjunction with a separate "notice" clause. The notice clause will specify the manner in which you must give notice of the breach to the agent. Typically, a notice clause requires written notice, sent either by registered or certified mail, return receipt requested, or by overnight delivery by FedEx or UPS. Regular, first-class mail is not usually sufficient, nor is written notice by email or text message, unless the contract specifically allows those methods. If you don't properly send the notice of breach, the period of time for cure does not start to run, and you cannot sue for breach of the contract. So you have to make sure to check the notice and cure clauses.

12

Attorneys and Retainer Agreements

You may not need a lawyer until you become successful. Most of the time, your talent agent can negotiate your employment contracts for you. Standard union contracts will not require a lawyer's input. If a particular contract is not a standard union contract and is more complicated, it should be reviewed by a lawyer. However, your talent agency may employ lawyers in-house or have lawyers they work with, who will do that review.

As you grow in your career, you may want your own lawyer. Your lawyer can negotiate, draft, and review your contracts. A lawyer can also help you if your rights are violated. Maybe a production company fails to pay you for your acting services or you get injured during a job. Perhaps somebody takes your photograph and uses it for a commercial purpose without your permission (a violation of your right of privacy), or you pitch a movie idea to a producer, who then makes the film but cuts you out of the project with no pay and no credit (a breach of contract). For unpaid compensation or work-related injuries, the union will represent and protect you, but for violations of your right of privacy or breaches of contract, you will need a lawyer to help you and give you advice.

You should also think about the different paths of your career. Many actors branch out into producing their own projects. When you become a producer, there are numerous legal issues involved (see chapters 15–22). You will need a production company formed. You will need to negotiate with unions and abide by union contracts. You will need to understand employment, insurance, privacy, defamation, and tort laws. As a producer, you will be the one hiring actors and crew, so you will have to negotiate and write lots of contracts. You will also need to understand federal and state securities laws that govern the raising of financing for your project, banking laws if you borrow money, and tax laws affecting the payment of wages and costs on the project. You will need to negotiate with film studios, television networks, film distribution companies, or theater companies to market, display, or perform your work. An entertainment lawyer is indispensable for producers.

Lawyers are expensive. If you hire a lawyer on an hourly rate, you will be charged several hundred dollars for each hour of the lawyer's services. But many entertainment lawyers will represent actors and charge a percentage of the actor's gross income, just like an agent or a manager. Lawyers typically charge 5%.

If you are or become well-known or famous, you may find that you can substitute a lawyer for either your talent agent, manager, or both. Once you have achieved that level of success, producers, directors, studios, TV networks, and other employers will come to you with offers of roles. You may no longer need an agent to find work for you, and you may no longer need a manager to guide your career. But you will still need someone to help you with your contracts. A lawyer can do that. Although most entertainment lawyers are not talent agents and, therefore, cannot legally help you obtain work, they are licensed to practice law and can always negotiate and draft your contracts. Some famous actors (such as John Travolta[1] and Bill Murray[2]) are known for having only a lawyer, and either no agent, no manager, or neither.

CHOOSING THE RIGHT LAWYER FOR YOU

If you want a lawyer, how do you go about finding one? Your talent agent or manager can usually introduce you to an entertainment lawyer that they work with. That ensures that you get someone who will fit well into your team. Another way is to ask friends and colleagues. Find out who has a good lawyer and then ask that person to give you a referral to their lawyer. When contacting a busy lawyer, it is always good to smooth the way by saying, "My friend, Heather, said I should call you." A third way to find an entertainment lawyer is to read the trades—*Variety, The Hollywood Reporter, Backstage,* thewrap.com, and deadline.com, to name a few. Read the articles about actors getting roles. Frequently, the last paragraph of the article will identify the actor's agent, manager, and lawyer. Once you have the lawyer's name, you can find contact information through the state bar association.[3] Then send the lawyer a good cover letter or email, along with a headshot and résumé, and say you are seeking legal representation.

Once you have identified a lawyer you are interested in, set up a face-to-face meeting. A lawyer should be willing to meet with you for half an hour at no charge.

> Laurie is a working actor with a long résumé. She auditions for a regular role in a TV series and is offered the job. Laurie has a good talent agent, but the series contract is long and complicated. She feels like it would be a good idea to have an entertainment lawyer look it over. Laurie's friend, Curly, suggests a lawyer he knows, Mr. Dewey. Laurie calls Mr. Dewey and sets up an initial half-hour consultation. Laurie has several questions but doesn't get a chance to ask them because during the meeting, the lawyer takes several phone calls and keeps shouting instructions to his secretary about things to do. Laurie asks the lawyer about his experience representing TV actors, and he replies, "Oh, don't worry, I can handle it. I've handled many big business transactions. How different could a TV contract be?" At the end of the meeting, Mr. Dewey shakes Laurie's hand vigorously and says, "Welcome to Dewey, Cheatham, and Howe!"

Mr. Dewey is not a good lawyer for Laurie's needs. An important part of a successful lawyer-client relationship is good communication. Mr. Dewey did not exhibit good communication skills. Constantly taking phone calls during the meeting and shouting instructions to his secretary, indicates he was not really focused on Laurie. Also, Mr. Dewey is not an experienced entertainment lawyer. Practice in another area of business law does not equate to understanding the nuances of the entertainment business. Finally, Laurie was not even able to confirm that Mr. Dewey would represent her on a percentage fee basis, rather than an expensive hourly rate. Laurie needs to keep looking.

THE RETAINER AGREEMENT

When you find a lawyer you like, and that lawyer agrees to take you on as a client, the lawyer will have you sign a retainer agreement. This is the official contract governing your representation by the lawyer. Most state laws governing services by lawyers require them to have written client agreements.

Also, remember that a lawyer is legally your agent, and the extent of authority of any agent should be clearly set forth in a written contract. You can retain a lawyer to represent you on only a particular job or to be your lawyer generally. So let's look at the typical provisions in a lawyer's retainer agreement.

Legal Services

The retainer agreement should specify what services the lawyer will provide. It could be written in broad, general language, such as, "I will assist you with all legal matters relating to your involvement in any capacity in any entertainment projects or other matters relating to the entertainment industry." Or it could be written more specifically, such as, "I will assist you with all legal matters relating to your employment as an actor in film, television, Internet, commercials, and legitimate stage productions." You can even hire a lawyer to look over the contract on just one job. In Laurie's case, the scope of services could be described this way: "I will assist you with negotiating and drafting your employment agreement for your acting services in the TV series titled *The Road to Madagascar*." The important thing is for you and the lawyer to decide on the scope of the services and describe them properly in the retainer agreement.

Suppose you hire the lawyer for a limited purpose, say to negotiate one contract, but then you work so well together that you want to continue and broaden the relationship. To cover this situation, the retainer agreement might contain an additional services clause that reads something like this:

> You ("client") acknowledge that you may request me ("lawyer") to render services in addition to those set forth in this Agreement or in connection with other matters, whether or not related to the matters covered by the Agreement. You and I agree that in such event, and if I agree to accept such other matters, no new agreement between us shall be necessary, and this Agreement shall govern the relationship between you and me as to all services rendered by me.

Termination of the Relationship

Unlike a talent agent or manager contract, a contract with a lawyer will not be for some set period of time. You are free to end the relationship with your lawyer at any time. Likewise, the lawyer is also free to stop representing you at any time. The exception is if the lawyer is handling a court case for you. An attorney's ability to end that relationship will be restricted and may require permission of the judge overseeing the case.

As with ending a talent agent or manager relationship, terminating a relationship with an attorney will not end the obligation to pay his or her fees. If a lawyer is working for you on a 5% commission basis, he or she has the right to receive the commission for any legal work done for you during the term of the contract. This means that, as with your agent and manager, you need to negotiate for a sunset clause to fade out the payment of commissions to the lawyer over a period of time. If you are paying the lawyer's hourly rate, rather than a 5% commission, you will still be obligated to pay for all of the time spent on your matters before you or the lawyer terminated the relationship.

Fees and Costs

The agreement with a lawyer must specify how the lawyer is being paid. If your matters are handled on a commission basis, the agreement should contain a clause much like the compensation clauses in an agent or manager contract, stating that the lawyer will receive 5% of your gross compensation for every contract that the lawyer negotiates, drafts, or otherwise assists you with. However, unlike the commissions payable to agents and managers, the lawyer is not entitled to take 5% of *all* of your jobs. The lawyer should only take 5% of your compensation on jobs in which he or she is involved as your representative. If you do not seek his or her legal advice or services on a particular contract, the lawyer should not take a commission from your compensation from that contract.

If you are paying the lawyer's hourly rate, then the fee clause should state the amount of that hourly rate, for example: "You agree to pay me the sum of $500 per hour." It should also describe how the lawyer will charge that rate and how you will be billed. When billing on an hourly rate, lawyers keep detailed records of the time they spend. Most charge for each tenth or each quarter of an hour of their time. If the hourly rate is $500, the lawyer will charge you $50 for every six minutes (1/10th of an hour), or $125 for every 15 minutes (1/4 of an hour) that is spent working on your matters. Most lawyers send a bill once each month, describing in detail the work done and specifying the date and amount of time spent for each bit of work.

Finally, you can expect your lawyer to charge for costs. Typical charges include photocopy charges, postage, messenger service fees, and even long distance telephone charges. You can negotiate to put a maximum amount on costs per month or to require special approval to incur costs above a certain amount.

Disclaimer of Guaranteed Results

Lawyers are careful not to guarantee the outcome of any contract negotiation or other legal representation because they want to avoid legal malpractice claims. A lawyer is obligated to use the same skill and care as an ordinarily skilled lawyer in the same field of practice, and if that skill and care are used correctly, the lawyer is not responsible if a contract falls out or you lose a case. Even the best of lawyers have lost cases, and sometimes even a highly experienced and skilled lawyer finds that a particular contract simply cannot be successfully negotiated because the party on the other side is too entrenched in his or her position.

For these reasons, it is common for a retainer agreement to contain a clause clearly stating that the lawyer is not guaranteeing the outcome or success of any legal matter. Even if the lawyer has given you an estimate or opinion of the likelihood of success of negotiations, the cost of a given project, or the chances of winning a lawsuit, the retainer agreement will make it clear that such estimates and opinions are not guarantees. You should understand that a lawyer's predictions and estimates are merely good faith judgments based on facts and circumstances known to the lawyer at the time, and facts and circumstances can and do change. Just as a doctor never guarantees a cure, a lawyer never guarantees a win.

Arbitration Clause

Just as in talent agency and talent management contracts, a lawyer's retainer agreement will probably have an arbitration clause. If so, any dispute between you and the lawyer will be resolved by private arbitration and not by a court trial. The arbitration decision will be final and binding with no right of appeal. You can also expect the arbitration clause to eliminate any possibility of punitive damages and to provide that the winning party is entitled to recover reasonable attorney's fees from the losing party.

Disposing of the Client's Files

State laws, or the rules of state bar associations, may require lawyers to maintain their clients' file for a certain number of years (e.g., five or seven years). After this time has expired, a lawyer will want to dispose of that file to free up file room space for ongoing matters. The lawyer may even destroy the file, although most state laws or state bar rules will mandate that "intrinsically valuable" documents, such as original stocks, bonds, wills, deeds, notes, or court judgments, may not be destroyed without client consent. A retainer agreement may contain a clause about disposition of your client file. If so, you should make sure that you are given an opportunity to request and receive the file before it, or any of its contents, is destroyed.

Related to this is your right to pick up your file if your relationship with the lawyer comes to an end. The lawyer has a legal obligation to give you your file. Some lawyers will tell you that you cannot have the file until their bill is completely paid, but withholding your file likely violates the rules governing the lawyer's conduct in that state. For example, in California, when the relationship ends, the lawyer must promptly return all files to the client, whether or not the client has paid the bill.[4]

Malpractice Insurance

Not all lawyers carry malpractice insurance. Lawyers who do not handle cases in court may not have it. Entertainment lawyers who only represent clients in business transactions often will not carry such insurance. This is because there is less risk to the lawyer of a malpractice case arising from a contract negotiation, than there is from a lawsuit gone bad. Make sure you ask if the lawyer has malpractice insurance, and ask that the retainer agreement identify that. If you retain a lawyer to handle a lawsuit for you, you should definitely make sure that the lawyer carries malpractice insurance. There is nothing worse than having a lawyer negligently handle your lawsuit, resulting in your losing it and perhaps losing a great deal of money, only to find out that the lawyer has no insurance covering his negligence. Don't fall into that trap. If you hire a lawyer to negotiate your contracts, and then later need a lawyer to handle a court case, either get a different lawyer for the case or make sure the first lawyer has malpractice insurance.

Speaking of lawsuits, sometimes there are cases in which you do not need a lawyer at all or indeed are not allowed to have one, such as in small claims court. Suppose you do an acting job for which you will be paid only a few hundred, or even a few thousand, dollars. You do the work, but you don't get paid. All attempts at negotiating payment fail. Now you have to sue. But that does not mean you have to launch a major litigation. All states have some form of small claims court. In California, an individual can sue for as much as $10,000 in small claims court, and a business can sue for up to $5,000.

Small claims actions have cheaper filing fees, and they get to trial much more quickly than regular lawsuits. But in California's small claims court, you have to represent yourself. You are not allowed to have a lawyer represent you. Of course, your opponent will not have a lawyer either. The good news is that you will not incur big legal fees for a trial lawyer. The bad news is that you must feel confident enough to go to court on your own. However, you can and should have a lawyer coach you for the small claims trial, even though the lawyer cannot represent you in the courtroom.

Part 5

AT HOME AND ON THE JOB

13

Landlord-Tenant Law

Types of Tenancies, Rent Control Laws, Obligations of the Landlord, and Assignments and Sublets

Because the cost of real estate in most major cities is quite high, most actors rent. Actors also frequently book jobs out of town and need to sublet their apartments while they are working on location. As renters, actors need to know the basics of landlord-tenant law.

First, understand that there are similarities in landlord-tenant law in all states because the relationship between a landlord and tenant is basically a contract relationship, so general contract law will apply. But the relationship is also governed by the law of real property, which may be quite different from contract law. Second, each state will have specific laws relating to the obligations of landlords and tenants. This book cannot cover the laws of each state, so if you run into a significant problem with your landlord, you should consult a lawyer in your state. However, this chapter will give you an overview of the landlord-tenant relationship and the laws that commonly apply.

The landlord-tenant relationship is created when a real property owner or lessor (the landlord) agrees to convey the right to possess the property to a lessee (the tenant) for a certain period of time. This is typically done by a written lease agreement. (Note that the proper legal terms are *lessor* and *lessee* and not *leasor* and *leasee*—never mind what you may see as answers in crossword puzzles!) Once property has been delivered to the tenant under a lease agreement, the tenant has the right to the exclusive possession of that property against everyone else, except the landlord, who always retains a reasonable right to enter the property for maintenance and repairs or to show the property to prospective future lessees or potential buyers of the property. The lease agreement is usually written but can be oral if it is for a period of time shorter than one year. The tenant's right to possession is temporary; it is for the length of the lease period, and at the end of that period, the tenant is legally obligated to return the property to the landlord.

TYPES OF TENANCIES
There are several different types of tenancies. The names given to tenancies can be a bit confusing.

Tenancy for Years
The name of this tenancy makes you think that it must last for several years. But a tenancy for years does not even need to last for one year. Rather, a tenancy for years lasts for a particular, specified length of time, no matter how long or short. If there is a definite date for starting the tenancy and a definite date when it will end, it is a tenancy for years. A lease for one year is a tenancy for years because it specifies the length of time—one year. But a lease for six months is also a tenancy for years because it also specifies the length of time—six months. In fact, a tenancy for even a short period of time, such as one week or one month, is called a tenancy for years because the time period is specified.

> Ellen has just moved to Los Angeles to pursue her acting career. She finds a nice apartment in West Los Angeles and signs a lease. The lease begins on October 1, and ends the following September 30.

Ellen's lease creates a tenancy for years because it specifies the beginning and ending dates. When the lease runs out on September 30, Ellen's tenancy ends. Ellen then no longer has a legal right to possess the property. The right to possess the property reverts (or returns) to the landlord.

When a lease expires and a tenancy for years ends, the landlord and the tenant can decide if they want to make a new lease. If they make a new lease, it can be for the same period of time as the previous lease or for a shorter or longer period of time—whatever they agree. When Ellen's lease expires on September 30, she and her landlord could agree to renew the lease for another year, or they could agree to continue on a month-to-month basis. That would be a different kind of tenancy—a periodic tenancy.

Periodic Tenancy

A periodic tenancy continues for the same period of time, over and over. For example, a lease that states that the tenant will pay rent each month on the first day of the month creates a periodic tenancy because the tenancy continues from month-to-month automatically, until either the landlord or the tenant takes steps to end it. A periodic tenancy can be for any period of time, as long as it repeats indefinitely. It could be week-to-week, month-to-month, or even year-to-year. To end a periodic tenancy, most states require that one of the parties give a written notice to the other party of the desire to end it. The notice must be given in advance for the length of time equal to the period of the tenancy. If a tenant wants to end a month-to-month tenancy, the landlord must be given written notice at least one month before the date the tenant wants the tenancy to end.

A tenancy for years can be converted to a periodic tenancy. This would happen when the tenancy for years comes to an end and the parties agree (either by actual communication or by their actions) to continue the tenancy but without specifying the time length.

Ellen's lease is expiring on September 30. After living there for a year, Ellen has settled in nicely and wants to renew for another year, but her landlord, Palm Tree Properties, does not because it plans to sell the building in the near future. Ellen and Palm Tree Properties agree on a month-to-month lease rather than a new one-year lease. Ellen's original tenancy for years is converted to a periodic tenancy. Either Ellen or Palm Tree Properties can then terminate that tenancy by giving the other party one month's written notice.

This is the general way tenancies are converted from one type to another. But the particular state law may affect this in some way. In California, a statute provides that if the parties do not specify the period of time the lease will last, it is automatically a month-to-month lease. When Ellen's one-year tenancy ends on September 30, if she and Palm Tree Properties have no discussions at all, but Ellen offers the rent on October 1 and the landlord accepts it, Ellen has automatically entered into a month-to-month tenancy under California law.

Tenancy at Sufferance

This third type of tenancy is not a real tenancy at all. It is a legal situation created when a tenancy ends (either a tenancy for years or a periodic tenancy) and the tenant does not move out. Instead, the tenant wrongfully remains in possession of the property, even though the legal right to possession has ended. The name of this tenancy comes from an old definition of the verb *suffer*, meaning "to tolerate" or "to allow." In a tenancy at sufferance, the tenant remains in possession of the property only as long as the landlord allows or tolerates it, even though the landlord may not like it. The verb *suffer* usually means "to undergo or endure some pain or injury," and indeed when a tenant refuses to leave the landlord's property at the end of a tenancy, the landlord is forced to undergo or endure an injury—being deprived of the possession of the property. In this situation, the landlord can sue to evict the tenant and can also seek money damages—usually the fair market rent for the time the tenant has wrongfully stayed in possession. It is important to note that a tenancy at sufferance can only exist if the tenant remains in possession after the legal tenancy has ended *and does not pay any rent*. If the tenant offers rent to the landlord, and the landlord accepts it, a new tenancy is created—most likely a month-to-month tenancy.

RENT CONTROL LAWS

Residential tenancies can be affected by rent control laws. These are not common, however. Only California, Maryland, New Jersey, New York, Oregon, and the District of Columbia have rent control laws, according to the National Multifamily Housing Council. Oregon is unique because its rent control law, passed in 2019, applies statewide and not just in a particular city in the state.[1] Fortunately, the vast majority of actors live in two states that do have rent control laws. According to the Bureau of Labor Statistics, in May 2018, California and New York together had about 21,000 working actors. The next closest states, Georgia (Atlanta) and Illinois (Chicago), do not have rent control.[2]

Rent control laws generally do two things: keep landlords from increasing the rent by unreasonable amounts and keep landlords from arbitrarily evicting tenants. In Los Angeles, for example, once you have rented an apartment, you cannot be evicted simply because the landlord wants to kick you out. Naturally, if you do not pay the rent or breach the lease agreement in some other way, you can be evicted. But as long as you pay your rent on time and obey all the rules, the rent control law says you are entitled to keep living in that apartment. However, not all apartments in Los Angeles are rent controlled, so these rules will not apply to apartments that are not rent-controlled.

The Los Angeles rent control law also restricts the amount that the landlord can raise your rent, usually just a small percentage amount per year. There are some exceptions to these rules. The landlord can evict you if the landlord or a family member of the landlord will occupy the apartment, the landlord needs the unit for a resident manager, the landlord plans to demolish the apartment or otherwise remove it from the rental market (such as converting it to a condominium for sale), or the landlord is ordered by a governmental agency to vacate the building because of some legal violation. But if you are evicted for these reasons, you may be entitled to compensation, which will help cover your moving expenses.[3]

New York has a rent stabilization law for some, but not all, apartments in the city. A list of rent stabilized buildings and information concerning the rent stabilization law can be found at the NYC Rent Guidelines Board website.[4] New York's rent-controlled apartments can be protected not only for the tenant but also the tenant's lawful successor, such as a family member, spouse, or adult lifetime partner.

Chicago has no rent control law at present. In fact, the 1997 Rent Control Preemption Act is an Illinois state law that bans municipalities from imposing restrictions on rental rates. Illinois' current governor, J. B. Pritzker, said during his campaign that he favored repealing that law, and some state legislators have introduced bills seeking to do just that.[5] At the time of publication of this book, however, the law had not been repealed.

OBLIGATIONS OF THE LANDLORD AND THE TENANT

During the tenancy, the tenant is obligated to maintain the leased premises in good condition and is responsible for any damages to the leased premises. Most leases provide that the tenant must return the property to the landlord at the end of the lease term in the same condition as received, subject to "normal wear and tear."

Ellen has lived in her West Los Angeles apartment for five years but has now decided to move. The carpet was new when she moved in. She cleans the apartment well and has the carpets professionally shampooed, so they look really good. After she moves out, the landlord tries to keep her security deposit, claiming that she must pay for replacement of the old carpet.

Ellen does not have to pay for installing new carpet. She was entitled to normal use of the property, and the landlord must accept normal deterioration of the carpet.

The landlord is responsible to maintain common areas such as stairs, pools, and elevators. The landlord is also usually responsible to maintain, repair, or replace fixtures and appliances that are provided in the apartment, such as stoves and ovens, refrigerators, garbage disposals in the kitchen sink, and kitchen and bathroom fixtures. However, be aware that in some large cities (such as Los Angeles), the apartment may not come with large appliances such as stoves or refrigerators, and you may need to purchase them yourself.

Warranty of Habitability

In most states, the law implies a warranty of habitability for residential leases. Some states have specific statutes defining what *habitability* means. In California, an apartment is uninhabitable if it substantially lacks: effective waterproofing and weather protection of roof and exterior walls, including unbroken windows and doors; plumbing facilities in good working order, including hot and cold running water, connected to a sewage disposal system; gas facilities in good working order; heating facilities in good working order; an electric system, including lighting, wiring, and equipment, in good working order; and floors, stairways, and railings in good repair. To be habitable, the apartment building, grounds, and appurtenances (e.g., a garden or a detached garage) must also be clean and sanitary and free from debris, filth, rubbish, garbage, rodents, and vermin. There must also be adequate trash receptacles in good repair.

In addition to these requirements, the California law says that each rental unit must have all of the following: a working toilet, wash basin, and bathtub or shower in a room that is ventilated and allows privacy; a kitchen with a sink that cannot be made of an absorbent material such as wood; natural lighting in every room through windows or skylights; safe fire or emergency exits leading to a street or hallway; litter-free stairs, hallways, and exits; storage areas, garages, and basements free of combustible materials; operable dead bolt locks on the main entry doors of rental units, and operable locking or security devices on windows; working smoke detectors in all units of multiunit buildings, such as duplexes and apartment complexes; a locking mail box for each unit; and ground fault circuit interrupters for swimming pools and antisuction protections for wading pools in apartment complexes and other residential settings. As you can see, the law is quite comprehensive.[6]

If your landlord fails to maintain the apartment in a habitable condition, you have a couple of options.

First, you could reach an agreement with the landlord to allow you to make the repairs and deduct the cost from the rent.

Second, if your landlord will not agree, you may have a legal right anyway to repair and deduct. You make the repairs and deduct the cost from the rent, even *without* the landlord's agreement. Not all states allow this remedy, so check the law in your state before you do it. In most states, a tenant must first give the landlord written notice of the defects and allow the landlord a reasonable time to make repairs. A typical reasonable time period would be 30 days.

Even if state law allows a right of repair and deduct, there may be limits. In California, there are three requirements: (i) the defective conditions must affect the tenant's health and safety, (ii) the cost of repairs cannot exceed one month's rent, and (iii) the tenant cannot use this self-help remedy more than twice in any 12-month period.[7] There are also risks in using this self-help method. If the defects are not serious enough or are not of the type recognized by the state law, the landlord can sue you for failing to pay the entire rent and seek to evict you.

The third option is to simply abandon the uninhabitable apartment. This only applies when you can successfully argue that your landlord has breached the implied warranty of habitability. If so, you can abandon the premises and will owe no further rent to the landlord, even if the lease agreement has not yet expired. This remedy is known as a constructive eviction. If your landlord permits an apartment to be uninhabitable because of defective or broken systems or appliances or unsanitary conditions and fails to make repairs, then the landlord has breached the implied warranty of habitability.

In this situation, you have been constructively evicted. You have not been *actually* evicted, but you are *essentially* evicted because you cannot use the uninhabitable apartment as desired. If you actually move out within a reasonable time following the landlord's failure to make repairs, you can use the legal defense of constructive eviction and refuse to pay any further rent. However, if you stay at the apartment for more than a reasonable period of time after you have given the landlord notice of the bad conditions, you will be deemed to have accepted the situation, and the constructive eviction defense will not apply.

> Evan lives in an apartment where the rent is cheap, but the conditions are bad. The electrical system is flaky. Every time Evan runs the microwave at the same time as the air conditioner, the circuit breaker flips. The garbage bins are always overflowing. Evan has found cockroaches in his apartment and mice in the garbage bins. Evan sends an email to the landlord about these problems, but the landlord does nothing. After 30 days of no action by the landlord, Evan emails the landlord and says he is moving out and will not pay any further rent. The landlord files a suit against Evan, claiming rent for the remaining six months of the lease.

Evan's landlord breached the warranty of habitability. Because Evan moved out within a reasonable period of time after giving the landlord a chance to fix things, Evan is entitled to the defense of constructive eviction. The landlord will lose the case, and Evan will not have to pay any rent.

Constructive Eviction

The constructive eviction defense can also be used when the landlord has breached the "covenant of quiet enjoyment." This is a promise, implied by law, that the landlord will not unreasonably interfere with the tenant's right to use the leased premises. The covenant of quiet enjoyment includes your right to be free from excessive noise, but it also includes the right to be free of any interference by the landlord with your right to enjoy the space. For example, if the landlord allows unpleasant odors to permeate your apartment or conducts repairs or remodeling that creates a lot of dust or noise, that can breach the covenant of quiet enjoyment. Even the actions of third parties can be a breach of the covenant of quiet enjoyment, if the landlord has control over those third parties' actions.

> Grande Properties, Inc. owns two adjoining buildings. One is an apartment building. The other is a commercial building. Grande Properties rents the commercial building to a noisy nightclub that plays loud rock music from

early evening on into the wee hours of the morning. Stefanie lives in the apartment building. The noise from the nightclub interferes with her ability to sleep or even to listen to her TV or have a conversation. She tells Grande Properties that it has breached her covenant of quiet enjoyment, but the landlord does nothing to stop the nightclub tenant from making the noise. Stefanie moves out of her apartment. She does not owe Grande Properties any further rent because it has breached the covenant of quiet enjoyment, and Stefanie has been constructively evicted.[8]

Liability for Injuries

The previous paragraphs tell you about the tenant's and landlord's obligations to repair and maintain the premises and the building. But suppose you, or one of your guests, is injured at the property as the result of some defective condition. Who is liable for the injury—you, as the tenant, or your landlord? It depends on where the injury occurred.

You are liable for injuries to yourself or others that are caused by your own negligence or intentional conduct. If you have a torn carpet in your apartment that you know about but fail to repair, and your friend trips on that torn section and falls, breaking an arm, you are liable for that injury. This is an excellent reason to always carry renter's insurance, which can not only shield you from liability for injuries to others caused by your negligence but can also protect your belongings in the event of fire or other damage to or destruction of the apartment. (The insurance will not protect you against your intentional conduct, of course, so if you engage in a fistfight with your neighbor, any injuries sustained are completely on you.)

On the other hand, the landlord is liable for injuries to persons that are caused by a hidden danger in the premises of which the landlord is aware or defects in common areas under the landlord's control, such as stairways, hallways, courtyards, or swimming pools. The landlord is also responsible for injuries caused by repairs that were negligently made by the landlord.

Nuisances

Another obligation you have as a tenant is to be a good neighbor to other occupants of the property (such as residents of other units in the apartment building). A tenant cannot create a nuisance and cannot interfere with others' quiet enjoyment of their leased property. A "nuisance" is unreasonable conduct that substantially interferes with or disturbs the use and enjoyment of land. Examples include excessive noise (don't blast your music at midnight), invasive odors (cooking is allowed of course, but conducting chemical experiments in your apartment is not), and even smoke (hosting a cigar party once a week might not be a good idea). Whether the conduct is unreasonable is measured by the sensibilities of the average person.

Tenants in crowded cities are particularly attuned to these irritations and may well complain about neighbors who they perceive as violating their rights. One interesting situation occurred in 2007 in New York, involving the well-known rock star Bono, who got into a dispute with his neighbor, rocker Billy Squier, in the exclusive San Remo apartment building where the two men lived.[9] The San Remo was also home to such celebrities as Steve Martin, Steven Spielberg, and producers Scott Rudin and James L. Nederlander. Bono and his family lived on a floor higher than Squier's unit. Bono noticed smoke coming into his apartment from lower apartments in the building, and he complained. The use of fireplaces in the building was banned while the problem was studied. Squier had a fireplace in his apartment and was displeased at the ban. According to news reports at the time, renovations over the years to the 1930s-era building may have caused chimney ventilation problems. Although some tests indicated unhealthy levels of smoke emissions, contemporary news reports stated it was unclear whether the problems could be corrected or whether the building was so far out of compliance with modern building codes that corrections would be prohibitively expensive. Unfortunately, there are no later news reports on how or if this situation was resolved. But the dispute shows just how sensitive neighbors can be to perceived nuisances.

FIXTURES

To understand the law about fixtures, you must first understand the basic difference between real property and personal property. Real property is land and anything that is permanently attached to the land. Real property is immovable. Personal property is everything else. Personal property is any type of property that can be moved, such as cars, computers, furniture, clothing, food, and even pets. Personal property also includes intangible property, such as copyrights and trademarks, and shares in a corporation. One type of property can be converted into the other. If you go to Home Depot and buy lumber, nails, bricks, cement, and other building materials, you can then build a house on your land. The building materials are personal property when you carry them out of Home Depot, but once they become a house, they are real property because the house is attached to the land. Similarly, if you demolish a house—which is real property—the broken up materials have once again become personal property and can be carted away from the land.

A fixture is some item of personal property that has been attached to a building. A satellite dish can be a fixture when you attach it to the wall or balcony rail of your apartment. A cabinet that you bought at IKEA becomes a fixture when you screw it to the wall in your kitchen. So why is this important? Remember who owns the building where you rent your apartment—the landlord and not you. The law says that anything that is fixed to the land becomes part of the land and belongs to the landlord.

> Javier is a recording engineer. He builds a sound studio in the second bedroom of his apartment. He builds some shelves on the wall to hold speakers, and he builds a cabinet to hold the mixer board and other equipment. Javier has not consulted his landlord before doing this work. A year later, Javier rents an office and wants to move all of his cabinets and shelves to that office. The landlord claims that the shelves and cabinet are fixed to the building, which is fixed to the land, and they now belong to him.

Who owns the cabinet and shelves? The legal test of whether an item has become a fixture is, can the item be removed and the premises left in substantially the same condition as when the tenant arrived? If so, the tenant is entitled to remove the fixture before leaving the premises. If not—in other words, the premises would suffer some substantial damage by removing the item—it belongs to the landlord.

Even if the item is not legally deemed a fixture, and the tenant can remove it, the timing is important. It must be removed before the expiration of the lease. If the tenant waits until the lease has expired, he or she will have lost the right to remove the item.

The best thing to do is to avoid the dispute in the first place. Before you install anything in a rented apartment, reach an agreement with the landlord about whether you can remove it when you leave.

ASSIGNMENTS AND SUBLEASES

The last point to talk about in landlord-tenant law concerns assignments and subleases. What if you have a lease, but you need to get out early? Or what if you will be out of the apartment for a temporary but, extended, period of time?

> Marguerite has just moved to New York and has found a great apartment that she managed to lease, beating out a hundred other applicants. She signs the one-year lease and moves in. One week later, an audition comes up for a national tour of that hot Broadway musical Marguerite has been dying to be a part of. She goes to the audition, and she is cast! The tour rehearses in New York for a month and then hits the road for nine months. Marguerite doesn't want to give up that great apartment. Can she keep it? And does she have to pay the monthly rent and just leave it empty for the whole time she is on the tour, or can she rent it to someone else for those nine months?

Under the law, in the absence of some specific clause in the lease that specifically prohibits it, leases are freely assignable and sublettable. An *assignment* is a transfer of all of the leased premises for the entire remainder of the rental term. It is a complete transfer of the lease from one tenant to a new one. A *sublease* is a transfer of only part of the leased premises or a transfer of the whole leased premises but for only a part of the time remaining in the rental term. It is a partial transfer of the leased premises to a new, temporary tenant.

In Marguerite's case, her lease runs for one year. She will have lived there for only five weeks when the tour leaves town. If her lease does not have a clause prohibiting it, she can *sublet* the entire apartment while she is gone. It is a sublease because she is turning over possession of the whole apartment to another tenant, but only for a portion of the remaining lease term. When Marguerite returns from the tour, there will still be a little less than two months left of the one-year lease term. Her subtenant will move out, and she will move back in.

By contrast, if Marguerite decides to give up the apartment altogether, and the lease does not forbid it, she can find a new tenant and *assign* the entire lease to that person. Then the new tenant will take over the entire apartment for the entire remainder of the one-year term, and Marguerite will no longer have any interest in the lease at all. She will need to find a new apartment when she returns to New York.

Many residential lease contracts do have restrictions on assignments and subleases. Some prohibit these transfers. Others allow transfers, but only with the landlord's consent. These restrictions are generally upheld by the courts, but they are interpreted strictly. To prohibit both an assignment and a sublease, the landlord must specifically state in the lease that both are prohibited.

If transfers are permitted, but only with the landlord's consent, the question can arise as to whether the landlord must consent or can refuse to consent. The law on this varies from state to state.

About half of the states require the landlord to act reasonably and in good faith in deciding whether to consent to the transfer. The landlord cannot arbitrarily or unreasonably refuse to consent to an assignment or sublet. He or she can only refuse to consent if there is a commercially reasonable objection to the new tenant. A "commercially reasonable objection" would be something that might put the landlord at risk of not getting paid the rent (e.g., the new tenant is unemployed or has a bad credit report) or the tenant has a bad reputation with prior landlords (perhaps the tenant has been evicted before or has caused damage to other apartments).

The other half of the states permit the landlord to refuse consent arbitrarily or even unreasonably to an assignment or sublease. In those states, the landlord has an absolute right to just say "no." California is one of the states permitting a landlord to refuse arbitrarily or unreasonably to permit an assignment or sublease.

In New York City, a law gives tenants the right to request permission to sublet from the building owner, and the owner may not unreasonably refuse such permission. However, the procedures are strict.[10] The tenant must inform the owner by certified mail, return receipt requested, no less than 30 days prior to the proposed subletting. The request must contain the following:

a. the term of the sublease,
b. the name of the proposed sublessee,
c. the business and permanent home address of the proposed sublessee,
d. the reason for the sublet request,
e. the tenant's address for the term of the sublease,
f. written consent from any cotenant or guarantor on the lease, and
g. a copy of the proposed sublease (along with a copy of the lease, if available), acknowledged by the tenant and subtenant as a true copy of the sublease.

The landlord has 10 days to ask for additional information, which the tenant must provide, so long as the request is not unduly burdensome. If the landlord fails to respond to the sublet request within 30 days, the landlord is deemed to consent. If the landlord unreasonably withholds consent, the tenant may proceed with the sublet. If the owner commences a legal action challenging the sublet and the tenant prevails in demonstrating that the withholding of approval was unreasonable or that the landlord acted in bad faith, the tenant may recover his or her attorney's fees. If the landlord accepts the sublease, he or she is also entitled to charge the original tenant a "sublet allowance," effective with the commencement of the sublet. In other words, for the time of the sublet, the landlord can raise the rent, within the limits of the law (in recent years this has been limited to a 10% increase). The increase is rescinded once the subtenancy ends and the original tenant returns. The original tenant is allowed to pass the sublet allowance along to the subtenant, plus up to an additional 10% (at the original tenant's discretion) if the unit is furnished.

Assignment in New York is much more restricted. A landlord can withhold consent to an assignment even without cause. If the landlord refuses consent for a reasonable basis, the tenant simply cannot assign the lease. However, if the landlord unreasonably refuses consent, the tenant is entitled to be released from the lease 30 days after a request to be released is given to the landlord.

Suppose you want to sublet or assign your lease, and either there is no restriction against this in your lease (in which case you can just do it), or there is a restriction but the landlord consents. Does this mean that if your subtenant or your assignee (the new tenant) fails to pay the rent, you have no responsibility? No, it does not. You remain liable for the rent for the whole term of your lease contract. On an assigned lease, if the new tenant fails to pay, the landlord can sue both the new tenant and you, the old tenant. On a sublease, if the subtenant fails to pay, the landlord can choose to sue both of you or to look only to you (the original tenant) for the rent. For this reason, it is a good idea to choose your subtenant or assignee carefully. Make sure that person is responsible and will reliably pay. The last thing you want is to be out on tour and get a phone call from your landlord demanding the rent.

What if you live in California or one of the other states where a landlord can arbitrarily refuse to consent to a sublease or assignment? Are you stuck? There is a legal loophole. There is a doctrine in contract law called the "duty to mitigate damages." Any time a contract is breached, the innocent, non-breaching party has a legal obligation to take reasonable steps to reduce the damage. The innocent party cannot just sit back and let the damages pile up. In a lease situation, this means that if a tenant breaches the lease and moves out, the landlord cannot just let the premises sit empty for the remainder of the lease term. The landlord has a legal obligation to mitigate the damages or, in other words, must take reasonable steps to try to find a new tenant. If no new tenant can be found, then the landlord can sue the breaching tenant for the entire lost rent. But if a new tenant is found, the landlord can only sue the breaching tenant for the difference, if any, between the rent that was required under the old lease, and the rent that is being paid by the new tenant.

> Adrian lives in Los Angeles. He has just signed a one-year lease on a new apartment. His rent is $1,500 per month. But one month later, he books a supporting lead role on a television series that shoots in Atlanta. Adrian needs to move to Atlanta for the next eight months. Adrian's landlord, Hollywood Homes Corporation, refuses to allow either a sublease or an assignment. Adrian decides to just break the lease and move out anyway. After all, the money he will earn shooting the series is much more than even the full amount of rent he would owe on the lease. Can Hollywood Homes Corporation sue Adrian for $1,500 multiplied by 11 months (i.e., $16,500)?

No, the landlord cannot do that. Hollywood Homes Corporation must try to mitigate the damages by finding a new tenant. Fortunately, housing is in short supply in Los Angeles, so it is not difficult for a landlord to re-rent an apartment.

> Hollywood Homes Corporation rents the apartment one month later to a new tenant, but the new tenant will pay only $1,400 per month. There is a shortfall to Hollywood Homes Corporation of $100 per month.

Hollywood Homes Corporation can sue Adrian for $2,500—the entire $1,500 for the one month that the apartment was empty before the new tenant moved in, plus $100 per month for the remaining 10 months of his lease after that.

On the other hand, if the new tenant will pay more rent than Adrian—say $1,600 per month—the most that Hollywood Homes Corporation can sue

Adrian for is $500, which is the difference between the amount Adrian would have paid for 11 months ($16,500), and the amount Hollywood Homes Corporation will receive from the new tenant for the remaining 10 months ($16,000).

Even though you might not have a legal reason to break your lease, you might not suffer large liability exposure if you do so. The landlord's legal duty to mitigate damages gives you an extra buffer against a lawsuit. In many cases, if the landlord can re-rent the apartment quickly and for the same or greater amount of rent as you were paying, the landlord will not even bother suing you. It is just not worth the time or trouble for the landlord to do so.

14

Employment Law for Actors

Discrimination in the Workplace, Sexual Harassment, Workplace Safety, and Immigration Laws

As an actor, most of the time you will work as an employee. You will provide your acting services at the location of the film studio, TV network, theater, or other company that has cast you, and you will work according to the direction and requirements of the project's producers and director. You need to understand the basics of employment laws, including laws on discrimination, workplace conditions, and sexual harassment.

EMPLOYMENT AT WILL

Historically, employment relationships were governed by the common law doctrine of "employment at will." This meant that, in the absence of a contract that specified the particular length of employment or the grounds for firing the employee, either the employer or the employee could terminate the relationship at any time, for any reason, or even for no reason at all. Today, the employment relationship is not only subject to the terms of any employment contract but is also regulated by both state and federal laws that have markedly eroded the employment-at-will doctrine.

When you are cast in a project, you will usually have a contract. The employment will not be "at will." Rather, the length of the employment will be determined by the particular job or project as expressed in the contract. If you are cast in a stage play that has a limited run or specific tour length, the job will end when the show closes. On the other hand, if you are cast in a long-running

Broadway show, the employment may be for an indefinite period of time. But even then, your Equity contract will normally provide that either you or the producer can terminate the employment on two weeks' notice. If you are playing a role in a film or you are working on a commercial, you will be employed only for the dates specified in the contract. But if your role is a regular character in a TV series, your contract may specify that you are bound for as long as the series continues (up to a maximum of seven years in California).

Even in these various situations, the producer of the project may have the right to terminate your contract early if you breach some obligation in the contract. This could be something as obvious as failing to show up for rehearsals or performances, but it could also include general dissatisfaction by the producer with your work because most contracts will have a clause specifying that your acting services will "comply with all directions, requests, rules and regulations of Producer, whether or not the same involve matters of artistic taste or judgment."

> Zachary is producing a medium-budget, action film with several well-known actors in the lead roles. The final scene in the film is a shoot-out in an abandoned airplane hangar. Because of scheduling complications, that scene is scheduled as the first scene to be filmed. All of the actors are present and are called to the set. One of the lead actors refuses to come out of his dressing room trailer. The director goes to speak with him, and then Zachary tries to convince him to come to the set but to no avail. The actor will not come out and will not explain why. Because Zachary cannot afford to wait, the actor is fired. The next day, a replacement is brought in to play the role. Later, drug paraphernalia is discovered in the actor's trailer, but Zachary is not sure if drugs were the cause of the actor's strange behavior.

In this case, the actor has failed to comply with the producer's directions, so the producer has the legal right to fire him.

An actor also has the legal right to terminate the contract if the producer breaches it. Most of the time, however, the only breach by a producer that would justify an actor terminating the contract is a failure to pay the actor's compensation. If that does occur, the actor can refuse to provide further work and can sue (or file a complaint with the state's government employment agency) to recover the unpaid wages.

Now let's look at the laws that affect the hiring process and can restrict the ability of an employer to terminate an employee's job.

LAWS PROHIBITING EMPLOYMENT DISCRIMINATION

The Civil Rights Act of 1964

This landmark law prohibits discrimination in employment on the basis of race, sex, color, religion, and national origin.[1] The law applies to employers engaged in interstate commerce who have 15 or more employees.[2] Many state laws are modeled after and may expand on the Civil Rights Act. The Civil Rights Act affects both the hiring and the firing processes. Employers cannot refuse to hire someone solely because of the person's race, sex, color, religion, or national origin. The employer also cannot fire someone solely on the basis of these categories.

Most of these categories have obvious meanings, but employment discrimination based on "sex" is more uncertain. Roughly half the states have laws protecting sexual orientation from employment discrimination, but until recently the federal government did not. According to the Equal Employment Opportunity Commission (EEOC), which is the federal agency that investigates violations of the Civil Rights Act and enforces the rights of employees, sex includes sexual orientation.[3] Thus, the EEOC says it would be illegal for an employer to refuse to hire someone simply because that person is gay, lesbian, bisexual, or transgender. Most federal courts had disagreed with the EEOC's interpretation and held that sex does not include sexual orientation and that employers were free to discriminate based on sexual orientation. However, on October 8, 2019, the US Supreme Court heard argument on three cases on this issue.[4] On June 15, 2020, the Court issued a single opinion on all three cases and held that Title VII of the Civil Rights Act of 1964 forbids an employer from firing an individual for being homosexual or transgender. The Court swept away any uncertainty on this issue by saying, "An individual's homosexuality or transgender status is not relevant to employment decisions." Importantly, the Court further held that "sex" (or sexual orientation) does not have to be the only reason for the discrimination. The Court said, "An employer violates Title VII when it intentionally fires an individual employee based in part on sex. It doesn't matter if other factors besides the plaintiff's sex contributed to the decision." With this decision, the

Court settled the question, so it is now clear that employers cannot discriminate based on either sex (gender) or sexual orientation.

How does the Civil Rights Act apply to actors? A play, film, or TV script will describe certain characters, and the actors cast must match those descriptions. Generally speaking, gender is fixed; male characters must be played by male actors, and female characters played by female actors. Of course there are exceptions, particularly in certain stage productions (an all-female *Hamlet* perhaps?), but in film and TV, gender is usually not flexible. Race and color are not so fixed, and much of the time a character can be played by an actor of any race or color. Certainly, religion and national origin should have no relevance to which actor can play a given role. And returning to sex, an actor's sexual orientation should also be irrelevant. Thus, the Civil Rights Act certainly applies to casting of actors, at least within the artistic parameters dictated by the project's script. If you audition for a role and circumstances indicate that you have been denied the role simply because of your race, color, religion, national origin, or sexual orientation, you may have been the victim of illegal employment discrimination. Likewise, if you are cast in a role but then are replaced or fired for reasons related to these protected categories, that would also be illegal. In either case, you may want to contact the EEOC or state employment agency about the issue.

Pregnancy Discrimination Act

Women's employment rights are protected by an additional law—the Pregnancy Discrimination Act.[5] This law says that employers must treat women affected by pregnancy the same as other nonpregnant workers who are similar in their ability or inability to work.

The US Supreme Court explained the application of this law a few years ago in the case of *Young v. UPS*.[6] Peggy Young worked as a part-time driver for United Parcel Service (UPS). Her responsibilities included pickup and delivery of packages that had arrived by air carrier the previous night. In 2006, after suffering several miscarriages, she became pregnant. Her doctor told her that she should not lift more than 20 pounds during the first 20 weeks of her pregnancy or more than 10 pounds thereafter. UPS required drivers like Young to be able to lift parcels weighing up to 70 pounds (and up to 150 pounds with assistance). UPS told Young she could not work while under a lifting restriction. Young consequently stayed home without pay during most of the time she was pregnant and eventually lost her employee medical coverage. Young sued and claimed discrimination under the Pregnancy Discrimination Act. Young said that UPS acted unlawfully in refusing to accommodate her pregnancy-related lifting restriction. She alleged that her coworkers were willing to help her with heavy packages, and she also said that UPS accommodated other drivers who were "similar in their . . . inability to work." UPS responded that the "other persons" whom it had accommodated were drivers who had become disabled on the job, those who had lost their Department of Transportation certifications, or those who suffered from a disability covered by the Americans with Disabilities Act (see the discussion of this law in this chapter). UPS argued that because Young did not fall within any of those categories, it had not discriminated against her on the basis of pregnancy but had treated her just as it treated all "other" relevant "persons." The trial court dismissed Young's case. She appealed all the way to the Supreme Court.

The Supreme Court disagreed with UPS. It held that a woman can make out a case of pregnancy discrimination by showing that she belongs to the protected class (she is pregnant), that she sought accommodation for her condition, that the employer did not accommodate her, and that the employer did accommodate other employees similar in their ability or inability to work. The employer can then respond by showing that it relied on "legitimate, nondiscriminatory" reasons for denying the accommodation. But those reasons normally cannot be just a claim that it is more expensive or less convenient to add pregnant women to the category of the other employees whom the employer accommodates. The Supreme Court went on to say that if Young could show that UPS accommodated most nonpregnant employees with lifting limitations but categorically failed to accommodate pregnant employees with lifting limitations, she would have a case. The court added that because UPS had multiple policies that accommodated nonpregnant employees with lifting restrictions, its reasons for failing to accommodate pregnant employees with lifting restrictions implied that UPS was engaged in intentional pregnancy discrimination.

The Pregnancy Discrimination Act protects women actors in two ways. First, they cannot be refused a role for the sole reason that they are pregnant, unless there are legitimate, nondiscriminatory reasons for refusing to accommodate their condition. Such reasons might include that the role requires physical stunts or other activity that would be dangerous or impossible for a pregnant woman to perform or that the role requires partial or full nudity for an artistic reason that would be inconsistent with a pregnancy condition. Second, the Act would prevent a woman who is already playing a role from being fired if she becomes pregnant. Rather, the producer of the show would be required to reasonably accommodate her condition, in the same way as the producer would accommodate other actors who had a temporary disability that affected their performance in some way. These protections can be illustrated by two cases of pregnancy discrimination against actresses.

In 1996, Hunter Tylo was hired to play the role of the new vixen in the upcoming season of the popular television series, *Melrose Place*, produced by the Spelling Entertainment Group. Tylo's character was intent on seducing the on-screen husband of the series star, Heather Locklear. Tylo became pregnant before filming for the season began, and the producers fired her before she had shot even a single episode. She sued under the Pregnancy Discrimination Act. The producers argued that her contract contained a clause permitting them to fire her if there was a material change in her appearance. They argued that her pregnancy would make her too fat to portray the sexy vixen. However, the evidence at trial revealed two major factors in Tylo's favor: Locklear had been pregnant during a prior season, and the producers had accommodated her pregnancy by using body doubles and creative camera angles to hide Locklear's pregnancy; and actress Lisa Rinna, who replaced Tylo in the vixen role, had recently announced she was pregnant and was permitted to continue working on the show in her role.[7] In other words, the employer accommodated other actresses' pregnancies but had refused to give the same accommodation to Tylo. The jury found in favor of Tylo and awarded her almost $5 million.

The other case involved Brandi Cochran, who was a model on the TV gameshow, *The Price Is Right*. Cochran had been one of the models on the show for seven years, from 2002 to 2009. She became pregnant in 2008. She alleged that the producers had spoken of her in glowing terms before she became pregnant, but that after she informed the producers that she was expecting twins, they treated her differently, making comments about her weight gain and her eating habits and removing her from the show's website. Cochran's son was stillborn in February 2009, and her daughter was born prematurely a month later. Because of these complications, it was a year later before she asked to return to the show. She alleged that producer Kathy Greco told her that she was not being invited back. She sued, claiming that she would still have had her job had she not become pregnant. The producers rejected her claim and said they were satisfied with the five-member model pool working with host Drew Carey at the time. At trial, the jury found that the producers had violated the Pregnancy Discrimination Act and awarded Cochran $775,000 in compensatory damages and $7.7 million in punitive damages.[8] The producers appealed the jury's verdict, arguing that their artistic choices were protected by the First Amendment. They further argued that their First Amendment right to free speech should prevail over Cochran's right to be free from pregnancy discrimination. The appeals court rejected that argument, saying the producers could not claim that the failure to rehire Cochran conveyed a protected First Amendment message unless they could identify what that message was. In other words, the producers would have to prove what message they wanted to convey by refusing to give Cochran her job back. The appeals court ordered a new trial, but the case settled before the trial began.[9] The amount paid by the producers to Cochran was not disclosed, but it can be assumed that it was a sizeable sum.

Americans with Disabilities Act

Similar to the Pregnancy Discrimination Act is the Americans with Disabilities Act (ADA).[10] This law requires employers to offer "reasonable accommodation" to employees or applicants with a disability who are otherwise qualified for the job they hold or seek. To have a case for violation of the ADA, a person must show that he or she has a disability, is otherwise qualified for the employment in question, and was excluded from employment solely because of the disability.[11] What is a disability under the ADA? The law defines this as any physical or mental impairment that "substantially limits one or more of major life activities."[12] If an employee with a disability can perform the job with reasonable accommodation for the disability, and if the employer can do that without undue hardship on the employer's business, then the accommodation must be made.[13] Examples of such accommodations would be: wheelchair ramps, flexible working hours, and improved training materials. The ADA also applies to job applications and physical examinations that are required for employment. The employer must make modifications to applications and the selection process so those with disabilities can compete.

Actors with disabilities cannot be barred from roles on that basis. There are numerous examples of successful actors, giving excellent performances, regardless of their disabilities. One well-known example is Michael J. Fox, who suffers from Parkinson's disease. Despite his condition, he has appeared in numerous guest star and recurring roles on such television series as *The Good Wife* (for which he was nominated for an Emmy five times) and *Designated Survivor*. Equally well-known is Peter Dinklage, star of *Game of Thrones* (for which he has won both Emmy and Golden Globe awards). Dinklage's first film was *Living in Oblivion* (1995), in which he played an actor frustrated with the limited and caricatured roles available to actors who have dwarfism. Since then, he has proven that his dwarfism is completely irrelevant as he has turned in one brilliant performance after another. Another fine actor was the late Clark Middleton, who was diagnosed with juvenile rheumatoid arthritis when he was four years old. He did fine work in two series—NBC's *The Blacklist* and Hulu's *The Path*. And one must not forget Academy Award winner Marlee Matlin who has demonstrated time and again that hearing loss is no bar to a highly successful acting career. Of course, these are just four examples of the numerous actors with disabilities who are working every day. And the ADA protects all such actors. If you are an actor with a disability, do not be afraid to ask for reasonable accommodations in auditions and performances. The law entitles you to ask and to receive such accommodation.

Age Discrimination in Employment Act

This law protects individuals older than age 40 from workplace discrimination that favors younger workers.[14] A prospective employee cannot be refused employment solely because he or she is older than 40, and an employee cannot be terminated from a job solely because he or she is older than 40. Proving a case under this law is tough. The employee must not only prove that the discrimination was based on age bias but must also show that the discrimination was the *sole* reason for the adverse employment action.

Age bias is rampant in the entertainment industry. Younger actors work more regularly than older actors. Of course, actors who have become stars or names continue to work as they get older, but even they feel the pressure of aging. Oscar winner Anne Hathaway said that she began to feel it when she was still in her early thirties. She told *Glamour* magazine, "When I was in my early twenties, parts would be written for women in their fifties and I would get them. Now I'm in my early thirties and I'm like, 'Why did that 24-year-old get that part?' I was that 24-year-old once. I can't be upset about it, it's the way things are."[15]

Entertainment industry executives also tend to be young, and older workers are frequently replaced by younger ones. In a way, this focus on age is understandable because the primary target audience for entertainment products is young. The most desirable demographic of consumers is 18–34. This age group is the largest cohort and is generally thought to spend much more on entertainment products than people older than that. Because this is the group the industry wants to sell to, it is often thought that the people who develop and market entertainment products must also be young, so they understand the desires of the target demographic. It is also generally thought that young consumers do not want to watch films or TV programs filled with older actors, just like they don't typically listen to music by older artists. They want to identify with the entertainment they consume, and that means that younger actors and other artists are more in demand than older ones.

But the law says that an employer cannot discriminate based on age. Unfortunately, that law is widely ignored in the entertainment field, and because it is difficult to prove age discrimination, the situation is not likely to change, in practical terms. Still, it's good to be aware of the Age Discrimination in Employment Act in case you feel that you have definitely been the victim of age discrimination.

LAWS PROHIBITING SEXUAL HARASSMENT

Now we come to the subject of sexual harassment. The US Supreme Court has interpreted the Civil Rights Act's prohibition against sex discrimination to include prohibitions against sexual harassment. There are currently two forms of sexual harassment: quid pro quo, and hostile work environment. *Quid pro quo* (which is Latin for "something for something") is sexual harassment involving demands for sexual favors in return for job opportunities, promotions, salary increases, or other tangible benefits. *Hostile work environment* harassment occurs when a workplace is permeated with discriminatory intimidation, ridicule, or insult so severe as to alter the conditions of the victim's employment and create an abusive working environment.

It is important to understand that sexual harassment is not limited to op-posite gender harassment. It is still sexual harassment even if the offender is the same gender as the victim.

To hold an employer responsible for sexual harassment conduct by the employees, the plaintiff must show that the employer knew, or should have known, about the conduct and failed to take any action to stop it.

An infamous example of quid pro quo sexual harassment in the enter-tainment industry is the so-called "casting couch." It is unfortunately true that people in power in the industry have demanded sexual favors in return for offering roles or other employment to actors. In 2017, the publicity sur-rounding allegations of sexual harassment against once-powerful Hollywood producer Harvey Weinstein caused many famous actresses to come forth and talk about their casting couch experiences. But this is nothing new. Such inci-dents of quid pro quo sexual harassment have been occurring since the earli-est days of Hollywood. Nor is the problem limited to actresses. Male actors have been victimized as well.[16] However, this conduct is definitely illegal. The charges brought against Weinstein reflect a newer attitude in the entertain-ment industry toward this heinous conduct, but it still occurs. Do not allow yourself to be a victim. If you are pressured for sexual favors in return for employment, seek legal advice or seek assistance from the EEOC.

Turning to hostile work environment harassment, a potential area of violation occurs when there is required nudity or simulation of sexual acts, either on stage or in film or TV. A recent positive development to protect ac-tors in these situations is the rise of intimacy directors, who can rehearse and block intimate scenes. Pioneered by Tonia Sina, who developed the method of intimacy direction in 2004, and who, with Alicia Rodis, cofounded the nonprofit Intimacy Directors International (IDI) in 2016, the goal of inti-macy direction is to standardize the process of intimate scene blocking and rehearsal. Jessica Renae, managing director of IDI, told Backstage.com that intimacy direction, "lays down a roadmap for actors to follow. We talk about consent, we talk about where hands are supposed to go—what is the story we're trying to tell? This way, when actors are in the moment and rehears-ing, they know exactly what they are consenting to at all times, and they're never left up to the variable of what another actor feels like doing that day."[17] In 2019, SAG-AFTRA announced its aim to standardize the practice of inti-macy direction on all union projects.[18]

On the other hand, the hostile work environment sexual harassment also presents a difficult case in certain segments of the entertainment business because of creative freedom. In 2006, the California Supreme Court tossed out a lawsuit by a former writer's assistant on the television show *Friends*. The female assistant had complained that the male writers of the show regularly spoke graphically about their sexual preferences and experiences, which she found offensive. The court ruled against her, saying that California law "does not outlaw sexually coarse and vulgar language or conduct that merely offends." The court further said that the sexual environment was not illegal based on "the totality of the undisputed circumstances, particularly the fact the 'Friends' production was a creative workplace focused on generating scripts for an adult-oriented comedy show featuring sexual themes."[19] This case has been often cited as establishing that where creativity is involved, including First Amendment rights to free speech, there must be a more flexible attitude toward a sexualized work environment. Still, the law is the law, and in view of the "#MeToo" movement and more enlightened views on sexual conduct in the entertainment industry, a hostile work environment case might be successfully pressed in the future.

SAFETY IN EMPLOYMENT

Safety in the workplace is mandated for actors from two sources. First, for union productions, the various actors' unions require producers to maintain certain workplace conditions, including safety. Second, a federal law, the Occupational Safety and Health Act, mandates that employers provide safe conditions to their employees.[20] Under this law, employers must not only ensure safe conditions but must also keep records of work-related incidents. Employers cannot fire employees who report violations. The Occupational Safety and Health Administration (OSHA) is a federal agency that is charged with enforcing this federal law. OSHA inspects workplaces for unsafe conditions and can issue fines for violations of the law.[21]

In 2011, OSHA cited 8 Legged Productions LLC, the production company for the Broadway stage production of *Spider-Man Turn Off the Dark*, with three serious violations of workplace safety standards following four separate incidents in 2010 that caused injuries to cast members. OSHA's investigation determined that actors were exposed to the hazards of falls or being struck during flying routines because of improperly adjusted or unsecured safety harnesses. An additional fall hazard stemmed from unguarded open-side floors that lacked fall protection. Finally, the company failed to shield actors from being struck by moving overhead rigging components. OSHA fined the production $12,600.[22]

In 2009, OSHA investigated an incident at Walt Disney World. An actor was fatally injured in August of that year from injuries sustained during the *Pirates of the Caribbean* tutorial stage show when he hit a concrete wall on a new stage. OSHA recommended that employees rehearse on new stages before their first live performance.[23]

The low amount of the fine for *Spider-Man* and the mere recommendation for *Pirates* actually reveal how little is being done by the courts and OSHA to protect actors. Actors must speak up and enlist the help of their unions. SAG-AFTRA has a 24-hour hotline for emergencies, and actors should not hesitate to use it if they believe the producer is crossing a line. If you have any concerns about unsafe conditions on a set or stage, you should report those to the producer immediately, and if no action is taken or you still feel conditions are unsafe, you should report the matter to both SAG-AFTRA and OSHA. Your health and safety are important. Do not let a producer bully you into accepting workplace conditions that might jeopardize them or production schedules.

What if you are injured on the job or you become ill because of workplace conditions? You are entitled to have your medical bills covered by the employer's insurance, and you may be entitled to other compensation as well. This insurance is known as workers' compensation insurance and is required to be carried by all employers. This requirement is generally covered by state law, rather than federal law, so it differs from state to state, but all states do have such a requirement. If your employer does not have this insurance, it is a serious violation of law, and the employer can be fined by the state labor department. You also need to understand a limitation imposed by the workers' compensation laws. The insurance coverage is your exclusive remedy. If you sustain a work-related injury or illness, you can recover damages only through the insurance. You cannot file a lawsuit against your employer. There are limited exceptions to this, which vary from state to state, but for most situations, the employer cannot be sued.

IMMIGRATION LAWS AND LEGAL RIGHT TO WORK

Finally, we turn to a brief discussion of immigration laws and their effect on actors' employment. Federal law makes it illegal for employers to hire someone who is not authorized to work in the United States.[24] All newly hired employees are required to fill out the federal I-9 Employment Verification form and provide forms of identification that prove their right to work. You have probably filled out this form many times and provided copies of your passport, Social Security card, or similar proof of right to work. An employer who violates this law faces severe penalties. Monetary penalties for knowingly hiring and continuing to employ unauthorized workers range from $375 to $16,000 per violation, with repeat offenders receiving penalties at the higher end.[25]

If you are a US citizen or a have a green card (meaning you are legally a permanent resident of the United States), you are entitled to work for any US employer. But if you are a citizen of another country, you may need a work visa to work in the United States. Many actors in US film, television, and stage productions are from Canada, the United Kingdom, Australia, and other countries around the world. They need to obtain a work visa from the US Customs and Immigration Service before they can legally work for a US production.

The most common type of work visa for actors is an O-1B visa. These are for persons who have "extraordinary ability in the arts or extraordinary achievement in motion picture or television industry."[26] Actors who have established themselves in their home countries can provide evidence of their professional work history and "acclaim," including their résumé of productions, reviews of their performances, nominations or awards won, and similar accolades.

Actors who are not as well-established or are just starting out may still be able to obtain an appropriate work visa, called a P visa, if they meet the qualifications. There are several categories. The P-1 visa can be issued to artists who are members of an internationally recognized entertainment group. A "group" is two or more persons, and "internationally recognized" is defined as "having a high level of achievement in a field evidenced by a degree of skill and recognition substantially above that ordinarily encountered."[27] The P-2 visa applies to artists or entertainers, individually or as a group, who will be performing under a "reciprocal exchange program." This is a program between at least one organization in the United States (including management organizations) and at least one organization in one or more foreign states that provides for the temporary exchange of artists and entertainers.[28] The

P-3 visa is for artists or entertainers, individually or as a group, who come to the United States "for the purpose of developing, interpreting, representing, coaching, or teaching a unique or traditional ethnic, folk, cultural, musical, theatrical or artistic performance or presentation."[29]

The O visa is more desirable because it allows for work in many fields, it does not require the artist to maintain a home in the foreign country, and it can lead to permanent residence in the United States. The P visa is strictly a temporary visa, requiring an existing job and lasting for the length of that particular employment only, which cannot exceed one year.

Application for these visas requires legal expertise and takes time. You should not attempt to obtain a work visa on your own because there are many technical requirements and pitfalls. You should always consult and work with a qualified immigration lawyer.

If you are hired to work in a production that will tour internationally, or you are cast in a production that is based in another country, similar work visa laws will apply in those foreign countries. Obtaining these visas is often expensive, so you should make sure that your contract specifies that all fees and costs of obtaining necessary foreign work visas will be paid for by the producer or production company.

Part 6

HOW TO PRODUCE
AND PROTECT YOUR
OWN PROJECTS

15

Business Organizations, or Why You Don't Want a Sole Proprietorship or Partnership

In today's world, it has become much easier and more affordable for actors to produce their own projects. Many actors produce web series for the Internet. Some actors produce stage productions. Others make short or even feature-length films to showcase their talent as actors (and frequently their talents as writers and directors as well). In the past, the cost of shooting films required actors to team up with a motion picture production company or studio. Sylvester Stallone launched his A-list career by writing the screenplay for *Rocky* and then refusing to allow anyone to produce it unless he played the lead role. Still, he could not afford to do it on his own. He had to make deals with Chartoff-Winkler Productions and United Artists. But today, any actor with a digital camera, basic sound recording equipment, and editing software can make a film.

If you have an interest in venturing into production—either stage or film—there are a number of laws you need to know to protect yourself from lawsuits and to protect your finished product from theft. You will need to have a business organization through which the production is created. You will need to know how to negotiate and prepare contracts, not only with your actors but also with your crew, and later with the network, film studio, or theater that distributes or showcases your production. You will need to know how to work with SAG-AFTRA if you are making a film or Internet series or with Equity if you are producing for stage. You need to know about certain torts, such as defamation, and rights of privacy and publicity, to avoid getting sued. You need to understand production insurance, errors and omission insurance, and workers' compensation insurance. And you need to know some copyright law and trademark law so you can prevent your intellectual property from being illegally used or copied.

So let's get started.

BUSINESS ORGANIZATIONS AND WHY YOU NEED ONE

You should never produce a project under your own individual name. Doing so can subject you to tremendous liability. You can buy insurance to protect yourself in case someone is injured during the production, but you cannot buy insurance to protect yourself against breaching a contract, such as failing to pay the costs of production.

There are four basic types of business organizations. Two of those—sole proprietorships and partnerships—are not suitable for production vehicles. The other two—corporations and limited liability companies—are suitable, but the choice of which to use requires some thinking and planning. We will cover corporations and limited liability companies in chapter 16. First, let's see why sole proprietorships and partnerships are not good.

Sole Proprietorships

A sole proprietorship is the simplest form of doing business. It is a one owner business. For many small businesses, there are several advantages in operating as sole proprietorships, but there is a serious disadvantage also.

The first advantage is that there is little paperwork involved in opening a sole proprietorship—usually just a business license and a fictitious business name statement. Most cities will require the owner to obtain a business license, so that the city can collect a business tax, which is usually a small percentage of the business income. The fictitious business name statement is filed with the appropriate local government office. This document identifies the true owner of the business. If the business name is something other than the true name of the owner, a fictitious business name statement is needed, so that the public can find out who actually owns the business.

Amanda Actor wants to produce a short film. She decides to call her production company AA Films, and she will run it as a sole proprietorship. Because the name of the production company is different from her actual name, Amanda must file a fictitious business name statement with the county clerk's office to identify that she is the sole proprietor of AA Films.

If anyone who does business with Amanda's production company or any member of the public wants to know who is the true owner of AA Films, they can look up the fictitious business name statement at the county clerk's office to see that Amanda Actor owns the business.

The second advantage of a sole proprietorship is complete control of the business. Because it is owned by one person, the owner does not have to consult with anyone else about business decisions.

The third advantage is that the accounting of income, and the payment of income tax, is simple. All income of a sole proprietorship is income of the sole proprietor—the owner. The sole proprietor simply reports all of that income as his or her own and pays the appropriate income tax on that income.

So far, so good. But what about the disadvantage? It's a big one. The sole proprietor has unlimited liability to creditors. If the business loses money, and the assets of the business are insufficient to pay the business debts, the sole proprietor is still fully responsible to pay those debts. The sole proprietor's personal assets are at risk and can be taken by creditors to pay the business debts.

Amanda Actor's short film will take place entirely in one location, a restaurant. Amanda casts the five necessary actors, organizes a crew, rents camera and sound equipment, and makes a deal to rent a restaurant on a Monday, when the restaurant is normally closed. The equipment rental cost is $2,000. The restaurant rental is another $500. Amanda is shooting nonunion, so she does not have to pay her actors SAG-AFTRA rates, but she still agrees to pay each actor $100. The crew will not work so cheap. Combined, the camera operator, sound operator, lighting gaffer, and makeup artist will cost $800. Amanda also purchases production insurance, which includes both general liability and workers' compensation coverage, for $500. Her total production cost is $4,300.

Amanda has a private investor who agrees to fund the whole cost, but Amanda schedules the film shoot to occur before she has actually received the investor's money. The film shoot goes successfully. Unfortunately, the investor backs out, and now Amanda is facing a bunch of bills with no money to pay them. She has only $2,300 in her own bank account.

Because Amanda is a sole proprietor, she has unlimited, total liability for the production debt. She will have to use all of the money she has in the bank to pay the bills, and she will still be unable to pay the equipment rental company. If it sues her for the $2,000 and obtains a judgment, Amanda is liable for that judgment. If she fails to pay it, the equipment rental company can garnish her wages at her place of work—meaning they can force her employer to pay a percentage of her wages to the equipment rental company rather than to Amanda. The company can also report the judgment as a bad debt, which will seriously damage Amanda's credit, making it harder to her to get credit cards, borrow money to buy a car, or take other actions that require credit.

These problems are bad enough. But they can get worse if there is a lawsuit against the business.

Amanda orders pizza delivery to feed her cast and crew lunch during the one-day shoot. Amanda's production insurance covers loss or damage to equipment, and personal injuries that might occur on set, but Amanda did not really anticipate any problems, so she bought the minimum coverage of $200,000.

The pizza delivery guy is working part-time to pay for his college education. He is a music major, playing the cello, and he is really talented. He has already been offered auditions with major symphony orchestras. But as he steps onto the set with his boxes of pizza, he trips on an electrical cord that the gaffer has carelessly failed to secure with tape. The pizza guy falls hard, breaking his wrist. This injury ruins his career as a cellist. He sues AA Films for his medical bills and all the wages he will lose because he can no longer be a professional cellist—total damages of $1 million. He wins the case.

Even though it was the negligence of the gaffer that caused the accident, Amanda is liable under the legal doctrine of *respondeat superior*—the employer must answer for the faulty conduct of the employees. Amanda hired the gaffer, so she is vicariously liable for his negligence. The production insurance is inadequate to pay the pizza guy's judgment, and because Amanda is operating AA Films as a sole proprietorship, she is personally liable for the $800,000 shortfall. She will undoubtedly have to file bankruptcy, and that will follow her around for years to come, causing all kinds of business and financial difficulties.

As you can see, it is a bad idea to engage in production as a sole proprietor. The risk of unlimited personal liability for production debt and lawsuit judgments is just too great.

Partnerships

The next simplest type of business organization is a partnership. To have a partnership, there must be at least two people who own the business together. There can be more than two partners. Indeed, there can be as many partners as the partners desire to have, but there must be at least two partners. (If there is only one person, then the business is a sole proprietorship, of course.)

Forming a partnership can be quite easy. All that is required is for two or more persons to agree to operate the business together, manage it jointly, and share the profits or losses. This agreement can be either written or oral. Some partnerships have extensive written contracts that define the partnership and the duties and responsibilities of the partners. Other partnerships operate on a simple oral contract.

In addition to an agreement to share profits or losses of the business, in a partnership, all partners have joint ownership of the business and its property. This means that each partner has an equal ownership interest in the business with all other partners. All partners together own the business and its assets and property.

This does not mean that all partners' percentage interests must be equal. It is perfectly acceptable and normal for some partners to have a larger percentage interest and some to have a smaller percentage interest. As long as all partners agree, the ownership of a partnership can be divided in unequal percentages.

In a partnership, no matter how the finances are divided up, all partners generally have an equal right to manage the business. This can be an advantage because it means all partners have a voice in making business decisions. It can also be a disadvantage if there are many partners because it may be more difficult to reach agreement. If there is an even number of partners (e.g., 2, 4, or 6), it may even be impossible to make business decisions because the number of partners in favor of doing something may be equal to the number of partners against doing that thing, resulting in a deadlock.

As discussed, partnerships are easy to form. There is little paperwork required. There may not even be a written partnership agreement, although there can be one. Partnerships are also fairly easy to close down. If a majority of partners vote to dissolve the partnership, then the business will close after a winding-up period. The winding-up involves paying all debts of the partnership and then distributing the remaining money and property to the partners, according to their respective ownership interests.

There are other events that can cause a partnership to come to an end, besides a vote of the partners. If a partnership goes bankrupt, that will usually bring an end to the partnership. The death or retirement of a partner may cause the termination of a partnership, and a vote by the partners to expel one or more partners may bring the partnership to an end. However, as long as the partnership has more than two partners, the partners can agree that these events will not end the partnership. If there are only two partners, then of course the death, retirement, or expulsion of one of them must terminate the partnership because there cannot be a partnership with only one person.

There are tax advantages to a partnership that are similar to a sole proprietorship. For income tax purposes, a partnership is not considered to have a legal existence separate from the partners. The partnership does not pay any separate income tax on the income generated by the partnership business. Instead, the income passes through to the partners, in their respective ownership percentages, and they each pay their own income tax directly on the amount of income they receive.

> Amanda Actor has thought through the risks of making her short film as a sole proprietor, and she thinks maybe she needs a more experienced hand. Peter and Paul Producer are brothers who have made several short films that have proven popular on YouTube. Amanda asks Peter and Paul to help produce her short film, and they agree. Amanda, Peter, and Paul agree to plan and produce the film together, to jointly make all artistic and business decisions, and to share the anticipated profits from showing the film on YouTube and other Internet video sites. Because Peter and Paul have more experience than Amanda, they decide that Peter and Paul will each receive 35% of the anticipated profits, and Amanda will receive the other 30%.

Whether they realize it or not, Amanda, Peter, and Paul now have a partnership because they have agreed to operate the production together, manage it jointly, and share the profits. It is still a partnership, even though the profits will be divided unequally.

Does Amanda's new partnership work better as a production entity than her sole proprietorship would have? No, not at all.

Like a sole proprietorship, the main disadvantage of a partnership is that the partners have unlimited liability to creditors. If the partnership is unable to pay its debts, or if a lawsuit is filed against the partnership and a large judgment is awarded, the assets of the partnership may be insufficient to pay. In that case, the personal assets of each of the partners is at risk.

This problem is actually even greater than a sole proprietorship because the rule is that each partner is an agent for each of the other partners. As discussed in chapter 9, an agent is someone who is authorized or has the legal power to act on behalf of someone else. In a partnership, each partner has the power to act on behalf of the partnership as a whole, and the power to act on behalf of each of the other partners. One partner can enter into a contract with a third person, and all partners will then be bound by that contract.

> Paul decides that the short film will be much more marketable if they have a name actor playing the lead role. He contacts a talent agent he knows and makes a deal for a minor star actor to play the lead. The star's fee for the one-day shoot is $50,000. Amanda disagrees with this plan, but Peter and Paul out-vote Amanda, and Peter signs the contract with the star on behalf of AA Films.

As a partner, Amanda is now equally liable with Peter and Paul for payment of the star's $50,000. If the film fails to earn enough money from YouTube revenues, the personal assets of Peter, Paul, and Amanda will be on the hook for the star's fee, as well as for all other production costs.

Each partner has a fiduciary duty to each other partner. As discussed in chapter 9, a fiduciary duty is the highest level of trust in the eyes of the law. In a partnership, this means that all partners must work together in good faith for the benefit of the partnership and all the partners. No partner can take any action that would harm the partnership or the other partners. No partner can set up a business that would compete with the partnership. No partner can take any property or money belonging to the partnership. All partners must inform each other of any information that is important to the partnership business. Each partner has an obligation to account to each other partner for all partnership income, assets, and profits.

> As it turns out, AA Films' short film is really good, and it does indeed become popular on YouTube, earning significant revenues. In fact, it earns far more than any of Peter and Paul's prior films. But Peter and Paul are less than honest. They breach their fiduciary duties to Amanda and abscond with all the revenues, leaving Amanda with all the production debts, including the $50,000 fee owed to the star.

Even though Amanda voted against hiring the star, she is personally obligated for the debt because the contract was made on behalf of the partnership. The star can sue her for breach of contract. Amanda has a right to sue Peter and Paul for their share, but only if she can find them, and they have disappeared with all the money. Once again, Amanda finds herself in bankruptcy.

In our next chapter, we will retrieve Amanda Actor from the dark hallways of the bankruptcy court and give her another chance. This time, she will choose a better type of business organization to protect herself from unlimited liability.

Business Organizations, or Why You Want a Corporation or Limited Liability Company

Poor Amanda Actor ended up in bankruptcy when she tried to produce her short film as a sole proprietor. She also ended up in bankruptcy when she made a partnership with those two crooks, Peter and Paul. Let's give her another chance. This time, Amanda will select a business organization type that limits her liability and protects her personal assets. She has two choices: corporations and limited liability companies. Each has advantages and disadvantages that will be explored.

CORPORATIONS

In the world of big business, the most common type of business organization is the corporation. It is also a common business entity for entertainment projects. This is because a corporation provides its owners with a strong liability shield, which, as seen in chapter 15, sole proprietorships and partnerships do not.

A corporation is a legal person. It exists separately and independently from its owners, who are called the *shareholders*. The shareholders come together to conduct business as a single, legally recognized entity. The word *corporation* itself comes from the Latin word *corporare*, meaning "combine in one body." A corporation is a body of people. As far back as ancient Roman times, the law recognized corporations such as universities, political groups, guilds (or unions) of tradesmen or craftsmen, and even religious groups.

Corporations have a potentially unlimited life. Although shareholders can buy in, sell out, and die, the corporation itself can go on and on. According to some sources, the oldest commercial corporation in the world is the Stora Kopparberg mining cooperative in Falun, Sweden, founded as early as 1347. Another long-lasting corporation is the Hudson's Bay Company, incorporated in England in 1670 and still in business all over Canada.

A corporation has all the legal rights and duties of real persons. It can enter into contracts, buy and sell real and personal property, and both file lawsuits and be sued. A corporation has all the same rights guaranteed by the US Constitution to individuals in the United States. A corporation has the First Amendment right of free speech, and it cannot be deprived of its property without due process of law, meaning that there must be a regular court or other official, legal proceeding before a corporation's property can be taken from it.

Corporations are creatures of law. In each state, statutes have been enacted to allow the creation and operation of corporations. These statutes are usually quite extensive, covering everything from how to form a corporation, to how to conduct annual meetings of shareholders, to how a corporation must be managed, and even to the kinds of business records that a corporation must keep. New York was the first state to enact a corporations law in 1811, but that first act was limited to corporations engaged in manufacturing. During the remainder of the nineteenth century, many other states passed laws allowing for the creation of corporations that could conduct any type of business. All states now have such corporations laws.

Corporate Ownership

A corporation is owned by its shareholders. Each shareholder is issued one or more shares of the stock of the corporation. A corporation must have at least 1 shareholder, but small or medium-sized production companies may have anywhere from 2 to 10 or more shareholders. Large publicly traded corporations whose shares are bought and sold by the general public in the stock exchanges, such as the major film studios and television networks, have millions of shareholders.

Each shareholder's ownership interest in the corporation is the mathematical ratio of the number of shares owned by the shareholder, divided by the total shares issued to all shareholders. Thus, in a corporation with one shareholder, that shareholder owns 100% of the shares. But even a small production company is likely to have several shareholders, consisting of both the creators and financiers of the project. Let's work that math with Amanda Actor.

> Amanda forms AA Films as a corporation. She raises the money for her short film from her parents (Mary and Rob), her brother (Chad), and three college friends, who will also act in the film (Melanie, Marcia, and Charlotte). AA Films, Inc. thus has seven shareholders, including Amanda. It issues 100 shares of stock to its shareholders. Amanda holds onto 52 shares; each of the other six shareholders is issued 8 shares. Amanda owns 52% of AA Films, Inc., and each other shareholder owns 8%.

Corporate Management

Unlike sole proprietorships, where all business decisions are made by the single owner, and partnerships, where each partner has an equal vote in management issues, the shareholders of a corporation do not take an active role in management. Instead, the shareholders elect a board of directors. A corporation must have at least one director, but it can have as many directors as desired. A small production company might have only one or two directors. A large publicly traded film studio corporation may have many directors.

> Amanda sets up AA Films, Inc. to have three directors. The seven shareholders vote to elect those directors according to their number of shares. Amanda has 52 votes and each other shareholder has 8 votes. How many directors can Amanda elect?

A formula for calculating this is $X = S/T(D + 1)$ where:

X = the number of directors Amanda can elect

S = total number of shares owned by the shareholder

D = number of board seats up for election

T = total number of shares the corporation has outstanding

Amanda holds 52 shares out of 100. $S/T = 0.52$. There are three seats up for election, so we multiply 0.52×4, which is 2.08. Rounding down to the nearest whole number, we see that Amanda is assured of being able to elect two members of the board, which is a controlling number. She elects herself and her mother, Mary, to the board. Amanda now effectively controls the corporation.

The board of directors manages the corporation on a big-picture basis. It sets the overall business strategy but does not operate the corporation on a daily basis. The board of directors elects or appoints officers to run the corporation on a day-to-day basis. All of the officers of a corporation are involved in the daily management of the corporation, and they in turn hire all other employees. Several states require three primary officers: president, secretary, and treasurer. The president is the head of the corporation. The secretary is responsible for maintaining all official company documents and records. The treasurer is responsible for the finances of the corporation. Other state laws allow a corporation to have just a single officer.

AA Films' board of directors consists of Amanda, Mary, and Charlotte. The board elects the officers of AA Films, Inc.—Amanda as president, Mary as secretary, and Amanda's father, Rob, as treasurer.

Although those are all the officers needed for AA Films, Inc., many corporations have other officers as well. These include the chief executive officer (CEO, who may or may not be the same person as the president), chief operating officer, chief financial officer (who may be the same person as the treasurer), and one or more vice-presidents. If there is a CEO, that person is the top employee, the "captain of the ship." Some corporations have both a CEO and a president, and in that case, the president usually has less authority than the CEO. Large corporations may have several operating divisions, with a president or vice-president in charge of each division. For example, a major film studio might have a president of production, a president of marketing, a president of studio operations, and so on, with one or more vice-presidents under each of these presidents.

Right now, you are probably thinking, "Wow, corporations are kind of complicated." Not to worry. An actor doing his or her own project does not need as complicated a corporate structure as a major studio. Amanda's family and friends can do everything just fine for AA Films, Inc., and they will continue to do fine as long as they know the law and follow it.

So far we have talked about ownership and management of a corporation. Now we will see how a corporation is created in the first place.

The Articles of Incorporation

The corporation statutes in each state set the procedures for creating a corporation. These statutes all contain essentially the same procedure. A corporation is usually created by filing a simple document—often only one or two pages long—with either the Department of Corporations or the Secretary of State (the appropriate government office varies from state to state). This document is called the *articles of incorporation,* or sometimes the *certificate of incorporation.* The action of creating a corporation is called *incorporating.* The articles of incorporation contain a series of articles, or statements, that lay out the structure and powers of the corporation. The usual articles are:

1. *The name of the corporation.* A corporation can have any name, as long as it is unique and is not a copy of, or so similar to, another corporation's name that the public would be confused between the two. However, a corporation's name must include, as a suffix, one of the following: incorporated, inc., corporation, corp., company, or co. This is required to inform the public that the business is a corporation.

    Article 1 of Amanda Actor's articles of incorporation names the corporation as AA Films, Inc.

2. *The purpose of the corporation.* You don't want to restrict the purpose to something like, "production company," because you may want to expand the nature of your business later on. Most statutes allow you to state a broad purpose.

    Article 2 of AA Films, Inc. says, "The purpose of this corporation is to engage in any lawful act or activity for which a corporation may be organized."

3. *The name and address of the corporation's agent for service of process.* This is a real person who can be served with the court papers if a lawsuit is filed against the corporation.

    Article 3 of AA Films, Inc. says, "The name and address of this corporation's agent for service of process is: Amanda Actor, 1234 Wilshire Boulevard, Beverly Hills, CA 90210."

4. *The stock of the corporation.* This includes the number of shares of stock that the corporation is initially authorized to issue to shareholders, and the

classes of stock if there are different classes. Every corporation must have at least one class of stock, known as common stock. The corporation is not required to issue all of its authorized shares, but it must issue at least one share of common stock to at least one shareholder.

Article 4 of AA Films, Inc. says, "This corporation is authorized to issue only one class of shares of stock that shall be designated common stock, and the total number of shares that the corporation is authorized to issue is 1,000 shares of common stock." Although AA Films, Inc. could issue 1,000 shares, it actually issues only 100 shares to its seven shareholders. The other 900 authorized shares are reserved for later use.

The articles of incorporation are signed by the incorporator—the person who is preparing and filing the articles of incorporation with the state government. The incorporator is frequently a lawyer hired to do that work. Once the articles of incorporation have been filed with the state government office, the corporation exists. However, the initial paperwork required for the new corporation is not yet complete.

The Bylaws

These are the rules for operating the corporation. The bylaws can be many pages long. The bylaws cover such subjects as when and where the shareholders will have meetings, when and where the board of directors will have meetings and how many directors will sit on the board, what officers the corporation will have, what records and reports the corporation must prepare and keep, the procedure for amending or changing the bylaws if necessary, and any other rules that the shareholders or board of directors think are needed.

First Meeting of Board of Directors

Once the bylaws are written, the next step is to conduct the first meeting of the board of directors. The first directors are appointed by the incorporator.

The incorporator for AA Films, Inc. is Carl Counselor, the lawyer hired by Amanda Actor to form the corporation. He appoints Amanda as the first and sole director.

At the first meeting of the board of directors of AA Films, Inc., Amanda organizes the corporation by doing the following:

1. Amanda certifies that the articles of incorporation were legally filed with the appropriate state government office;
2. she adopts and approves the bylaws as the official rules of AA Films, Inc.;
3. she adopts the corporate seal—an actual metal stamp that contains the name of the corporation, the state where it was incorporated, and the date of its incorporation;
4. she adopts a form of stock certificate—a document that can be issued to the seven shareholders as evidence of their ownership interests in the corporation;
5. she authorizes AA Films, Inc. to open a bank account;
6. she approves the official address for the corporation's main business office—1234 Wilshire Boulevard, Beverly Hills, CA 90210;
7. she issues 52 shares of stock to herself, and 8 shares of stock to each of the other six shareholders; and
8. she elects the initial officers of AA Films, Inc.—herself as president, her mother as secretary, and her father as treasurer.

After this first meeting of the board of directors is finished, the shareholders (who were just issued their shares of stock during the board of directors' meeting) hold their first meeting. At this meeting, the shareholders elect the board of directors for the first year of operation of the corporation. These directors may be the same persons who were appointed the first directors by the incorporator, or they may be different persons. For AA Films, Inc., because the newly adopted bylaws state that there shall be three directors, the shareholders elect Amanda, Mary, and Charlotte as the directors for the first year of AA Films, Inc.'s operations.

Minutes of the Meetings

Are we finished with the formation of the corporation yet? Almost. The last step is for the newly elected secretary of the corporation to type up the minutes of the meetings. This is a detailed listing of everything that occurred in the meeting of the board of directors and in the meeting of the shareholders. You can think of the minutes as a "minute-by-minute" report. The secretary puts the minutes into the corporation's minute book—a permanent book (typically a three-ring binder) that will always maintain all minutes of all official meetings of the board of directors and shareholders.

Now the corporation has been fully formed.

The following chart lays out the steps for forming a corporation.

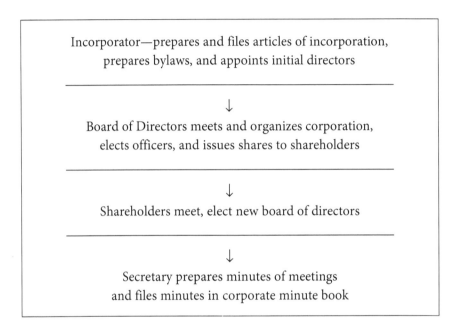

Incorporator—prepares and files articles of incorporation, prepares bylaws, and appoints initial directors

↓

Board of Directors meets and organizes corporation, elects officers, and issues shares to shareholders

↓

Shareholders meet, elect new board of directors

↓

Secretary prepares minutes of meetings and files minutes in corporate minute book

The Big Advantage: Limited Liability of the Owners

As you can see, even a simple corporation is a complex organization. There is a lot of paperwork involved in setting up and maintaining a corporation, and the ownership and management has multiple layers. Why then would anyone want to bother having a corporation? The answer is that there is a big advantage to this type of business organization—*limited liability of the shareholders.*

The shareholders pay the corporation a sum of money to buy their shares. If the corporation is sued and is ordered to pay a large judgment, the money paid by the shareholders—being part of the corporation's assets—can all be spent to pay that judgment. But the shareholders' personal assets are not at risk. They cannot be required to give the corporation any more money. No judgment creditor can try to take away or sell any of the shareholders' assets. Their houses, the money in their bank accounts, their cars and other personal property, in fact, all of their property, is protected from the corporation's creditors. The most money that a shareholder can lose is the money originally paid to buy his or her shares.

AA Films, Inc. has seven shareholders. Amanda owns 52 shares. Those shares were issued to her in consideration of her contributing her screenplay to the corporation. Mary, Rob, Chad, Melanie, Marcia, and Charlotte all have 8 shares each, for which they paid $100 per share ($800 per person). The total cash assets of AA Films, Inc. is $4,800, more than enough to pay the production costs of $4,300. All cast and crew are hired by AA Films, Inc., and AA Films, Inc. makes contracts with all its employees and all suppliers of equipment and production premises.

Now along comes that cellist pizza guy who falls and breaks his wrist. It is still the negligence of the gaffer that caused the accident, but this time the gaffer's employer is not Amanda. The employer is AA Films, Inc., so it is the corporation that is vicariously liable under the legal doctrine of respondeat superior. The pizza guy wins his case and obtains a judgment against the corporation for $1 million. The production insurance pays $200,000 of that, leaving $800,000 unpaid. Can Amanda, Mary, Rob, Chad, Melanie, Marcia, and Charlotte be ordered to pay any part of the judgment? No. A corporation has its own legal existence separate from the shareholders. The corporation is responsible for its own debts, and the shareholders have no liability for its debts. This time, Amanda stays out of bankruptcy because she and the other shareholders are protected by the liability shield provided by the corporation.

Raising New Funds

Another advantage of a corporation is the ease of raising money to expand the business. A corporation can issue and sell more shares of stock. Although this does mean that the percentage ownership of the current shareholders is reduced, the value of their shares is increased by the additional money brought into the corporation from the sale of new shares.

Amanda wants to hire that star actor to play the lead in her short film. The star's fee is $50,000. AA Films, Inc. has previously issued 100 shares of stock to its seven shareholders. But in light of the star agreeing to play the lead, a new investor, Maurice Moneybags, has agreed to put up the $50,000. The board of directors of AA Films, Inc. votes to issue another 500 shares and to sell them to Maurice for $100 per share (the same amount paid per share by the existing shareholders). AA Films, Inc. has now raised the necessary $50,000, and there are now 600 total shares issued and outstanding.

The new ownership of AA Films, Inc. is as follows: Maurice owns 83%, Amanda owns 8.67%, and each of the other six shareholders owns 1.33%. Although Amanda has given up majority ownership of the shares, AA Films, Inc. is now more valuable (its cash assets before paying production costs are now $54,800 rather than $4,800), and its prospects for making money from the short film are much greater.

Two Disadvantages of Corporations

The advantages of a corporation look pretty good, but there are a couple of significant disadvantages to organizing a production company as a corporation.

Double Income Tax

The first disadvantage is the potential for double tax on the corporation's income. In a sole proprietorship, the income of the business is the personal income of the sole proprietor. The sole proprietor pays income tax on that income. In a partnership, the income passes through to the partners, in their respective ownership shares, and each partner pays his or her own income tax on that share of income. But because a corporation is a separate legal person, it is responsible for paying its own income tax on all income it receives. By itself, this would not be a problem. The difficulty arises when we consider how shareholders make money from a corporation.

There are two ways for shareholders to earn income from a corporation in which they own shares. In large, publicly traded corporations whose shares trade on the stock exchanges, the best way to make money is to "buy low, sell high"—buy the shares at a low price and then sell them at a higher price. But there is no such public market for the shares of a small production company. For small corporations, the shareholders make their money by receiving *dividends*. A dividend is a distribution to shareholders of some or all of a corporation's profits.

AA Films, Inc.'s short film is a great success on YouTube. It earns revenues in its first year of $200,000. After paying for the $54,300 costs of production, it has a net profit of $145,700. The corporation pays a 21% income tax on that net profit,[1] so it pays $30,597 in income tax. It distributes the remaining $115,103 to its eight shareholders by paying dividends, in accordance with their percentage ownership of shares. Maurice gets 83% ($95,535.49), Amanda gets 8.67% ($9,979.43), and each of the other six shareholders gets 1.33% ($1,598.01).

AA Films, Inc. paid its own income tax of $30,597 on its net profits. It then distributed the rest of its income to its shareholders as dividends. However, those dividends are now income to the shareholders. Maurice must now pay income tax on his dividend of $95,535.49, Amanda must pay income tax on her dividend of $9,979.43, and the other shareholders must each pay income tax on their dividends of $1,598.01 each. But didn't the corporation already pay income tax on that same money? Yes, it did. The income gets taxed twice, once when it is in the hands of AA Films, Inc., as its income, and again when it passes to the shareholders by dividends, as their income. This double tax is a disadvantage of a corporation.

Potential Shareholder Liability

The other disadvantage of a corporation is the possibility that a court may allow creditors to "pierce the corporate veil." The corporate veil is the legal rule that a corporation has its own existence separate from its shareholders. It is because of this legal separation of existence that the shareholders have limited liability to creditors. As long as the corporation is treated as a separate entity, this corporate veil conceals and protects the shareholders from personal liability. However, it is possible to lose that concealment if the corporation is not properly operated and maintained.

When will a court pierce the corporate veil? The courts have identified many factors that weigh into the decision. Those factors include (among others): (i) *commingling* (mixing together or combining) money and property between the corporation and the shareholders; (ii) failing to conduct proper annual meetings of shareholders and board of directors and failing to prepare and maintain minutes of those meetings; (iii) an absence of corporate assets (all assets are actually owned by the shareholders) or *undercapitalizing* the corporation; and (iv) failing to prepare and maintain proper paperwork for loans, property transfers, or payment of debts.

The important point is this: If a corporation is to be selected as the form of organization for a production company, then all of the formalities of organizing, operating, and maintaining the corporation must be observed. The corporation cannot be treated as just the alter ego—a substitute personality— of the shareholders. The corporation must be treated as a truly separate legal person. That way, the limited liability of the shareholders will be preserved.

LIMITED LIABILITY COMPANY

Last but not least, let's take a look at using a limited liability company as a production vehicle.

Just like corporations, limited liability companies (LLCs) are authorized by statutes in each state. Unlike corporations, which have been used in the United States for more than 200 years, LLCs have only been in existence since 1977, when Wyoming passed the first law allowing creation of LLCs. All states now have laws providing for the organization of LLCs.

The LLC is a hybrid business organization form. It has the management and tax advantages of a partnership, but it has the limited liability advantages of a corporation. An LLC is not a perfect form of business organization—it does have disadvantages as well—but for many businesses, the advantages definitely outweigh the disadvantages.

Ownership and Creation of an LLC

Like a corporation, an LLC is a legal entity of its own, separate from its owners. The owners of an LLC are called *members.*

Also like a corporation, an LLC is created by filing a simple form with the appropriate state government office (such as the Secretary of State or Department of Corporations). The document is called the *articles of organization.* Very much like a corporation's articles of incorporation, the LLC's articles of organization: state the name of the LLC; describe its business in general terms; identify the agent for service of process; and state the LLC's principal office address.

LLC Management

In some states, the articles of organization have an additional requirement, quite different from what you would find in a corporation's articles of incorporation. In those states, the LLC articles of organization must state the method of managing the LLC. The two choices are *member managed* or *manager managed.* Similar to a partnership, the members of an LLC all have an equal right to participate in managing the LLC. However, the members can choose to have one or more members manage the LLC on behalf of all members. Member managers operate much like a partnership. In a partnership, the partners together (or sometimes a few managing partners) make all business decisions together. Likewise in an LLC, the member managers make the business decisions for the LLC. Alternatively, manager-managed LLCs operate much like a corporation's board of directors. The managers are hired by the members and make the business decisions for the LLC.

The nice thing about LLCs is that once the articles of organization are filed and the LLC is formed, there is no further required paperwork. There are no required meetings of the members, and no required minutes of meetings. There are no bylaws to create. Many state LLC laws require a written operating agreement, but in other states this is not required. Because the required paperwork to form and maintain an LLC is much simpler than for a corporation, the LLC is favored by many businesses.

LLC Taxation

An LLC can be set up to be taxed either like a corporation or like a partnership. If partnership tax status is chosen, then the LLC itself does not pay taxes. All income of the LLC will pass through to the members, in proportion to their ownership interests. Each member then pays his or her own income tax on the income received. This avoids the problem of double taxation that can occur with a corporation.

Disadvantages of an LLC

So what are the disadvantages to an LLC? There are four.

1. As with a partnership, the more members there are, the more people are involved in business decisions. This problem can be reduced by choosing to have the LLC managed by member managers or hired managers rather than by all members.
2. If the LLC wants to raise more money, it may be difficult. Just as with a partnership or sole proprietorship, an LLC cannot truly seek investors. It cannot issue shares like a corporation could. The only ways for an LLC to get more money (other than from business operations and cash flow) are to require the members to make additional contributions of capital, take

in new members (which would require consent of all existing members), or borrow the money from a bank or private lender.

3. An LLC might be subject to lawsuits in many states. For jurisdiction purposes, an LLC is considered to be a citizen of every state in which its members live. If there are members living in many different states, then the LLC can be sued in any of those states, even if the principal office of the LLC is located in only one state. For example, if an LLC only has offices in California but has members who live in New York, Florida, and Texas, the LLC could be sued in any of those four states. This can make defending lawsuits more expensive and difficult.

4. If an LLC is sued, its liability veil can be pierced and the members can be held personally liable for the judgment (or any other LLC debts), just like a corporation whose corporate veil is pierced. There are no required meetings of members and no required minutes of meetings, so the failure to maintain those formalities is not a factor in piercing an LLC veil. But all the other factors that would cause a corporation's veil to be pierced still apply. Commingling money and property between the LLC and the members, failing to provide sufficient money or property to the LLC to allow it to operate (undercapitalizing the LLC), or failing to prepare and maintain proper paperwork for loans, property transfers, or payment of debts between the LLC and its members can all be factors that would cause a court to find that the LLC is just the alter ego of the members.

MAKING THE RIGHT CHOICE

There is a lot to consider when deciding whether to use a corporation or an LLC for a small production company. It is definitely a good idea to seek advice from an experienced entertainment lawyer. But if you decide to produce your own projects, you certainly should choose either a corporation or an LLC as your form of business, and you should never choose to operate as a sole proprietorship or partnership. You want that liability shield, and you only get that with a corporation or an LLC.

17

Copyright Law for Actors

Creativity is big business. In the global economy, consumers spend nearly $2 trillion each year on entertainment, including buying books, music CDs or digital downloads, computer games, DVDs, and artwork such as paintings and sculptures; watching movies and television; attending concerts and stage shows; and accessing the Internet. Inventors create new products, such as smartphones, tablets, and computers, advanced computer-friendly televisions, new devices and software for playing music, and Internet websites, all to make it easier for consumers to enjoy that entertainment. Companies engaged in the business of entertainment (and business in general) actively protect their creative works by copyright, and brand their products and services by trademarks.

Intellectual property is the engine that drives this worldwide machine. There are four types of intellectual property: copyright, trademarks, patents, and trade secrets. The first two are the most important to you as an actor-producer, so this chapter will cover copyrights, and the next chapter will cover trademarks. You need to know some law of copyrights because you want to secure and protect your ownership of any content you produce. You also want to understand how to properly license your copyrights for use by others, so you can make money from your projects. Trademark law is important for you to understand because you will want to own and protect the titles of your projects (titles cannot be copyrighted but can be trademarked), protect your production company name, and build awareness and consumer loyalty for your products.

WHAT ARE COPYRIGHTS?

Under the US Copyright Act (and copyright laws of most developed countries), copyright consists of a collection of legal rights that are owned and controlled by an author. Copyright is automatically created in certain works of authorship when those works are "fixed in a tangible medium."[1] When a "work of authorship" is created in some permanent form that can be perceived by the senses—seeing it, hearing it, or touching it—the copyright is instantly attached to the work. For example, a screenplay or stage play is fixed in a tangible medium when it is written, either by handwriting or by typing, either on paper or in a computer file. A motion picture is fixed in a tangible medium when it is recorded on film or on a digital medium. Music is fixed in a tangible medium when it is written as sheet music or is played and recorded in some permanent way, such as a digital file on a computer, smartphone, or other device.

A Short History of Copyright

The first copyright law in the world was in England in 1710. The long title of the statute was, "An Act for the Encouragement of Learning, by vesting the Copies of Printed Books in the Authors or purchasers of such Copies, during the Times therein mentioned." The word *copyright* literally means an author has the right to control who makes copies of the work. As the title of this first statute indicates, the first copyright law only protected books. Authors were granted exclusive control over their books for a period of 14 years. As time went on, the protection of copyright was extended to many other creative works, including maps, paintings, and sculptures.

In the United States, the Constitution gave Congress the right to regulate both copyrights and patents. The first federal copyright statute took effect in 1790. Like the English statute, the duration of the copyright protection was only 14 years, but US law included a right to renew the copyright for another 14 years if the author was still living after the first 14 years. The statute protected not only books but also maps and charts—important in a time when much of the world was still unexplored and unmapped, and maps and sea charts had great economic value.

In 1831, the US copyright statute was extended to include protection for musical works. The duration of the copyright was also extended, to 28 years with a right to renew for another 14 years. In 1864, copyright protection was extended to dramatic works such as stage plays, stage musicals, and operas. This protection included, for the first time, the right of an author to control who could publicly perform the dramatic works.

The invention of photography led to extending copyright protection to photographs in 1870. Also in 1870, for the first time in the United States, copyright protection was given to works of art, such as paintings, drawings, and sculptures. At the same time, authors were given the right to control who could make derivative works—works derived from the original work—such as translations of books into other languages or stage dramas taken from novels. The right of music composers to control the public performance of their music didn't come along until 1897. Motion pictures first became protectable in 1894. In 1909, US copyright law was revised and the duration of copyright was extended again, for 28 years with a right to renew for another 28 years. Sound recordings could not be copyrighted at all, until the law changed in 1972 to allow that.

A major revision of the US copyright law occurred in 1976 (and the new law became effective in 1978).[2] Under this version of the law, pantomimes and choreography gained copyright protection for the first time. There was also a major change in the duration of copyright. No longer was there a first period of time and a right to renew. Instead, the duration of copyright became the life of the author plus an additional 50 years after the author's death. For corporations that owned copyrights (such as the Warner Bros. movie studio), the new duration was a single term of 75 years. This change in US law brought it into alignment with the copyright duration in other countries of the world.

Over the next 20 years, there were several more minor changes to the copyright law, including granting protection to computer programs, architectural works, and the digital transmission of sound recordings (such as radio stations streaming over the Internet). There was also one more significant change in the duration of copyright. In 1998, Congress extended the duration by 20 years. Copyright protection in the United States now lasts for the life of the author plus another 70 years after the author's death or 95 years for corporate owners of copyrights.[3]

In 2018, the first important new copyright law in decades became law—the Music Modernization Act.[4] This law creates a new blanket license for music streaming services like Spotify, Apple, Pandora, and so on, so they can stream music without having to negotiate individual licenses with all the individual artists. It is also a "compulsory" license, which means that artists cannot refuse to give those licenses to the streaming services (in 2014, Taylor Swift famously pulled her recordings from Spotify because she felt the royalties it paid were too low). But in return for the license being compulsory, the law creates a whole new system of setting the royalty rates based on the market value of the music, rather than arbitrary rates set by the Copyright Office. It will take some time for these new rates to be established and take effect, but it should result in a lot more money going to artists. The new law also protects sound recordings made before 1972, which were not protected by copyright before, so the streaming services had been playing those old recordings without paying any royalties. Finally, the law grants rights to sound engineers and producers to be paid a portion of the royalties that the streaming services pay.

The Public Domain

The 1976 Copyright Law eliminated many formal requirements for copyright ownership that had existed in the previous law. One critical requirement had been that copyright owners in the United States had to make sure each copy of their works displayed a copyright notice—usually the symbol ©, together with the author's name and the year copyright protection began. If any copy of the work was distributed to the public without this notice, the author lost copyright protection and the work fell into the public domain. The 1976 Copyright Law no longer requires this copyright notice, so the risk of a work accidentally falling into the public domain has been greatly reduced.

What is meant by the public domain? When a previously copyrighted work enters the public domain (such as when the copyright finally expires), it becomes free for use by anyone. It can be copied, distributed, performed, or displayed by anyone without permission from the former copyright owner. Also, anyone can use the work as the source for a derivative work. Let's look at that last point in more detail.

Mark Twain published his novel *Tom Sawyer* in 1878. The duration of copyright at that time was a total of 28 years, because the novel was published when the US copyright law provided for a first term of 14 years and a renewal term of another 14 years. The 28 years expired in 1906 and *Tom Sawyer* entered the public domain. The next year, in 1907, the Kasem Company, a film production company, produced a silent movie of *Tom Sawyer*. In 1917, another film company, the Oliver Morosco Photoplay Company, made another silent movie version of *Tom Sawyer*. In 1930, Paramount Pictures produced the first version of *Tom Sawyer* with sound. Because the novel had passed into the public domain in 1906, it was thereafter free for use by anyone. The Kasem Company was free to make its 1907 movie version of the novel without permission from Twain. Likewise, both the Oliver Morosco Photoplay Company and Paramount Pictures were free to make their own movie versions of the novel without permission from Twain's heirs,[5] the Kasem Company, or anyone else. Many other movie and television versions of *Tom Sawyer* have been made since 1930, including a musical version in 1973 and an animated version in 2000 in which all the characters were animals. All of these different versions are possible because the novel—the source material for all the movies—is in the public domain.

What Can Be Copyrighted?

In the United States, there are eight types of creative works that can be protected by copyright:[6]

1. literary works (such as books, magazines, newspapers, poetry, and computer software);
2. musical works, including any accompanying words (this covers both melodies and song lyrics);
3. dramatic works, including any accompanying music (such as screenplays, stage plays, operas, and stage musicals);
4. pantomimes and choreographic works (stories told with movement, and dances);
5. pictorial, graphic, and sculptural works (such as paintings, drawings, photographs, maps, and sculptures);
6. motion pictures and other audiovisual works (such as movies, television, animation, and computer games);
7. sound recordings (such as recordings on tape, disc, or digital file); and
8. architectural works (generally this is limited to creative works of architecture and does not cover standard designs, shapes, or features).

If you produce a film, an Internet series, or an animated work, you will have copyright ownership of several types: the screenplay is protected as a dramatic work; the film, series, or animation is protected as an audiovisual work; and if you incorporate original music in the work, the music is protected separately as a musical work. If you produce an original play, the play script is protected as a dramatic work. If you produce a new musical play, the book is protected as a dramatic work and the songs are protected as musical works.

As stated previously, copyright exists automatically when a work of authorship is fixed in a tangible medium. There is no paperwork required to own the copyright, nor is there any need to register the copyright. Simply creating a work that falls into one of the eight categories listed automatically gives you ownership of the copyright in that work.

However, there are significant good reasons to register a copyright, so when you produce a project you should make sure to do so. Registration is not expensive. You can register by filling out the appropriate forms online at the Copyright Office website (www.copyright.gov) and paying the filing fee (current fees are either $35 for a single author of a work that is not a "work made for hire" or $55 for a standard application, which includes a "work made for hire"). Registering gives notice to the world that you own the copyright, and it establishes the date on which the work was created.

Failing to register has two big disadvantages. First, if someone infringes your copyrighted work (uses it without your permission), you cannot sue them until you have registered the work.[7] Second, if you register only after an infringement has occurred, you cannot win any statutory damages (explained later in this chapter) or recover your attorney's fees for any infringing acts that occurred before your registration (unless your registration was within three months after the first publication of the work).[8] So register your copyrighted works as early as possible. It is a good idea to consult with an experienced entertainment attorney to make sure you understand the procedures for registration and do it properly.

The Exclusive Rights of a Copyright Owner

Once a creative work has been copyrighted, what rights does the copyright owner have? There are six exclusive rights that are controlled by a copyright owner.[9] They are:

1. Right to make copies of the copyrighted work,
2. Right to distribute the copies to the public,
3. Right to make derivative works based on the copyrighted work,
4. Right to perform the copyrighted work for the public,
5. Right to display the copyrighted work for the public, and
6. Right to transmit the copyrighted work in a digital medium (this applies to sound recordings only).

With these six rights, a copyright owner can control what is done with the creative work and also what is not done. When you own a copyrighted work, it is important to control the use of that work to be properly paid for the use.

For example, consider J. K. Rowling, the author of the *Harry Potter* novels. As she wrote them, Rowling automatically created and, therefore, owned the copyright in each novel. She then gave a license to book publishers Bloomsbury Publishing (in the United Kingdom) and Scholastic Press (in the United States), giving them the right to make copies of the novels and sell those copies to the public. She then gave a license to the Warner Bros. motion picture studio, giving it the right to make movies based on the novels. She also granted a license to Penguin Random House Audio Publishing, giving it the right to create recordings of someone reading the books and to sell those audiobooks to the public. Later, she granted a license to create and produce (and cowrote with Jack Thorne) the hit stage show *Harry Potter and the Cursed Child*, which extends the Harry Potter story. By controlling the way her books were used and sold to the public, and the derivative works based on the books, not only did Rowling make money from her creative works but so also did her licensees—the print and audiobook publishers, movie producers, and stage producers. All of that was possible because of the legal concept of copyright.

Now let's see how licensing these exclusive rights could work for you as an actor-producer.

Monique is an actor who decides to make a short film, showcasing her talent. She writes a script, gathers other actors, finds a director and crew, and makes the film. Now she wants to get her film out to the viewing public. First, she enters it into various film festivals. She gives a license to each film festival for the right to show the film in the festival. She also creates a poster for the movie, with a photo of herself and her co-lead actor, to publicize the film. The film wins some awards at these festivals and gains some notoriety. Now she puts the film on YouTube. She signs up as a YouTube Partner so she can make money from the advertising that accompanies the film. The film proves popular and garners hundreds of thousands of views. It catches the attention of an independent production company, which wants to expand the film into a full length feature film. Monique gives a license to the production company to write a new script and produce the feature film. A condition of that license is that Monique will play the lead in the feature film, just as she did in the short film.

Monique owns the copyrights in the short film's screenplay, in the film, and in the poster for the film. She has controlled this short film in many ways. None of the film festivals could show the film or display the poster without a license from Monique. That license gave the festivals the right to perform the film for the public and publicly display the poster. She makes money by licensing the film to be publicly performed on YouTube and shares in revenues from advertising. She gives a license to the production company to make longer versions of both the screenplay and the film, both of which are derivative works—the new script and the feature film are derived from the short film script and short film.

Fair Use

An important exception to the copyright owner's exclusive right to control the use of the work is the doctrine of fair use. For certain purposes, anyone can use a copyrighted work without obtaining any license or other permission from the copyright owner and without paying anything for the use.[10] This fair use only applies to:

1. *Criticism or comment.* Example: a television entertainment news reporter reviews Monique's short film and shows a clip of the movie.
2. *News reporting.* Example: a newspaper reporting on one of the film festivals provides an excerpt of the dialogue from Monique's film.
3. *Teaching (including multiple copies for classroom use).* Example: a teacher provides copies of Monique's screenplay to teach movie story structure.
4. *Scholarship or research.* Example: a professor writing a new textbook on the short film world includes a copy of the poster for Monique's film and discusses its story.
5. *Parody (a subcategory of "criticism or comment").* Example: a comedian does a sardonic riff on Monique's dialogue in his stand-up comedy routine.

If a copyright owner files a lawsuit against someone for infringement—use of a copyright without permission or license from the copyright owner—the defendant can offer the defense that it was a fair use. In deciding the case, a court will examine several questions:

1. What was the defendant's purpose in using the copyrighted work? (This includes deciding whether the use was for a commercial or noncommercial purpose.)
2. What kind of work is the copyrighted work? (A creative work such as a screenplay, film, or music will be given more protection than a less creative work, such as an encyclopedia.)
3. How much of the copyrighted work was used? (The more that is used, the less likely it was a fair use.)
4. What was the effect of the defendant's use, if any, on the market value of the copyrighted work?

If the court determines that the defendant's use fell within the fair use exception, the copyright owner cannot stop the defendant's use of the work and will not win any money damages for that use.

COPYRIGHT INFRINGEMENT

Suppose someone uses Monique's short film or screenplay without permission and without it being a fair use.

> Harry Hacker downloads a copy of Monique's film from YouTube, edits it to remove Monique's producing credits and other identifying characteristics, and replaces those credits with new ones identifying the work as being produced by Harry Hacker. He then uploads the changed film to YouTube and other websites in an attempt to profit from Monique's work.

Monique may want to sue Harry Hacker for copyright infringement. Let's take a look at what that means.

An infringement of a copyright can occur even if the copyrighted work is not copied exactly. There can be distinct differences between the two works. Exact copying is not required. Copyright infringement has occurred if there is *substantial similarity* between the two works. Generally, if an ordinary person observing the two works would recognize the copy as having been taken from the copyrighted work, then the copyrighted work has been infringed. It is not even necessary for a large portion of the copyrighted work to be copied. Copying a small but significant portion may be enough to constitute infringement.

A famous case involved the film *Amistad*, directed by Steven Spielberg. Barbara Chase-Riboud wrote a novel titled, *Echo of Lions*, about a true-life revolt on the Spanish slave ship *L'Amistad*. Chase-Riboud's manuscript was submitted to Spielberg's Amblin Entertainment for consideration as a movie. Amblin executives met with Chase-Riboud but passed on the project. Chase-Riboud's legal filings also alleged that David Franzoni, the screenwriter on *Amistad*, had once been hired by another company to adapt Chase-Riboud's book. Both Spielberg and Franzoni denied having ever read her book. The lawsuit did not allege that the entire novel was copied or even substantial portions of it. Rather, it alleged that 12 things from the novel were used in the movie, including the appearance in both the novel and the movie of a fictional black abolitionist who aided in the Africans' legal case.[11] After a series of settlement discussions, the case was dismissed by Chase-Riboud. News reports said it was not clear if Chase-Riboud had received any financial payment.[12]

Remedies for Infringement

If a copyrighted work is infringed, what remedies can the copyright owner obtain? There are basically three types: actual damages, statutory damages, and injunctions.

Actual damages means the money that the copyright owner has lost because the defendant used the copyrighted work without permission and without paying any money for a license. The actual damages are measured by the profit that the defendant made from illegal use of the copyright. The defendant is allowed to prove the amount of money spent in making the illegal copies.[13] In other words, the profit that the copyright owner can win is the net profit—the total amount of money earned by the defendant (the gross profit), minus the cost of making the copies, such as cost of materials, printing costs, and similar expenses. If the defendant happens to be a famous artist or author, he or she can also prove that fame increased the amount of money earned with the illegal copies; in other words, that a less famous person selling the illegal copies would not have earned as much.

What if the defendant made absolutely no profits at all, so there are no actual damages? In that case, a copyright owner can still win statutory damages.

The amount of statutory damages is set by US Copyright Law. There is a big range—the amount of statutory damages is "not less than $750 or more than $30,000 as the court considers just."[14] In other words, it is up to the judge or jury to decide how much to give the copyright owner for the infringement. Judges and juries look at many factors to make this decision, including the public interest in protecting copyrights, the value of the copyrighted work, the effect on the market for the copyright owner's work, and the defendant's financial situation. The defendant's "state of mind" is also an important factor. If the defendant intentionally infringed the copyright, the judge can increase the award of statutory damages to as much as $150,000. But the reverse is also true. If the defendant was not aware and had no reason to believe that he or she was infringing a copyright, the judge can reduce the statutory damages to only $200.

When a copyrighted work is being infringed, the copyright owner wants to put a stop to that. This can be accomplished with an injunction, which is a court order that the defendant stop the infringing conduct.[15] To further protect the copyright owner, the court can also order the defendant to turn over to the court all copies that have been made and all machinery, films, recordings, computers, or digital files that can be used for making copies.[16] The court can then order all illegal copies and devices for making copies to be destroyed.

As this chapter has illustrated, when you produce creative content, you own a valuable piece of intellectual property—the copyright in the work. You can earn money by licensing that copyright to others in various ways. You can also protect against theft of your work by invoking your right to sue for infringement. As an actor-producer, you will devote a lot of time, energy, and money to creating your projects. Make sure you get the most value from them by registering the copyrights, licensing the copyrights properly, and protecting against infringement.

18

Trademark Law for Actors

We encounter trademarks all the time in everyday life. Any word, picture, phrase, slogan, or any combination of these can be a trademark. A trademark is used to identify goods in the marketplace and to distinguish the goods of one seller from those of another seller.

You probably think of trademarks as applying only to products, like Nike and Adidas, for sports shoes and clothing; Wilson and Spalding, for sports equipment; and Coca-Cola and Pepsi, for soft drinks and other beverages. But trademarks also identify services. In the entertainment industry, this covers services provided by film studios, television networks, production companies, Internet services, music services, legitimate stage theaters, and many others. Some examples of service marks are Google, YouTube, Paramount Pictures, NBC, Netflix, Imagine Entertainment, Universal Music Group, and the Shubert Theatre.

Importantly for your work as an actor-producer, trademarks also protect titles of projects. The creative content you produce can be protected by copyright law, but the titles of those projects cannot. A title cannot be registered as a copyright,[1] but it can be protected as a trademark.

You have surely noticed the symbol ® on many products. That symbol means that the trademark or service mark is registered with the US Patent & Trademark Office. Sometimes, companies use the symbols ™ or ℠ instead of the ®. If a trademark is not registered with the US Patent & Trademark Office, it is illegal to use the ®.[2] But companies still want to let the public know that they use certain words, pictures, or slogans as trademarks, so they use the ™ symbol, which simply means "trademark." Similarly, companies with unregistered service marks use the ˢᴹ symbol to let the public know that their words, pictures, or slogans are service marks.

ACQUIRING OWNERSHIP OF A TRADEMARK

Ever since ancient Roman blacksmiths put their own distinctive marks on armor they made, merchants have been using trademarks to identify their goods. But how does someone become the owner of a particular trademark? Registering the trademark with the US Patent & Trademark office is not required for ownership of a trademark. A trademark is created and owned simply by adopting, or choosing, words, pictures, slogans, or phrases, and then using those words, pictures, and so on, in the marketplace to identify the goods. The first person to use a trademark for his or her goods becomes the owner of that trademark. The more a trademark is used, the stronger it becomes because more and more people recognize it and associate it with a particular business.

The ownership of an unregistered trademark is limited to the geographic market area in which the trademark is used. Someone else, in a different area, can use the same trademark for his or her goods. The public is not likely to be confused because the selling area for the two competing goods is separate.

> Michael has a small film production company called "Archangel Films" in Austin, Texas. Three years later, Norton starts up a production company in Atlanta, which he calls "Archangel Productions." Neither Michael nor Norton have registered their service marks. Michael finds out about Norton's company and sues for trademark infringement.

Michael cannot win that lawsuit. A trademark is infringed only if the public is likely to be confused and think that the services or goods of one company are in fact the services or goods of the other company. Although the names of Michael's and Norton's production companies are similar, there is no likelihood of public confusion because the service marks are used in separate markets in cities that are hundreds of miles from each other, so there is no trademark infringement.

Has this rule changed in the Internet age? Every company now has a website, and websites can be accessed from anywhere in the world. Does that mean there is no longer a geographic limit to a company's "market area"?

> Michael's website advertises his availability for hire as a producer/director. He also mentions that one of his short films, *Ocean Memories*, won an award in the Atlanta Film Festival. Elaine, a producer in Los Angeles, needs an independent producer to shepherd a production that is shooting in Atlanta. She wants to hire Michael, but Elaine mistakenly types "archangelprods.com" in her computer instead of "archangelfilms.com" and up pops Norton's website.

Because both Archangel Films and Archangel Productions have websites, Norton's service mark is now likely to cause confusion with Michael's, even though the two companies are far distant from each other. Remember that the first person to use a trademark becomes the owner of that trademark. Michael used his service mark first. His ownership is stronger than Norton's. If Michael now sues Norton for trademark infringement, he has a much better chance of winning the lawsuit.

Remember that in this example, neither Michael nor Norton had registered their service marks with the US Trademark Office. Suppose Michael did register? Is that an advantage, or is it just a needless expense? Registration is expensive, currently between $225 and $325 per trademark registered. But yes, there is a big advantage in registering. Federal registration expands the geographic ownership area for the trademark, and the registrant obtains ownership of the trademark in the entire United States, even if the business has only one physical market location in one city. If Michael had registered his service mark, Archangel Films, immediately on opening his business, he would have been able to immediately sue Norton for trademark infringement when Norton opened Archangel Productions three years later, and Norton would have to select a different company name.

When you produce projects, you create several trademarks. The title of the film, TV show, Internet series, or stage play is a trademark; the name of your production company is a trademark; even your characters' names can be trademarks. You want to make sure you protect those trademarks. Even if you do not register them with the Trademark Office, always use the ™ symbol next to your trademarks in all advertising, publicity, or any other use of your project in the marketplace.

DURATION OF TRADEMARKS

Once someone becomes the owner of a trademark, how long does that trademark last? The easy answer is that a trademark lasts as long as it is still being used in the marketplace to identify the goods or services. For example, Coca-Cola was first registered as a trademark in 1893, and it is still being used today—more than 125 years later!

The federal trademark registration itself does need to be renewed every 10 years. This is easily done by filing required paperwork with the US Trademark Office. But even if the registration is not renewed, the trademark ownership will continue as long as the trademark continues to be used in the marketplace.

However, a trademark can be lost. One way is if the trademark is abandoned. Abandonment is presumed if the trademark is not used in commerce for two years. If the trademark is abandoned, the rights of the trademark owner cease, and the trademark then becomes free for use by anyone else.

FAIR USE OF TRADEMARKS

Is it ever legal to use another company's trademark without getting permission? Yes, if it is a type of fair use. The most common fair use of trademarks occurs in advertisements, where one product is compared to a competing product. One of the most famous of these advertising campaigns was the Pepsi Challenge. Beginning in 1975 and continuing for almost three decades, Pepsi-Cola ran a series of television commercials in which a person tasted two colas, without knowing what they were. After the person chose the cola that tasted best, the brands were then revealed to show that the person chose Pepsi over Coca-Cola (naturally, the person's choice always turned out to be Pepsi because it was a Pepsi commercial!). Because Pepsi was using Coca-Cola's trademark for the purpose of comparing its product to the competing product, Coca-Cola could not sue Pepsi-Cola for trademark infringement. Pepsi's use of the Coke trademark was fair use. But another type of fair use applies to you as a producer—the artistic use of a trademark in a film, television show, Internet series, or even a video game.

A case involving the *Grand Theft Auto: San Andreas* video game illustrates artistic fair use of a trademark.[3] The game is set in the fictional city of Los Santos, but Los Santos looks like actual neighborhoods in Los Angeles because the game developers visited Los Angeles, took photos, and used actual locations as the basis for the game. The game scenery shows liquor stores, ammunition stores, casinos, tattoo parlors, bars, and strip clubs. One of the strip clubs shown in the game is called the Pig Pen. The plaintiff, ESS Entertainment, owned an actual strip club in Los Angeles called the Play Pen. ESS Entertainment's trademark showed the nude silhouette of a woman standing in the *P* of the word *Play*. The video game representation of the Pig Pen strip club also showed the nude silhouette of a woman standing in the *P* of the word *Pig*.

ESS Entertainment sued, arguing that the similar names and the similar drawings of the nude woman silhouette in *Pig* and in *Play* were likely to confuse the public into thinking that the Play Pen either sponsored *Grand Theft Auto: San Andreas* or approved of the fictional Pig Pen strip club in the game. ESS Entertainment lost the lawsuit. The court said the use of a trademark in an artistic work is protected by the First Amendment as freedom of expression. The court explained that an artistic work's use of a trademark is legal unless the use of the mark "has no artistic relevance to the underlying work." As long as the use has some artistic relevance, it is a fair use and is not infringement of the trademark, unless it actually misleads the public "as to the source or the content of the work."

As an example, if you produce a film in which two actors are sitting on a dock at a lake, drinking Corona beers as they carry on a dialogue, you can show the Corona trademark because there is probably some artistic relevance to the characters drinking beers in the scene, and viewers of the film are unlikely to be confused and think that Corona was the producer of the film. On the other hand, if one of the characters says something derogatory about the quality of the Corona beer, that could raise a different problem—not a claim of trademark infringement, but a claim of trade libel, which is a tort (see chapter 19 for a discussion of tort claims arising from productions). Although the First Amendment might still protect your freedom of expression in this case, it is expensive to be sued. So if you plan to disparage a product, it is better not to use an actual trademark to do so.

WEBSITE ADDRESSES ARE TRADEMARKS

As an actor, you should, of course, have a website. You will also want a website for your production company. At the very least, you should have a separate page on your actor website that presents your production services and projects. Your website address is also known as a domain name, and a domain name can be protected as a trademark. You can prevent others from using either your professional name or your production company name as a domain name. Even if the domain name used by someone else is similar but not identical to your domain name, you may still be able to prevent their use of their domain name. This is done by filing a dispute with the World Intellectual Property Organization (WIPO). You can find information about this on its website.[4] However, you should consult an entertainment lawyer to assist you with this process.

TRADEMARK INFRINGEMENT AND TRADEMARK DILUTION

Other than fair use, the use of someone else's trademark without permission may be an infringement. The legal test that a judge will apply to determine if a trademark has been infringed is *likelihood of confusion*. If the public is likely to be confused by the defendant's use of a trademark, and that trademark is owned by another (the plaintiff), then the defendant has infringed the plaintiff's trademark. What kind of confusion are we talking about? The public might believe that the defendant's goods or services are actually those of the trademark owner. The public might also believe that the trademark owner sponsors the defendant's goods or services or approves of those goods or services.

One famous case involved a woman named Samantha Lundberg, who opened a coffee shop in the small town of Astoria, Oregon, that she named Sambuck's. Her surname before marriage had been Buck, so she argued that Sambuck's was actually her own name. The Starbucks Coffee Company disagreed and sued her for both trademark infringement and trademark dilution.[5]

To win its case for infringement, Starbucks did not have to prove that any consumers were *actually* confused into thinking that Sambuck's was either a Starbucks coffee shop or that Starbucks somehow approved of or sponsored Sambuck's. All Starbucks had to prove was that the two trademarks, Starbucks and Sambuck's, were so similar that consumers were *likely* to be confused. The court found that there was likely confusion. A survey conducted by Starbucks found that more than 85% of persons who were shown the Sambuck's Coffeehouse name immediately thought of Starbucks, and 70% said there was a high degree of similarity between the two terms.

Starbucks also successfully proved that the Sambuck's trademark diluted the strength of Starbucks' trademark. The owner of a famous trademark can sue for dilution, which is any use of the trademark that will reduce its strength or fade its fame in the public's mind. In a trademark dilution lawsuit, it does not matter if the plaintiff's goods are in competition with the defendant's goods. They can be completely different. It also does not matter if the defendant's trademark is confusingly similar to the plaintiff's trademark. Likelihood of public confusion is not the test in a trademark dilution lawsuit. Rather, the test is only that the distinctiveness of the famous trademark is impaired by association with another similar trademark. This is known as *dilution by blurring*. Dilution can also occur if a defendant creates an association in the minds of consumers that is inconsistent with the preexisting good reputation of the plaintiff's mark. This is *dilution by tarnishment*. The court found that Lundberg's use of Sambuck's and consumers' association of the Sambuck's mark with the Starbucks mark would eventually diminish the distinctiveness of the Starbucks mark, so there was dilution by blurring. The court also said that there was no evidence that the Sambuck's coffee shop enjoyed the same "premium reputation that the Starbucks brand currently enjoys," and so there was also dilution by tarnishment.

Remedies for trademark infringement include money damages (the court orders the defendant to pay over to the plaintiff all of the defendants' profits made by using the trademark illegally and can also award the plaintiff any additional damages that the court finds have occurred) and an injunction (the court orders the defendant to stop the infringing conduct).

Don't Get Sued, or How to Avoid Committing Torts

As discussed in chapter 15, when you produce projects, you will need to purchase production insurance to protect you against general liability for accidents occurring on your film set or on stage. You will need workers' compensation insurance to protect against your cast and crew being injured or becoming sick because of workplace incidents or conditions. Usually, a comprehensive production insurance policy will also include workers' compensation coverage. In addition to these, you will also need a type of insurance called errors and omissions. This protects you against unintentional copyright or trademark infringement claims (it will not protect you against intentional infringement) and against claims for defamation or violation of rights of privacy.

Defamation and violation of privacy rights are torts. They can be inadvertently committed because of the content or subject matter of your script. Let's examine those torts more closely.

DEFAMATION

In Shakespeare's *Othello*, the character Iago makes this famous speech about reputation:

> Good name in man and woman, dear my lord,
> Is the immediate jewel of their souls:
> Who steals my purse steals trash; 'tis something, nothing;

'Twas mine, 'tis his, and has been slave to thousands:
But he that filches from me my good name
Robs me of that which not enriches him
And makes me poor indeed.

What was true in Shakespeare's time is just as true today: once a good reputation is lost, it may be difficult to regain. The tort of defamation is meant to prevent someone from damaging another person's "good name." There are two kinds of defamation: libel, which is committed by writing, and slander, which is committed by speaking. Statements made on websites fall in the category of libel because they are written. Broadcasts (TV and radio), films, web series, and stage plays that contain defamatory content are also considered libel and not slander, even though the audience "hears" the content because it is the written script that forms the basis for the audio content.

Both forms of the tort are committed when a defendant makes a false statement of fact about the plaintiff that harms the plaintiff's good reputation. The statement must be one of fact and something that can be proven to be either true or false. It cannot be an opinion because the First Amendment protects everyone's right to express their opinions, even if doing so might hurt someone's reputation.

In the production context, there is a risk of committing defamation any time a real person is portrayed or referred to in the story. There is also a risk, although less so, if a character has the name of a real person and is sufficiently similar to the real person that the public could reasonably believe the real person was the model for the character.

For example, in the film *Reality Bites*, star Ethan Hawke portrayed a rebellious slacker named Troy Dyer. In 2005, following the release of a 10th Anniversary Edition DVD of the film, a man named Troy Dyer sued Helen Childress (the screenplay writer), director Ben Stiller, producers Danny De-Vito, Michael Shamberg, and Stacey Sher, and Universal City Studios for defamation and false light invasion of privacy (this tort will be discussed), based on the allegedly unflattering representation of Troy Dyer in the movie. The 10th Anniversary Edition DVD included a running commentary on the film by Childress and Stiller, in which Childress stated the characters in the film were based on her friends at USC film school—including the plaintiff Dyer.

Dyer claimed his work as a financial consultant in Wisconsin had been affected by the negative association with the movie character. In defense, Childress claimed that Dyer gave her express permission to use his name for the fictional Troy Dyer. Childress asserted the use of Dyer's name was an inside joke because the fictional Troy Dyer was dissimilar to the real Dyer, who was "straight laced, mature, [and] conservative." Dyer denied that he ever gave Childress permission to use his name or likeness. After the release of the 10th Anniversary Edition DVD in 2004, Dyer was besieged by inquiries from potential clients as to whether he was the fictional Troy Dyer. That's when he sued.

The defendants argued that they were protected by the First Amendment because the film addressed broad topics of interest to the public, including the issues facing Generation X at the start of the 1990s. Thus, they said, the film involved the right of free speech in connection with a public issue or an issue of public importance. The court disagreed. It said:

> Here, the specific dispute concerns the asserted misuse of Dyer's persona. However, the representation of Troy Dyer as a rebellious slacker is not a matter of public interest and there is no discernable public interest in Dyer's persona. Although *Reality Bites* may address topics of widespread public interest, the defendants are unable to draw any connection between those topics and Dyer's defamation and false light claims. . . . In sum, assuming the issues facing Generation X at the start of the 1990s are of significant interest to the public, Dyer, a financial consultant living in Wisconsin who happened to have gone to school with Childress, was not connected to these issues in any way. Thus, the defendants failed to meet their initial burden of showing the activity underlying Dyer's lawsuit was in furtherance of the defendants' constitutional right of free speech in connection with a public issue or an issue of public interest.[1]

The serious mistake made by defendants in that case was using the name of an actual person and then portraying him in a false way, harming his reputation. This lawsuit could have been avoided in two ways. First, Childress could have simply used fictional names in her screenplay, rather than actual names of her classmates at USC. Second, if Childress really wanted to use Troy Dyer's name, the producers should have obtained a release from Dyer in which he gave them the right to use his name and gave up any right to sue. (See discussion of releases in this chapter.) Eventually, the case was settled, and presumably Troy Dyer was paid (an undisclosed amount).

You are not protected from defamation claims just because your project is based on a true story or even is a docudrama or documentary. In 2009, A&E Television Networks produced, broadcast, and released on DVD a multipart documentary called, *The History of Sex*. During the section covering the twentieth century, the documentary discussed the HIV/AIDS epidemic. The off-camera narrator was heard saying, "AIDS had exacted a deadly toll on gay men and [intravenous] drug users as well as hundreds of thousands of heterosexuals in Africa and Haiti. But it wasn't publicly acknowledged by [President] Ronald Reagan until well after Rock Hudson died of the disease in 1985." As those words were spoken, the documentary showed a back view of two men walking down the street at night, apparently holding hands. Just before the narrator said "drug users," the screen showed Miles Whitaker on the street at night, shaking a cup and nodding at people walking by. Just before the narrator said, "heterosexuals," the documentary cut away from Whitaker and showed a front view of two men walking arm in arm at night, including a clear shot of the left profile view of Whitaker for approximately three seconds. The documentary did not mention Whitaker's name, say he had HIV/AIDS, or say he was a homosexual or intravenous drug user. Whitaker sued for defamation, invasion of privacy, and intentional infliction of emotional distress.[2] While A&E claimed First Amendment protection, the court refused to dismiss the case, saying,

> A&E's documentary concerning the history of sex and specifically its discussion of the HIV/AIDS epidemic was, as Whitaker concedes, clearly a matter of public interest. However, A&E's act of speaking on the AIDS epidemic is not the principal thrust or gravamen of Whitaker's complaint. The principal thrust or gravamen of Whitaker's causes of action is the assertedly false portrayal of Whitaker as an intravenous drug user and HIV/AIDS sufferer. A&E does not suggest Whitaker is a public figure, and therefore, whether he is an intravenous drug user who is an HIV/AIDS sufferer is not a matter of public interest.

As this case illustrates, even if you are making a documentary, you have to be careful not to make people appear to be something they are not. Any person who appears on camera and is recognizable should sign a release. If you cannot get a release from someone, then do not use that footage, or use your editing software to edit that person out.

The tort of defamation includes a legal wrinkle when a celebrity or public figure is the person who is suing. Because such persons have intentionally put themselves into the public eye and are therefore legitimately the subject of public discussion, the Supreme Court has held that they must clear a higher hurdle to win a defamation lawsuit. A celebrity or public figure plaintiff must prove that the false statement was made with actual malice, which means the defendant made the statement either knowing that it was false or with a reckless disregard for the truth. It's a tough standard to prove, but in the right case it can be met.

In 1994, television and radio stations owned by Capital Cities/ABC in New York broadcast the following news report:

> The FBI is investigating a beating and abduction in Cheektowaga last night. Today, investigators are questioning John Prozeralik, the owner of John's Flaming Hearth Restaurant, in Niagara Falls, New York. Prozeralik was either tricked or forced to the Howard Johnson's in Cheektowaga according to police, where he was beaten with a baseball bat or pipe, and tied up. Today, the FBI is investigating the possibility that Prozeralik owed money to organized crime figures.[3]

Shortly after the report was broadcast, Prozeralik and his attorneys notified the television station that Prozeralik was not the victim in this story. The reporters then verified that the actual victim was David Pasquantino. The TV stations broadcast a retraction during the evening newscasts:

> Tonight, we have developments on two fronts in the abduction that ended yesterday in a Cheektowaga motel. First, the victim is not, and I repeat, is not, John Prozeralik, the operator of John's Flaming Hearth Restaurants. The FBI earlier today said and confirmed the victim was Prozeralik, but our independent investigation is revealing he was not involved.[4]

The court later found that this retraction was also false and misleading because in fact the FBI had never confirmed that the victim was Prozeralik.

Prozeralik sued Capital Cities/ABC for defamation. At trial, the evidence showed that naming Prozeralik as the victim had no basis in fact. A reporter testified that during their morning meeting about the incident and the possible identity of the victim, who was thought to be a Niagara restaurateur, one of the reporters said, "I wonder if it was John Prozeralik. . . . That's the first name that comes to mind." The court said, "This was a purely speculative question. The only connection was that Prozeralik happened to be one of many Niagara restaurateurs."[5]

Prozeralik was a public figure because he was a well-known restaurateur. As a public figure, he had to prove that the TV and radio stations had actual malice when they broadcast the report. The court said that he met that burden. In fact, there was no dispute that the night before the Capital Cities/ABC broadcasts, the actual victim, David Pasquantino, had been correctly identified by name in the evening broadcast of a rival television station. Capital Cities/ABC's own witnesses testified that the only reason their news employees speculated about Prozeralik's name was because they believed that the organized crime abduction victim was a Niagara restaurateur. But the court said, "Prozeralik was one of countless restaurateurs in the region but had no connection whatsoever to the crime, the criminal or the story, except for defendant's employees' rootless speculation and then glaring projection of his name into the public's eye."[6] Because the news employees had a high degree of awareness that their story was probably false, or at least must have entertained serious doubts about its truth, the court said they had actual malice in broadcasting it.

As these cases demonstrate, there is real potential to be sued for defamation if a project is about a real person, uses a real person's name, or shows a picture of a real person. So if you intend to make a project about a real person, use any real person's name, or use images showing a real person, you should obtain a release of claims from that person. A typical release of this type will read as follows—the "Granted Rights" are the rights given to you as the producer of the project to use the real person's name and image in the project:

I [the real person] agree hereby to release and discharge you [the producer], your employees, agents, licensees, successors and assigns from any and all claims, demands or causes of actions that I may now have or may hereafter have for defamation, invasion of privacy or right of publicity, infringement of copyright or violation of any other right arising out of or relating to any utilization of the Granted Rights. It is further understood and agreed that the Granted Rights may be used in any manner and by any means, and either factually or with such fictionalization, portrayal, impersonation, simulation and/or imitation or other modification as you, your successors and assigns, determine in your sole discretion.

This release not only gives you the right to use the person's name and image, it also shields you from being sued if you decide to fictionalize or dramatize the person's story, character, or anything else about the person.

INVASION OF PRIVACY

What about claims of invasion of privacy? Those claims were part of both the *Dyer v. Childress* and the *Whitaker v. A&E Television Networks* cases. So what is invasion of privacy? It is actually four separate legal claims. The first occurs when a person is placed in a false light. The second happens when private facts are disclosed to the public. The third occurs when someone intrudes on a person's private space. The fourth is committed when a person's name or picture is used for commercial purposes without the person's permission. Let's look at each of these four types of invasion of privacy.

False Light

This was the type of claim in both *Dyer v. Childress* and *Whitaker v. A&E Television Networks*. The tort is committed by portraying someone in a way that is not only false but is likely to be offensive to any reasonable person. In *Reality Bites*, the fictional Troy Dyer was a rebellious slacker. The real Troy Dyer was a mature, conservative, and respected financial consultant. The portrayal in the movie was false and would likely have been offensive to any reasonable person in Dyer's position. In the A&E documentary, Miles Whitaker was portrayed as a drug user and HIV/AIDS sufferer, when in fact he was neither. Any reasonable person would agree that these false facts are offensive.

Public Disclosure of Private Facts

The tort of defamation protects against false statements that hurt a person's reputation. What if the statements are true, but the person would prefer to keep them private? Does the law offer any protection? A recent case in

Canada illustrates that in the age of the Internet, there are numerous opportunities for this tort to be committed.

A young woman and young man were in a romantic relationship during
their final year of high school. They broke up before the woman moved to
another city to attend university, but they continued to communicate regularly. The young man asked the woman to make a sexually explicit video of
herself to send to him. At first, she refused. He persisted for several months
and reassured the woman that no one else would ever see the video. Finally,
she relented and sent him a sexually explicit video. He promptly posted it
online and shared it with several of his friends. The video was online for three
weeks before it was eventually removed. The young woman was emotionally
distraught, suffered loss of sleep and loss of appetite, and eventually required
hospital treatment. Notice that the young woman was not defamed because
the video was true and was made by her. But she had intended it to be kept
private for viewing only by her former boyfriend. The Canada court found
that her privacy had been violated by the public disclosure of the private
video, and she was awarded $100,000 in damages.[7]

How could this tort be committed by your production? If you make a film,
stage play, or other project about a true story, using only true facts, you cannot be sued for defamation because there are no false facts. But if those true
facts were previously private, and your project reveals them to the public, you
may have invaded the privacy of the person, or persons, involved.

> Sylvester grew up in the city. He joined a gang and began drinking and using
> drugs. One night, he and his friends were involved in a fight with a rival gang.
> Sylvester ran away from the fight, but after he had left, a member of the rival
> gang was killed. Sylvester and his friends were charged with the homicide. Syl-
> vester was eventually acquitted. He later moved to a small town, changed his
> name, married, had a family, and became a respected member of the commu-
> nity. Thirty years after the events, a filmmaker discovered the story of the crime
> and trial from old news reports and made a documentary about it, revealing
> Sylvester's new name and current location. Sylvester's reputation in his small
> town was destroyed.

The filmmaker in this fictional example could be sued by Sylvester for the
public disclosure of private facts. The facts had long since faded from public
view, but the documentary brought them back to light.

Intrusion

This tort occurs when someone intentionally intrudes, physically, electronically, or otherwise on the private space, solitude, or seclusion of another person or the private affairs or concerns of the person.

A famous example was the lawsuit by Fox Sports reporter Erin Andrews against the owner of the Nashville Marriott hotel. While staying at the hotel in 2008, Andrews was secretly filmed in the nude by a peephole camera installed by a stalker. The hotel was held to also be responsible for the intrusion because hotel staff had told the stalker which room Andrews was staying in and then had agreed to the stalker's request to be put in an adjacent room. Andrews won a jury award of $55 million.[8] The hotel defendants later settled for an undisclosed amount paid to Andrews.[9]

Use of Name or Picture for Commercial Purpose

The final type of invasion of privacy is the tort of misappropriation of name or likeness. Some states, such as New York and California, have passed laws that prohibit using a person's name or picture for advertising or other commercial purposes, unless that person gives permission. In other states, although there are no statutes forbidding this, judges have ruled in various cases that using someone's name or picture for advertising without permission is an invasion of privacy.

One famous case involved a former model, Russell Christoff, who had done a standard portfolio shooting job for the Nestlé Company. His contract stated that if any of the photos were actually used on a product, he would receive appropriate payment. Sixteen years later, he discovered that his face had been used on the product label of Taster's Choice coffee for more than five years. He sued and won $15 million at the trial. After a series of appeals, the case was apparently settled in 2010, for—you guessed it—an undisclosed amount.[10] This case reveals the necessity of getting a release from anyone whose name or image you intend to use in your projects. The failure to do so could prove costly indeed. It also shows that even if you get a release, you must then honor its terms and do, or pay, what you have agreed. (This case is also a good lesson for you as an actor. Even if you have given a release, or signed a contract, for use of your name and image, make sure you get the compensation that is agreed. If you do not or if the contract is somehow breached, talk to a lawyer.)

A related claim that applies only to celebrities is the right of publicity. This is the right of a famous person to control the commercial use of his or her fame. Using a celebrity's name or image without permission can violate his or her right of publicity.

Gary Saderup, an artist who made drawings of celebrities, was sued when he put one of his drawings of The Three Stooges on T-shirts and sold them. The court found that although he may have had a First Amendment right to create an artistic drawing of The Three Stooges, he had violated the comedians' right of publicity when he used his drawing for the purpose of exploiting their fame by putting the drawing on commercial products.[11]

By contrast, in 2014, Lindsay Lohan sued over the alleged use of her likeness to portray the character called Lacey Jonas in the game *Grand Theft Auto 5*. Her case was dismissed by the New York court in 2016 because it found that the game maker, "never referred to Lohan by name or used her actual name in the video game, never used Lohan herself as an actor for the video game, and never used a photograph of Lohan."[12] Even though the game character looked much like a photograph of Lohan, it was not Lohan's actual image, so her publicity right was not violated.

One of the most notorious cases happened in 2007, when well-known television actress and comedienne Carol Burnett sued 20th Century Fox Film Corporation for copyright infringement, trademark infringement, and violations of her rights of publicity and privacy. All of those claims came from an episode of the animated series, *Family Guy*. Near the beginning of the episode, character Peter Griffin enters a porn shop with his friends. Upon entering, Peter remarks that the porn shop is cleaner than he expected. One of Peter's friends explains that, "Carol Burnett works part-time as a janitor." The screen then switches to an animated figure resembling the "Charwoman" character created by Burnett in her television series, *The Carol Burnett Show*. The Charwoman is shown mopping the floor next to seven blow-up dolls, a rack of XXX movies, and a curtained room with a sign above it reading "Video Booths." As the Charwoman mops, a slightly altered version of *Carol's Theme* from *The Carol Burnett Show* is playing in the background. The scene switches back to Peter and his friends. One of the friends remarks, "You know, when she tugged her ear at the end of that show, she was really saying goodnight to her mom." Another friend responds, "I wonder what she tugged to say goodnight to her dad," finishing with a comic exclamation, "Oh!"

The federal court dismissed Burnett's copyright and trademark claims on the theory that the scene was a parody and was therefore protected under the First Amendment, as well as under the fair use parody exception of the Copyright Act.[13] The court did not rule on the merit of Burnett's claims of violation of rights of privacy and publicity, but Burnett did not pursue those claims any further.[14]

Once again, you can avoid being the target of lawsuits for violation of rights of privacy or publicity if you obtain signed releases from all persons who appear, or are referred to, in your projects. A release is simple to prepare and usually not difficult to obtain, whereas a lawsuit is always complicated and expensive.

TRADE LIBEL

Finally, if the script for your project disparages some actual product, there is the potential issue of trade libel. Trade libel is similar to defamation, but instead of harming the reputation of an individual person, trade libel harms the reputation of a company or its products. Trade libel is a false statement about the quality of a company's products or services that causes the company a financial loss. If your script calls for characters to trash a product's quality or reputation, you should make sure both the products and the company are fictional. This is not the time to rely on your right of artistic expression and use an actual company or its products or trademarks. Make up some fake labels or packaging and avoid the lawsuit.

20

Get It in Writing! Contracts You Will Need When Producing

You have formed a corporation or an LLC to serve as your production company; you are ready to obtain production insurance, workers' compensation insurance, and errors and omissions insurance to protect yourself from lawsuit liability during production; you have protected your trademarks either by registration with the US Trademark Office or by using the ™ symbol to identify all unregistered trademarks; and you have scoured the content of your script to make sure you will not defame any person or company and will not violate anyone's rights of privacy or publicity. You are now ready to move forward with production of your project. This chapter will discuss the various contracts you will need to acquire rights for plays or screenplays or true-life stories. We will also talk a bit about signatory agreements with unions.

ACQUIRING RIGHTS

Perhaps you will write your own play or screenplay for your project. But if writing is not in your skill set, you will need to acquire a script from someone else. You will need a contract giving you the right to produce the play, film, or screenplay. As you know from chapter 17, the exclusive rights of a copyright owner include the right to control public performances of the copyrighted work, and the right to make derivative works—works based on the copyrighted work. Plays and screenplays are both copyrighted works. To produce a play on stage, you need a license from the playwright to publicly perform the play. To turn a screenplay into a movie, you need a license from the writer to make a derivative work (i.e., the motion picture version of the screenplay).

Screenplay Rights

There are two ways to acquire the rights to a screenplay.

The first is simply to make a contract with the screenwriter, giving your production company the right to produce the screenplay as a film. We will discuss the terms of such a contract. The second way is to hire a writer to write a screenplay for you. This method falls under a section of copyright law called a "work made for hire."

When you hire someone to provide creative services that result in a "work of authorship"—a copyrightable work—you become the owner of that copyright. The Copyright Act says that a work made for hire is either (i) a work prepared by an employee within the scope of his or her employment; or (ii) a work specially ordered or commissioned.[1] When a motion picture is produced, all of the actors and crew will be employees of the production company, and all of their creative contributions will be owned by the production company as works made for hire.

Screenwriters can also be employees, but generally only if they are regularly employed on a long-term basis by a production company to write not just one script for one project, but many scripts for many projects (or many episodes of a TV series or Internet series). Most of the time, screenwriters are not employees but are independent contractors. They are hired to write a single script, either based on their own idea, on an idea of the producer, or on some preexisting work (like a short story, novel, nonfiction book, or magazine story). Their screenplay is a "specially ordered or commissioned" work. This is a work made for hire under the Copyright Act, and the employer can become the owner of the copyright in the screenplay. To acquire the copyright in a specially ordered or commissioned work, there must be a written contract with the screenwriter. If the contract is only an oral one, the copyright will not transfer to the employer but will instead be retained by the screenwriter.

Stage Play Rights

If you are producing a stage play, the work made for hire concept does not apply. Even if you specially order or commission a play to be written for you, you will not become the owner of the copyright. The playwright will retain the copyright in the play. This is because the Copyright Act provides that a specially ordered or commissioned work must fall within one of nine particular categories: a contribution to a collective work, a motion picture, a foreign language translation, a supplementary work, a compilation, an instructional text, a test, answer material for a test, or an atlas. Stage plays are not among those nine categories, so a play cannot be a work made for hire. Because you cannot acquire the copyright in the play, you must have a license agreement with the playwright, giving you the right to produce the play on stage.

SCREENPLAY RIGHTS AGREEMENTS

Let's take a look at a contract acquiring the right from a screenwriter to produce a film from the screenplay. The basic terms the contract needs to cover are compensation, credit, the rights you are acquiring, and warranties.

Compensation

There are usually two parts to an agreement for a screenwriter's compensation: the basic amount being paid to acquire the right to produce the screenplay and the back-end share of profits, if any.

The basic compensation can range from a low amount for a short film, low-budget feature film, or Internet series to high six figures for major motion pictures. If you are producing only a short film, you should try to negotiate basic pay of less than $1,000. If you are producing a low-budget feature, perhaps you should expect to pay as much as $5,000–$10,000.

An alternative way of setting the pay, rather than negotiating a specific dollar amount, is to agree on a percentage of the budget for the project. This can ensure that you don't overpay for the script. A typical deal would be to pay the screenwriter 1–3% of the project budget. For example, if the budget for your short film is $5,000, you might pay the screenwriter 2%, or $100. If you are making a feature film with a budget of $200,000, that 2% fee would be $4,000.

If you want to offer the screenwriter a share of profits, the range should be 2–5% of net profits. Net profits can be defined as all revenues earned by the producer (you) from the film, minus (i) the actual cost of making the film, (ii) all profit participation payments to other cast or crew who are sharing in profits, (iii) all taxes payable on revenues received by the producer, and (iv) any SAG-AFTRA or other union or guild residuals payable to actors, director, or other crew.

Credit

Credit is a highly negotiated subject for screenwriters. The Writers Guild of America (WGA) specifies screen credit in three ways: "written by" credit when both the story and the screenplay were original with the screenwriter; "screenplay by" credit when the story originated with someone else (either an original idea of the producer, or a screenplay that is based on a novel, short story, or true story); and "story by" credit if the screenwriter originated the story but did not write the screenplay.

You can use these categories as guides for negotiating credit with your screenwriter. If your production is not governed by the WGA because your screenwriter is not a member of that union, you are free to negotiate any credit that is agreeable to you and the screenwriter. Screenwriters will want a "written by" credit because that is the best, but if you have created the story, or if the project is based on a preexisting work, you will want to only give "screenplay by" credit to the screenwriter.

Rights Acquired

You want to make sure you acquire the broadest possible rights in the screenplay, so that you have the flexibility to market the finished film in any way you desire and also have the right to make future projects based on the film, if it turns out to be successful. Here is typical language for a rights-acquired clause:

> Author assigns and sells to Producer, entirely and exclusively, in perpetuity and throughout the universe all right, title and interest in the Screenplay, including but not limited to all motion picture rights, all television rights, DVD, Internet, and home video rights, and all allied and incidental rights whether now known or hereafter conceived, including but not limited to motion picture and television sequel and remake rights, music and music publishing rights, soundtrack album and other soundtrack exploitation rights, merchandising rights, theme park rights, other sound or digital recording rights, computer assisted media rights, radio rights, stage rights, and promotional and advertising rights. The rights granted include the right to distribute, transmit, exhibit, broadcast, manufacture and otherwise exploit all works produced in any and all media and for all devices whether now known or hereafter devised, and in any and all markets, as well as the right of Producer in its discretion to make any and all changes in, additions to and deletions from the Screenplay.

You also want to put in a clause about work made for hire because even if the screenwriter wrote the script long before any discussion with you about producing it, you are paying to acquire the script and it is essentially a specially ordered or commissioned work. So add this language to your rights-acquired paragraph:

Any materials written or contributed by Author are intended by Author and Producer to be a "work made for hire" by the Author pursuant to Sections 101 and 201 of Title 17 of the United States Code. In the event any such materials are determined not to be a "work made for hire," then Author hereby exclusively and irrevocably assigns to Producer, in perpetuity, all rights (including without limitation, all copyrights and renewals and extensions thereof) in and to such materials. The termination of this Agreement for any reason shall not affect Producer's ownership of the results and proceeds of Author's services hereunder or alter any warranty, representation, covenant or undertaking on the part of Author hereunder.

Warranties and Indemnification

Finally, you want to have a clause in the contract that protects you from lawsuits if it turns out that the screenwriter lifted the ideas for the screenplay from someone else, cowrote the screenplay with someone else and didn't tell you about that, or the content violates someone's right of privacy or publicity or defames someone. Here's a sample warranties and indemnification clause:

Author hereby represents and warrants that: (i) the Screenplay was written solely by and is original with Author (except to the extent that any material is in the public domain or is supplied to Author by Producer, or is added to the Screenplay by Producer); (ii) neither the Screenplay nor any element thereof infringes the copyright in any other work; (iii) to the best of Author's knowledge, neither the Screenplay nor its exploitation will violate the rights of privacy or publicity of any person or constitute a defamation against any person, or in any other way violate the rights of any person; (iv) Author is the sole owner of all rights assigned to Producer free and clear of any liens, encumbrances, other third party interests of any kind, and free of any litigation or any claims, whether pending or threatened, (v) Author has full right and power to make and perform this Agreement without the consent of any third party; and (vi) the Screenplay has not previously been exploited as a motion picture or television production. Author shall indemnify Producer against any liability, loss, damage, cost or expense (including reasonable outside attorneys' fees) incurred by reason of any claim arising in connection with any of the foregoing.

The contract terms just discussed cover a screenplay. But you might also need to acquire the rights to make a motion picture version of a novel, nonfiction book, or short story. The terms of that kind of contract are similar and will cover the same basic points: compensation, credit, and rights acquired. Compensation is entirely negotiable and might range from a few thousand dollars for the rights to a short story to tens of thousands of dollars (or more) for a novel or nonfiction book, depending on its popularity and how many copies it has sold. Credit given to a book or short story writer is typically in the form of, "Based upon the novel [or book or short story] titled "___" by [name of the author]."

TRUE STORY RIGHTS

If your film project is based on a true story, you need to acquire the life story rights of all real persons involved. The same types of terms will apply to this contract, including compensation, credit, rights acquired, and warranties.

As with acquiring motion picture rights to a book or short story, the compensation is entirely negotiable. Prices range from low four figures for relatively unknown stories to high six figures for life stories of famous people.

Credit will typically be "Based on the life of," "Based on a true story," "Inspired by a true story," or similar wording.

The warranties given by a real person should specify that the story is true, and that the story is owned by him or her and has not previously been sold to anyone else. It is particularly important to get a warranty that the story is true. In recent years, there have been some unfortunate examples of true life stories turning out to be entirely made up, which has been embarrassing for the producers.

The rights-acquired clause of the contract should not only include the right to make the life story into a movie but also the right to fictionalize the story and add or subtract events as necessary to make the story dramatic. The life story owner must waive any right to sue for defamation, invasion of privacy, or any other rights. You may also want the life story owner to agree to consult with you and the screenwriter.

STAGE RIGHTS CONTRACTS

What if your project is not a film but is a stage play? That's a different kind of contract completely. The playwright will keep the copyright, and you will only obtain a license to produce the play.

If the play has been published by one of the recognized play publishing companies, such as Samuel French, Dramatists Play Service, or Music Theatre International, that company will provide you with the license agreement and will set the royalty for the license fee, which varies depending on various factors, including how many seats are in the theater where you will perform, ticket prices, and how many performances you will have.

If the play is a new play, or has not been published, you will need to negotiate a license directly with the playwright (or agent, if he or she has one). Terms that you might need to negotiate include:

1. *Royalty rate.* This is usually a flat amount per performance and is based on number of seats in the house, ticket prices, and number of performances.
2. *Credit for the playwright.* This can include name credit only or might include a required biography in the program.
3. *The right to extend.* You will want the right to extend the length of the license for more performances if the show is a hit.
4. *Obligations of the playwright.* If the play has not been previously produced, you may want the right to consult with the playwright about casting, the right to require rewrites before or during rehearsals, or the right to have the playwright attend rehearsals and perhaps the opening performance.
5. *Publicity.* You may want to negotiate publicity that the playwright will participate in, such as newspaper, Internet, radio, and TV interviews.
6. *Future productions.* Finally, if the show turns out to be a hit, you will want the right to be the producer of future productions in other theaters, so you should negotiate for that.

WORKING WITH UNIONS

If you are producing a film, TV, or Internet series project, you may need to hire actors who are members of SAG-AFTRA. To do that, your production company must become a signatory to the appropriate SAG-AFTRA agreement. There are different agreements for all kinds of projects, from new media (Internet), music videos, and corporate/educational films, to feature films and TV productions. The SAG-AFTRA website contains information for producers and assistance in signing up.[2] Once you have signed the agreement, you can begin the process of cast clearance, which is checking each actor you want to cast, to make sure that the actor is a member in good standing of the union. Once the cast is cleared, you are ready to begin rehearsals, table reads, or principal photography.

Besides your production company being a signatory with SAG-AFTRA, you may also be using a union crew. If your director is a member of the Directors Guild of America (DGA), you will need to become a DGA signatory. Other unions represent other crew positions, so you might need to also sign up with International Alliance of Theatrical Stage Employees, Moving Picture Technicians, Artists and Allied Crafts (IATSE), which represents camera crews, art directors, costume designers, make-up artists and hairstylists, studio lighting technicians, set painters, and script supervisors, or the Teamsters, which represent drivers of all kinds of support vehicles.

What if you are using SAG-AFTRA actors but no union crew? You can proceed with production without signing with any other unions. However, if your project is bigger than a low-budget film and the other unions become aware of you, they might try to organize your workers and force you to sign all the crew to union contracts. If you are shooting nonunion, it is best to keep a low profile.

If your project is on stage, and you want to use actors who are members of Actors' Equity, you need to sign contracts with that union. Information can be found on the Actors' Equity website to get you started, but you will need to follow up with your regional Equity office.[3]

Get It in Writing!
Cast and Crew Contracts

As an actor, you know that you should always have a contract when you do a job. As a producer, you also need contracts with everyone who is working on the project. Contracts not only get people committed to the project, but they also help prevent disputes and protect you from any cast or crew later claiming to have a job or position that they do not have or claiming to have any kind of ownership or other interest in your project. Contracts also are necessary if you are making a copyrightable project, such as a film, TV show, or Internet series, because without written contracts, arguments can arise as to whether the work of your cast and crew is work made for hire. The last thing you need is a legal battle over your claim to the copyright.

In the last few years, two such legal claims have been fought, all the way up to the federal appeals court level. One claim was by an actor and the other by a director.

Cindy Lee Garcia was an actor who appeared in a short film that was uploaded by the film's producer to YouTube.[1] The facts related by the court are riveting:

> In July 2011, Cindy Lee Garcia responded to a casting call for a film titled *Desert Warrior*, an action-adventure thriller set in ancient Arabia. Garcia was cast in a cameo role, for which she earned $500. She received and reviewed a few pages of script. Acting under a professional director hired to oversee production,

Garcia spoke two sentences: "Is George crazy? Our daughter is but a child?" Her role was to deliver those lines and to "seem concerned."

Garcia later discovered that writer-director Mark Basseley Youssef (aka Nakoula Basseley Nakoula or Sam Bacile) had a different film in mind: an anti-Islam polemic renamed *Innocence of Muslims*. The film, featuring a crude production, depicts the Prophet Mohammed as, among other things, a murderer, pedophile, and homosexual. Film producers dubbed over Garcia's lines and replaced them with a voice asking, "Is your Mohammed a child molester?" Garcia appears on screen for only five seconds.

Almost a year after the casting call, in June 2012, Youssef uploaded a 13-minute-and-51-second trailer of *Innocence of Muslims* to YouTube, the video-sharing website owned by Google, Inc., which boasts a global audience of more than one billion visitors per month. After it was translated into Arabic, the film fomented outrage across the Middle East, and media reports linked it to numerous violent protests. The film also has been a subject of political controversy over its purported connection to the September 11, 2012, attack on the United States Consulate in Benghazi, Libya.

Shortly after the Benghazi attack, an Egyptian cleric issued a fatwa against anyone associated with *Innocence of Muslims*, calling upon the "Muslim Youth in America and Europe" to "kill the director, the producer[,] and the actors and everyone who helped and promoted this film." Garcia received multiple death threats.

Garcia sued Google, Inc., the owner of YouTube, claiming that she owned the copyright in her footage, and she demanded that the film be removed from the website. At first, the three-judge panel of the federal appeals court agreed with Garcia and ordered YouTube to remove the video. But in a rehearing by all nine judges of the appeals court, the decision was reversed. Garcia was found to not have any copyright interest in her performance. The court noted that under the Copyright Act, only works of authorship qualify for copyright protection. It then pointed out that if everyone who provided creative contributions to a motion picture could be called an author, then virtually everyone could claim ownership of their contribution. The court said this would be intolerable because the movie would be splintered, making "Swiss cheese of copyrights." The court found that such a result would "tie the distribution chain in knots," so it refused to find that Garcia had any copyright interest in her acting performance. However, it implied that she might have other claims against the producer, such as defamation or violation of her right of publicity.

It is not clear whether Garcia ever signed a written contract with the producer. If she had, and if that contract had contained a work made for hire clause, the lawsuit could have been avoided. Garcia would have had no claim to copyright if her contract stated that her services were provided to the producer as a work made for hire.

Certainly what the producer in that case did was wrong. You should *always* be honest with your actors about the nature of the project and exactly how their performance fits into it. And you should *never* manipulate an actor's performance in such a way that he or she is portrayed as saying or doing something as polarizing and dangerous as what happened with Garcia. But after being completely honest, you should also always make sure to get each and every actor to sign a written contract that contains a clause about work made for hire. Here's an example of such a clause:

> Actor hereby grants to Producer all rights of every kind and nature in, to and with respect to, the results and proceeds of Actor's services hereunder as a "work made for hire" for Producer. Actor acknowledges that Producer shall be the sole and exclusive owner of all right, title and interest in and to the Picture, including, without limitation, the copyright therein, and of all the results and proceeds of Actor's services and shall have the right to use, exploit, advertise, exhibit and otherwise turn to account any or all of the foregoing in any manner and in any media, whether now known or hereafter devised, throughout the world, in perpetuity, in all languages, as Producer, in its sole and unfettered discretion, shall determine. If for any reason it is determined that the results and proceeds of Actor's services hereunder are not a "work made for hire," then Actor hereby grants to Producer all right, title and interest in and to such results and proceeds, including copyright (and all rights therein).

Another case that involved a director also occurred with a short film, called *Heads Up*. The producer, Robert Krakovski, through his production company 16 Casa Duse, LLC, diligently obtained written contracts with all actors and all crew persons, and each contract did contain a clause about work made for hire. However, the director, Alex Merkin, never signed his contract. The producer nevertheless allowed the production to go forward even though that contract had not been signed. That turned out to be a costly mistake.

After principal photography wrapped, Krakovski gave Merkin a hard drive with the unedited film footage on it. Merkin did sign a Media Agreement in which he agreed that he would edit the film but not license, sell, or copy the footage without the permission of the producer. However, when Krakovski proposed changes to the Media Agreement to clarify that 16 Casa Duse owned the footage, Merkin replied that he was "not giving up any creative or artistic rights" he had in the project and "all of [his] creative work . . . is still [his] work and not the property of 16 Casa Duse, LLC."[2] The parties negotiated but could not reach any agreement, and Merkin threatened to take action if 16 Casa Duse used any of "his" raw film footage. Merkin later registered a copyright in the "raw footage" under his own name.

Krakovski hired a different editor and completed the short film. Krakovski then arranged a private screening at the New York Film Academy in New York, with a reception at a restaurant. Krakovski spent about $2,000 to reserve the restaurant. Merkin responded by threatening the New York Film Academy with a lawsuit if the screening went forward. The screening was canceled, and Krakovski lost his deposit at the restaurant. Krakovski then sued Merkin, seeking an injunction to prohibit Merkin from further interfering with the film and asking the court to cancel Merkin's copyright registration. The trial court granted the injunction, and Merkin took the case up to the federal appeals court in New York. Relying on *Garcia v. Google, Inc.*, the appeals court held that Merkin did not own any copyright in his directing services contribution to the film or in the raw footage. But here's where things get interesting. The court also ordered both Merkin and his attorney to pay 16 Casa Duse's attorney's fees and court costs—to the tune of $185,579.65! All this for a short film that likely had no real market value, being of interest only for film festivals and as a showcase for the talents of cast and crew. A costly exercise for everyone involved.[3]

These two cases illustrate the dangers of not getting the signature of each and every cast and crew member on a contract that contains a proper clause about work made for hire. Do not make that mistake. Put it in writing and get it signed!

Besides contracts with actors and key crew, such as the director, cinematographer, sound operator/mixer, and gaffer for motion pictures, or stage manager, designers, and running crew for stage productions, you should also make sure you have at least short contracts with all crew persons. These can be reduced to simply the job title, amount of pay, credit to be given (if any), dates of work, and, as always, a clause about work made for hire. Sample contracts for both film and stage are readily available from various sources on the Internet.

22

Get It in Writing! Using Music in Your Project

For any type of producing project, you may want to use music. Film, TV, and Internet projects need music in the background to set the mood, to enhance the action, or simply to smooth the transition from one scene to another. Sometimes a scene calls for the actors to actually sing a song or dance to a tune. Stage productions use music as well, again for scene transitions, to set a mood, or even to play in the background as the audience is seated, during intermission, and during curtain calls. Stage musicals incorporate music as part of the story itself.

No matter how you are using music, you must make sure you are using it legally, and that means getting an appropriate license agreement. Agreements for music used on screen differ from those for stage and are more complicated, so we will start with those.

SYNCHRONIZATION LICENSES

A synchronization license (usually called a sync license) is required to put music into any audiovisual work (film, TV program, game, etc.). The name of the license comes from the old method of putting sound together with film. Although many modern digital cameras record sound simultaneously with the images, film cameras do not. Sound is recorded separately, and later the film images and the matching sound must be put together in the editing process. The sound must be synchronized with the picture. Everyone has experienced watching a film where the sound is out of sync and the actors' lip movements do not match the words being spoken or sound effects do not match the action.

Likewise, music is recorded separately from the film and must be synchronized to the film images in editing. Because of this, the license to use music in a film came to be known as a synchronization license. When television came along, the sync license was adopted in that medium as well, to license the use of music in a TV show. Today, it applies to all audiovisual works, regardless of medium.

Sync licenses are negotiated with the owner of the copyright. In fact, you may need to negotiate with two separate copyright owners. Remember our discussion in chapter 17 about copyrights? When you have recorded music, there are typically two copyrights involved.

The first is the copyright in the music itself. That may be a song with lyrics or only a piece of instrumental music. The composer(s) of the music will own that copyright. It is common for composers to transfer their copyrights to a music publishing company, which then manages the marketing of the music, and in that case, it's the publishing company you will negotiate with for a sync license. If you are going to make a new recording of the music, specifically for your film, you only need to license the music copyright.

But what if you want to use a preexisting recording of a song or instrumental piece? That sound recording has its own, separate copyright. You will need to license that copyright as well, usually from the record company that created the recording.

How much does a sync license cost? The amount is dependent on many factors, including what type of project it is and where it will be marketed; how much of the music piece you want to use; how the music will be used in the film; and of course, how famous or popular the piece of music is. Although there are no set rates, you can anticipate that a license for music for a not-famous song by a little known composer, which is used in an independent feature or short film, may cost anywhere from less than $100 up to a few hundred dollars. Some experts suggest that you should allocate about 5% of your total project budget to music license fees. And don't forget that you will need to pay both the music copyright owner and the sound recording copyright owner if you are using pre-recorded music, so plan on doubling the negotiated license fee for all pre-recorded music.

If you are planning to make a short film or even a feature film that will only play in film festivals, you can specify "festival use only" in your music license agreements and that will reduce the cost. But if your film is then picked up for distribution, you will have to renegotiate for the wider use and that may be costly. You can preplan for this by asking for options in the license, so that you make an agreement up front on what the additional fees will be for distribution in theaters, TV, the Internet (such as Amazon, Netflix, Hulu, or any video streaming site), or on DVD.

You can also hold down license fee cost by working with new composers who are eager to get exposure for their music and may be willing to negotiate a low fee or even no fee at all. Other factors that may reduce costs include the territory where you will use your project (only in the United States? also in Canada? worldwide?); how long you want to use the project (only one year or forever?); and your total music budget and division of fees (is every composer being paid the same amount?).

The amount of the piece used is also important in negotiating the license fee. The more of the music you want to use, the more it will cost. If you can do with only a few seconds, that will be much less expensive than if you want to include the entire four-minute song.

The type of use will also determine the cost of the license. There are five basic types of music usage in an audiovisual project: visual vocal (this is where the song is sung on camera as a featured use; this is the most expensive license use type), visual instrumental (an on-camera, featured instrumental performance), background instrumental (background music only), background vocal (the song is sung, but the singer is not on camera, and although the viewer hears the music, the film characters do not), and source (background vocal, but the characters can hear the music and react to it). Using a whole song in either the opening or closing credits is another type of use (called theme or titles) and, as you might expect, will be quite expensive.

If you can afford it, you should hire a music supervisor to negotiate these sync license fees for you. Music supervisors negotiate with many companies for many songs, and they will know which songs are more or less affordable. They will also know the tricks and techniques for negotiating the lowest rates. Of course, music supervisors charge for their services, but they can save you a lot of money in license fees, so their salary is well worth the price.

Whatever you do, do not take a chance on using music in your project that is not licensed. That is just a ticket to a lawsuit. In 2014, YouTube star Michelle Phan was sued by Ultra Records for allegedly using songs in her videos without permission.[1] In 2004, Eminem sued Apple for using one of his songs in an iPod advertisement without a license, and it was reported that he settled that suit in 2005.[2] There are many other examples, but the point is, even the big guys can get sued for using music without a license. Don't let that be you. Get a proper sync license.

What if you do not have the budget for music sync licenses? You can still use music in your project if you get it from a royalty-free source. There are several of these on the Internet. However, make sure it is truly free. There are sources that let you download the music for free, but charge you a license fee to use it. Other sources require you to buy the music to download it, but you can then use it in an audiovisual work without paying royalties. What you really want is free royalty-free music. This means you pay nothing to download, do not need a license, and can use the music for any commercial purpose. YouTube has a free audio library where you can browse music by genre or mood and where you can find free sound effects. For some music, you must give attribution (credit) in your project, but for other music, attribution is not required. The Free Stock Music website is indeed free, and no attribution is required for use of any of the tracks found there.[3] And there are many other such websites.

COMPOSER AGREEMENTS

Perhaps you have graduated from small projects, and now your budget for your film, TV, or Internet project is more substantial. You might have enough money to hire a composer to write an original score for your film. If so, you will need a contract with that composer. The terms you will want to negotiate are the services to be performed, the compensation to be paid, the person responsible for covering recording costs, credit, due date for delivery, rights acquired (including a clause about work made for hire), and warranties and indemnifications (to make sure the music delivered is truly original and not copied from some other source).

Services to Be Performed

This includes more than just writing the music. You will want the composer to write the score, prepare all arrangements and orchestrations, record the music (if played by the composer on the composer's own instruments), rehearse and conduct the musicians (if recorded by several musicians or a whole orchestra in a recording studio), and mix down and produce recordings of the score in timed synchronization with the picture. You may also want the composer to come to the postproduction sound mixing sessions for your film to supervise the editing and mixing of the music with the film. You also need the composer to deliver to you a cue sheet. This is a list of the length of all the music used in the film and its location in the film by time code. You will need to deliver this cue sheet to any distributor of the film, and you will also need to provide it to your performance rights society so that you can be paid performance royalties for the use of the music in your film (see discussion about ASCAP and BMI performing rights societies).

Recording Costs

For most small (or even medium) projects, the fee paid to the composer will include recording costs. The composer will likely record all the music digitally on a computer and then deliver the final mixed score to you in a digital file. If, however, the music is going to be recorded by a group of musicians or an orchestra, recording costs can include compensation payable to third-party producers, musicians, vocalists, conductors, arrangers, orchestrators, copyists, synthesizer programmers, audio engineers, technicians, and others; transportation costs and living expenses for musicians or others to attend recording sessions; payments to a union or guild for musician services at recording sessions; payments for rehearsal hall or studio rentals, and for the rental and transportation of instruments and/or recording equipment; payments for tape, editing, mastering, mixing, and other similar functions; payments for reference dubs and equalizing time; and other costs and expenses. If the fee being paid to the composer is large enough, it may cover these expenses. If it is a smaller fee, you may need to cover these expenses out of your production music budget.

Compensation to the Composer

For a score for a small project, recorded digitally by the composer, you can expect the fee to range from a few hundred or few thousand dollars to as much as low five figures, depending on how much music you need. For a larger feature film, and for more well-known composers, the fee can increase to six figures or higher. There are two other components to compensation for composers as well. If a soundtrack recording is issued for public sale, the composer should be paid a percentage of the revenues the producer receives. Typical amounts are 25–50% of the producer's profits received from the soundtrack album. Also, the composer typically reserves the right to collect the so-called "writer's share" of public performance royalties (see the discussion about public performance royalties).

Rights Acquired

Your composer contract must include a rights-acquired clause, and you should make sure you designate the score as a work made for hire, so that your production company owns the copyright.

Credit

Credit is typically given to composers in the main credits of a film and is usually worded in some manner as, "Music Composed by Sam Smith."

Delivery Date

You need to specify the due date for delivery of the final, mixed, and recorded music. You don't want to be heading into sound mixing in postproduction and still be waiting for the recorded score to be delivered.

MUSIC FOR STAGE PRODUCTIONS

There are two issues to be considered for the use of music in stage productions. Is the music being used only for scene background, scene transitions, or audience seating, intermission, and exit background? If so, you will likely only need to make sure that the theater (or other venue) has a proper blanket license for playing music. On the other hand, if you want to incorporate music as part of the actual content of the play—you want actors to sing songs to advance the story, or you want to specify particular music titles in the dialogue and then play or sing those particular songs (or parts of them)—you may need a grand rights license from the composer. Let's look at blanket licenses first.

Blanket License for Public Performance of Music

One of the exclusive rights of the owner of copyright in a musical work is the right to control public performance of the music.[4] Think about all the places where you hear music being played: shopping malls, retail shops, grocery stores, restaurants, nightclubs, and even elevators. Of course, you also hear music when you attend any live concert, whether that is in a theater, nightclub, coffee shop, or huge arena. Because music cannot be publicly performed without a license from the composer/copyright owner, the saying goes that, "if the music is being played, someone is getting paid." But it would be impossible for every venue to negotiate separate public performance licenses from every composer in the world. So how do these venues get the permission to play music? It's done through a blanket license.

There are two large organizations in the United States that issue such blanket licenses—American Society of Composers, Authors and Publishers (ASCAP) and Broadcast Music Incorporated (BMI). These are performance rights societies.[5] Music composers join either ASCAP or BMI to get paid for the public performance of their music. They authorize their performance rights society to issue licenses to all venues that play music. A blanket license given by ASCAP or BMI to a venue authorizes the venue to play any music that is in the performance rights society's catalog. Between them, ASCAP and BMI control millions of songs, so a venue that has a blanket license from both organizations can play virtually any music that it wants.

ASCAP and BMI set the license fees for each venue and then collect the fees from all the locations. They then pay performance royalties to all the composers of all the music played in those venues (according to a complicated logarithmic calculation that is probably only understood by computer geeks at the societies!). ASCAP and BMI also issue licenses to radio stations, movie theaters, and TV networks, which also must pay performance royalties for music played on the radio or heard in any motion picture or TV show.

When you produce a stage production, you should check with the theater to make sure it has the proper ASCAP and BMI blanket licenses. If so, then you can use any music you like for scene background, scene transitions, and audience seating, intermission, and exit music. If there is no blanket license, and you use music anyway, you are actually responsible for negotiating your own public performance licenses with the composer(s) of the music. If you do not do so, you run the risk of being sued for copyright infringement. ASCAP and BMI do police venues that play music, so the risk of being caught is real. For example, in 2019, ASCAP sued the Nook nightclub in Austin, Texas, alleging that it was playing music without paying songwriter performance royalties.[6] The ASCAP representative said that it had contacted the venue more than 50 times about obtaining a license, but the nightclub never obtained one. And according to a news report in the *Omaha World-Herald*, BMI files about 10 lawsuits each year against various venues just in Nebraska and Iowa.[7] So even if your production is in a small theater in a small town, you could be found out.

What if you want to incorporate songs as part of the story of your play? In recent years, there have been many successful musicals built around a composer's song catalog: *Mamma Mia!*, *Jersey Boys*, and *Jagged Little Pill* are three examples. Other musicals are written using songs from numerous composers, such as *Motown the Musical*, *Rock of Ages*, and *Priscilla, Queen of the Desert*.[8] When songs are used to tell the story and advance the plot of a play, the songs are being used for dramatic rights, also called the grand rights. These rights must be negotiated directly from the song composers. Of course, this can be a complicated negotiation, one that you are ill-advised to attempt on your own. If you need the grand rights for music in a stage production, hire an experienced entertainment attorney to assist you.

Finally, let's return for a moment to music used in films. As we discussed, if you have the budget for it, you might hire a composer to write a film score specifically for your film. Assuming your contract with the composer gives your production company the copyright as a work made for hire, you are now the owner of music. You should consider having your production company become a member of either ASCAP or BMI so that you can collect music performance royalties when your film is screened in a theater, on TV, or anywhere on the Internet. Performance royalties can add up, and this can be a good source of income for your production company. You can even license your film score to be used by other audiovisual productions, which will not only earn you an initial license fee but will also increase the amount of music performance royalties you can receive. Because sooner or later, all audiovisual works seem to end up on the Internet, there is one other performing rights society in the United States that you will also want to sign up with—Soundexchange.com. That organization specializes in issuing licenses for performance of music on the Internet.

Glossary

acceptance: the expression of agreement to the proposal

age of majority: the age at which people become legal adults

agent: a person who is authorized, or has the power, to act on behalf of someone else

alter ego: another aspect of one's own self; a secondary personality

articles of incorporation: a document filed with a state government office to create a corporation

articles of organization: a document filed with a state government office to create a limited liability company

assignee: the third person who receives a transfer of contract rights

assignment: the transfer of a right or interest

assignor: a party to a contract who transfers contract rights to a third person

breach of contract: the failure by one or both parties to perform their contract obligations

bylaws: a document laying out the rules for operation of a corporation

capitalize: to supply a corporation with enough money or assets to conduct business

commingle: to mix together or to combine

common law: law that is derived from custom and judicial precedent rather than statutes

competence: the ability to do something successfully

competent: fit, able, or qualified

confidential: something spoken, written, or done in strict privacy or secrecy

consideration: something of value that is given in exchange for a promise

copyright: a collection of legal rights relating to creative works

corporation: an association of people or companies that has a separate legal existence independent of the owners

counteroffer: any new or different proposal that follows the offer

damages: the money equivalent for a detriment or injury

defamation: the false or unjustified injury of the good reputation of another

defendant: the person who is being sued in a civil lawsuit or is accused of a crime

derivative: something that has been derived

derive: to come from another source or origin

disaffirm: repudiate, reject, or declare to be void

dividend: a payment to a shareholder of a portion of a corporation's profits

doctrine: a principle or policy of the law

duress: compulsion by threat or force; coercion

eviction: a lawsuit to expel or remove a tenant from real property

evidence: proof of facts presented at a trial

fiduciary: a relationship of high trust and confidence

filch: to steal something

fixture: something attached to a building and permanently associated with that building

fraud: deceit, trickery, or lies done to obtain an unfair or dishonest advantage

incorporate: to form a corporation

infringe: to actively break a law or agreement; to encroach on another's rights

infringement: the use of intellectual property without permission from the owner

injunction: an order of the court instructing one of the parties to stop doing something or to do a particular thing

intellectual property: property that comes from the creativity of the mind

intrusion: going in without permission, invitation, or welcome

joint: two or more people joined together in ownership or obligation

jurisdiction: the power or authority of a court to hear a case; the power of a court to order the parties to a lawsuit to do something or stop doing something

landlord: a person or company who owns real property and rents it to another

lease: a contract that creates a leasehold estate

leasehold estate: a right to possess real property for a period of time

lessee: the precise legal term for a tenant

lessor: the precise legal term for a landlord

liable: legally responsible

libel: defamation in writing

license: a contract granting someone the right to use intellectual property

licensee: a person who receives a license from a licensor

licensor: a person who grants a license to another

majority: the age when a person is legally considered to be an adult

medium: the material or form used by a writer, artist, or composer

minor: a person who is younger than the age of full legal responsibility

misappropriation: to wrongfully take something

mitigate: to reduce the amount of damages resulting from an injury

mutual: done by each of two or more parties

mutuality: the activity that is done by two or more parties

negligence: the failure to use the care that a reasonable person would use in the same situation

offer: the first proposal to make an agreement

offeree: the person receiving an offer or counteroffer

offeror: the person making an offer or counteroffer

oral: spoken or communicated by speech

order: a decision or ruling by a judge

parody: to imitate a song, movie, or other creative work for purposes of humor or satire

party: a person who is involved in a lawsuit, either as plaintiff or defendant

personal property: any property that is not land or something attached to land or property that can be moved

plaintiff: the person who starts or commences a lawsuit

profits: financial gain, specifically the difference between the amount earned and the cost spent in producing, manufacturing, or selling something

public domain: being available to the public as a whole; not protected by copyright

punitive damages: money paid as punishment

real property: land and anything that is permanently attached to the land

representation: a statement of something asserted to be true

rescind: to retract, revoke, or withdraw from a contract

rescission: the revocation or cancellation of a contract

respondeat superior: "let the master answer for the servant." This legal doctrine holds an employer liable for the negligent acts of employees

revert: to go back or return

slander: defamation by oral speech

slogan: a short phrase used in advertising

sole proprietorship: a business owned by a single person

statute: a law enacted by the legislative branch of a government

stock: an ownership interest in a corporation

stock certificate: a document that is evidence of an ownership interest in a corporation

sublease: a transfer of part of the leased premises or a transfer of the entire leased premises for a part of the time remaining in the rental term

tangible: can be perceived by touch or other senses

tenant: a person or company who rents real property from the owner

tort: wrongful conduct that is neither a breach of contract nor (usually) a crime

trademark: any word, picture, phrase, or combination of those, used to identify goods

warranty: a promise in a contract that certain statements by one of the parties are true

Notes

CHAPTER 1

1. "SAG-AFTRA Minimums," SAG-AFTRA, accessed December 6, 2019, https://www.sagaftra.org/files/rate_sheet_low_budget_theatrical_8_13.pdf.

2. There are many articles available on the Internet about this situation. For example, see Jonathan Sim, "The Story of Eric Stoltz in 'Back to the Future'," *Geeks*, accessed December 7, 2019, https://geeks.media/the-story-of-eric-stoltz-in-back-to-the-future.

3. David J. Fox, "Kim Basinger Court Case Shines Light on Deal-Making: Trial: The 'Boxing Helena' lawsuit is the second recent high-profile dispute involving a star's defection from a project. 'The way the industry does business is what is on trial here.'," *Los Angeles Times*, March 1, 1993, https://www.latimes.com/archives/la-xpm-1993-03-01-ca-150-story.html.

4. Kathleen O'Steen, "Basinger files Chapter 11," *Variety*, May 27, 1993, https://variety.com/1993/film/news/basinger-files-chapter-11-107245/.

5. Adam Sandler, "Basinger 'Boxing' Suit Settled," *Variety*, December 17, 1995, https://variety.com/1995/film/features/basinger-boxing-suit-settled-99123537/.

6. "Bill Murray talks about his 1-800 phone number and what it takes for him to respond," *Today*, April 13, 2018, https://www.today.com/video/bill-murray-talks-about-his-1-800-phone-number-and-what-it-takes-for-him-to-respond-1209389635553?v=raila&.

7. Robert Schnakenberg, *The Big Bad Book of Bill Murray* (Philadelphia: Quirk Books, 2015), chap. B, Libby E-reader.

CHAPTER 2

1. Steve Ryfle, "Keanu sees red over 'The Watcher,'" *Hollywood.com*, March 19, 2001, http://www.hollywood.com/general/keanu-sees-red-over-the-watcher-57162056/.

2. "Keanu: I was tricked into making film," *The Guardian*, September 11, 2001, https://www.theguardian.com/film/2001/sep/11/news.

3. The entertainment industry newspaper, *Variety*, reported that, "Reeves ultimately received an additional $2 million for his 11 days of work on the pic." Tim Swanson, "Inside Move: 'Watcher' dogs Reeves," *Variety,* September 18, 2001, https://variety.com/2001/film/news/inside-move-watcher-dogs-reeves-1117852857/.

4. *Brooke Shields v. Gross*, 448 N.E.2d 108 (N.Y. 1983).

5. John Angelo Sergio, "Photo Coverage: The *Lion King* First International Tour Meets the Press," *BroadwayWorld*, February 8, 2018, https://www.broadwayworld .com/article/Photo-Coverage-THE-LION-KING-First-International-Tour-Meets -The-Press-20180208.

6. Josh Grossberg, "Keanu Reeves, Reticent 'Watcher'," *E News*, September 9, 2000, https://www.eonline.com/news/40426/keanu-reeves-reticent-watcher.

7. The maximum length of the actors' contracts in California is seven years because a California statute limits contracts for personal services to a seven-year term. Cal. Lab. Code § 2855(a).

8. Joe Flint, "'Modern Family' stars play hardball in salary dispute," *Los Angeles Times*, July 25, 2012, https://www.latimes.com/business/la-xpm-2012-jul-25-la-fi -ct-modern-family-20120726-story.html.

9. Jeanine Poggi, "Here's How Much It Costs to Advertise in TV's Biggest Shows," *AdAge*, October 2, 2018, https://adage.com/article/media/tv-pricing-chart/315120.

10. Amy Watson, "Cost of a 30-second TV spot during *Modern Family* in the United States from 2014/15 to 2019/20 TV season (in U.S. dollars)," *Statista*, November 18, 2019, https://www.statista.com/statistics/623379/modern-family -ad-price-usa/.

11. Laurie L. Dove, "What are TV upfronts?" *howstuffworks*, accessed December 6, 2019, https://entertainment.howstuffworks.com/what-are-tv-upfronts.htm.

12. Flint, "'Modern Family' stars play hardball in salary dispute."

13. Matthew Belloni, "'Modern Family' Cast Reaches Deal to End Salary Standoff," *The Hollywood Reporter*, July 27, 2012, https://www.hollywoodreporter.com/thr-esq/modern-family-cast-deal-salary-355527.

14. Michelle Regalado, "'Modern Family': How Much Does the Cast Really Make?" *Showbiz CheatSheet*, September 17, 2017, https://www.cheatsheet.com/entertainment/modern-family-much-cast-really-make.html/.

15. Lacey Rose, "Ellen Pompeo, TV's $20 Million Woman, Reveals Her Behind-the-Scenes Fight for 'What I Deserve'," *Hollywood Reporter*, January 17, 2018, https://www.hollywoodreporter.com/features/ellen-pompeo-tvs-20-million-woman-reveals-her-behind-scenes-fight-what-i-deserve-1074978.

CHAPTER 4

1. "Contracts & Codes," Actors' Equity, accessed December 6, 2019, https://www.actorsequity.org/resources/contracts/.

2. See chapter 19 for a discussion of the torts of misappropriation and violation of rights of publicity and privacy.

CHAPTER 5

1. Edward Jay Epstein, "Gross Hysteria," *Slate*, January 23, 2006, https://slate.com/culture/2006/01/how-the-studios-compensate-the-most-powerful-movie-stars.html.

2. Mike Fleming Jr., "STUDIO SHAME! Even Harry Potter Pic Loses Money Because of Warner Bros' Phony Baloney Net Profit Accounting," *Deadline*, July 6, 2010, https://deadline.com/2010/07/studio-shame-even-harry-potter-pic-loses-money-because-of-warner-bros-phony-baloney-accounting-51886/.

CHAPTER 6

1. Lesley Goldberg, "'Big Bang Theory's' Big Bucks: Why the Cast Will Earn $1 Million Per Episode," *Hollywood Reporter*, August 6, 2014, https://www.hollywoodreporter.com/live-feed/big-bang-theorys-big-bucks-723652.

2. *New media* as defined in the SAG-AFTRA contract means original content that will be transmitted on the Internet or for mobile devices. "New Media Contracts," SAG-AFTRA, accessed December 7, 2019, https://www.sagaftra.org/production-center/contract/884/getting-started.

CHAPTER 7

1. AGVA represents on-stage talent only for nonbook shows (i.e., nonscript). Book shows and revues with a book fall under the jurisdiction of Actors' Equity. "About AGVA," AGVA, accessed December 7, 2019, http://www.agvausa.com/aboutagva.html.

CHAPTER 8

1. "Join Equity," Actors' Equity, accessed December 7, 2019, https://www.actors equity.org/join/.

2. "Signatories," AGMA, accessed December 7, 2019, https://www.musicalartists .org/about-agma/signatories/.

3. "Steps to Join," SAG-AFTRA, accessed December 7, 2019, https://www.sagaftra .org/membership-benefits/steps-join.

4. KC Wright, "How to Join SAG-AFTRA," *Backstage*, March 2, 2017, https://www. backstage.com/magazine/article/join-sag-aftra-10720/.

5. SAG-AFTRA, "New Media Contracts."

CHAPTER 9

1. California Labor Code § 1700.4(a).

CHAPTER 10

1. I reviewed the 2012 Cathy Parker Management artist contract on behalf of a client.

2. Dan J. Kroll, "Kelly Ripa's agent 'discovers' losing in court," *Soap Central*, May 25, 1998, http://www.soapcentral.com/amc/news/980525-ripasuit.php.

3. Cathy Parker Management is now owned by Georgeanne Bruzzese and has been renamed CPM Talent Management. "About Us," CPM Talent, accessed December 7, 2019, https://cpmtalent.com/about-us. I do not know if the standard management contract has been changed.

CHAPTER 11

1. California Code of Regulations, tit. 8, §12001 (1989).

CHAPTER 12

1. Anita Busch, "John Travolta Leaves CAA, Keeps Other Reps," *Deadline*, November 10, 2017, https://deadline.com/2017/11/john-travolta-caa-exit-keeps -manager-lawyer-1202206245/.

2. *Today*, "Bill Murray talks"; Schnakenberg, *Bill Murray*, chap. B.

3. For example, in New York, you can find lawyers at "Attorney Search," New York State Unified Court System, accessed December 7, 2019, http://iapps.courts.state.ny.us/attorney/AttorneySearch. In California, find lawyers at "Attorney Search," State Bar of California, accessed December 7, 2019, http://members.calbar.ca.gov/fal/LicenseeSearch/.

4. California Rules of Professional Conduct, Rule 1.16(e)(1).

CHAPTER 13

1. Dees Stribling, "Oregon Passes 1st-in-Nation Statewide Rent Control," *Bisnow*, February 27, 2019, https://www.bisnow.com/national/news/multifamily/oregon-passes-1st-in-nation-statewide-rent-control-97729.

2. "Occupational Employment Statistics," *Bureau of Labor Statistics*, last modified March 29, 2019, https://www.bls.gov/oes/current/oes272011.htm (see the green map).

3. "RSO Overview," Los Angeles Housing Community Investment Department, accessed December 7, 2019, https://hcidla.lacity.org/RSO-Overview.

4. "Rent Stabilized Building Lists," *NYC Rent Guidelines Board*, accessed December 7, 2019, https://www1.nyc.gov/site/rentguidelinesboard/resources/rent-stabilized-building-lists.page.

5. Brian Rogal, "Rent Control Measures Move Forward in Uncertain Political Environment," *Bisnow*, January 31, 2019, https://www.bisnow.com/chicago/news/affordable-housing/rent-control-measures-move-forward-in-uncertain-political-environment-97278.

6. "Guide to Residential Tenants' and Landlords' Rights and Responsibilities," *California Department of Housing and Community Development*, accessed December 7, 2019, http://www.hcd.ca.gov/manufactured-mobile-home/mobile-home-ombudsman/docs/Tenant-Landlord.pdf.

7. California Civil Code § 1946.

8. This exact situation occurred in the case of *Blackett v. Olanoff*, 371 Mass. 714, 358 N.E.2d 817 (1977). The court held that the apartment tenants had been constructively evicted because the landlord had the right to control the actions of the nightclub owner but failed to do so. The landlord was not allowed to seek any rent from the apartment tenants who had moved out.

9. Allen Salkin, "Among the Rich, a New Dispute Over Air Rights," *New York Times*, May 16, 2007, https://www.nytimes.com/2007/05/16/nyregion/16bono.html.

10. See the New York Attorney General's publication, "Tenants' Rights Guide," NYC, accessed December 7, 2019, https://www1.nyc.gov/assets/buildings/pdf/tenants_rights.pdf.

CHAPTER 14

1. 42 U.S.C. § 2000e-2(a).

2. 42 U.S.C. § 2000e(b).

3. "What You Should Know about EEOC and the Enforcement Protections for LGBT Workers," *US Equal Employment Opportunity Commission*, accessed December 7, 2019, https://www.eeoc.gov/eeoc/newsroom/wysk/enforcement_protections_lgbt_workers.cfm.

4. *R.G. & G.R. Harris Funeral Homes Inc. v. Equal Employment Opportunity Commission*, US Supreme Court Docket No. 18-107, involved a transgender person who was fired; *Bostock v. Clayton County, Georgia*, Supreme Court Docket No. 17-1618, and *Altitude Express, Inc. v. Zarda*, Supreme Court Docket No. 17-1623, both involved a gay man who was fired.

5. 42 U.S.C. § 2000e(k).

6. *Young v. United Parcel Service, Inc.*, 135 S. Ct. 1338, 191 L.Ed.2d 279 (2015).

7. Ann W. O'Neill, "Actress Fired over Pregnancy Wins $5 Million," *Los Angeles Times*, December 23, 1997, https://www.latimes.com/archives/la-xpm-1997-dec-23-mn-1420-story.html; "Jury gets 'Melrose Place' pregnancy lawsuit," *Los Angeles Times*, December 16, 1997, http://www.cnn.com/SHOWBIZ/9712/16/melrose.suit/index.html.

8. Eriq Gardner, "'Price Is Right' Model Will Get New Trial in Pregnancy Discrimination Lawsuit," *Hollywood Reporter*, December 12, 2014, https://www.hollywoodreporter.com/thr-esq/price-is-right-model-will-756904.

9. *Cochran v. FreemantleMedia North America, Inc.*, California Courts, accessed December 7, 2019, http://www.courts.ca.gov/opinions/nonpub/B247541.PDF; Bea Karnes, "Former 'Price Is Right' Model Settles Lawsuit Out-of-Court," *Patch*, March 2, 2016, https://patch.com/california/hollywood/former-price-right-model-settles-lawsuit-out-court-0.

10. 42 U.S.C. § 12101 *et seq.*

11. "The ADA: Your Employment Rights as an Individual With a Disability," *US Equal Employment Opportunity Commission*, last modified May 9, 2019, https://www.eeoc.gov/facts/ada18.html.

12. 42 U.S.C. § 12102.

13. "Facts About the Americans with Disabilities Act," *US Equal Employment Opportunity Commission*, accessed December 7, 2019, https://www.eeoc.gov/eeoc/publications/fs-ada.cfm.

14. 29 U.S.C. § 621; "Age Discrimination," *US Department of Labor*, accessed December 7, 2019, https://www.dol.gov/general/topic/discrimination/agedisc.

15. Leanne Bayley, "It's GLAMOUR Day! Meet our new cover star, Anne Hathaway," *Glamour*, September 7, 2015, https://www.glamourmagazine.co.uk/article/anne-hathaway-glamour-october-2015-cover-star.

16. For more information see, Thelma Adams, "Casting-Couch Tactics Plagued Hollywood Long Before Harvey Weinstein," *Variety*, accessed December 7, 2019, https://variety.com/2017/film/features/casting-couch-hollywood-sexual-harassment-harvey-weinstein-1202589895/.

17. Alex Ates, "Intimacy Directors Should Be on More Sets, Says SAG-AFTRA," *Backstage*, August 1, 2019, https://www.backstage.com/magazine/article/sag-aftra-intimacy-director-on-set-standard-68685/?fbclid=IwAR0aeXgjyHdtqWN62cJUAbSmw4pdAzEaCuO0zMmsYKwW0_eIV5QhTpbS2UI.

18. "SAG-AFTRA to Standardize Guidelines for Intimacy Coordinators," SAG-AFTRA, July 21, 2019, https://www.sagaftra.org/sag-aftra-standardize-guidelines-intimacy-coordinators?fbclid=IwAR2numikBsO_rGCCcByf7_zPOG6hTswDCngq8jMzllrzCYxcLzWNNrsIZps.

19. *Lyle v. Warner Bros. Television Productions*, 38 Cal. 4th 264 (2006).

20. 29 U.S.C. § 651 *et seq.*

21. 29 U.S.C. § 666.

22. "US Department of Labor's OSHA cites *Spider-Man* Broadway musical production company following injuries to cast members," *OSHA*, March 4, 2011, https://www.osha.gov/news/newsreleases/region2/03042011.

23. "US Department of Labor's OSHA cites Walt Disney World following monorail collision and issues recommendation letter following actor's death," *OSHA*, December 23, 2009, https://www.osha.gov/news/newsreleases/region4/12232009.

24. 8 U.S.C. § 1324a.

25. "Form I-9 Inspection Overview," *US Immigration and Customs Enforcement*, last modified August 19, 2019, https://www.ice.gov/factsheets/i9-inspection.

26. "O-1 Visa: Individuals with Extraordinary Ability or Achievement," *US Immigration and Customs Enforcement*, last modified January 5, 2017, https://www.uscis.gov/working-united-states/temporary-workers/o-1-visa-individuals-extraordinary-ability-or-achievement.

27. "P-1B A Member of an Internationally Recognized Entertainment Group," *US Immigration and Customs Enforcement*, last modified July 17, 2015, https://www.uscis.gov/working-united-states/temporary-workers/p-1b-member-internationally-recognized-entertainment-group.

28. "P-2 Individual Performer or Part of a Group Entering to Perform Under a Reciprocal Exchange Program," *US Immigration and Customs Enforcement*, last modified July 15, 2015, https://www.uscis.gov/working-united-states/temporary-workers/p-2-individual-performer-or-part-group-entering-perform-under-reciprocal-exchange-program.

29. "P-3 Artist or Entertainer Coming to Be Part of a Culturally Unique Program," *US Immigration and Customs Enforcement*, last modified July 17, 2015, https://www.uscis.gov/working-united-states/temporary-workers/p-3-artist-or-entertainer-coming-be-part-culturally-unique-program.

CHAPTER 16
1. The standard tax rate for corporations under the 2018 federal tax law is 21%. 26 U.S.C. § 11(b).

CHAPTER 17
1. 17 U.S.C. § 102(a).

2. 17 U.S.C. § 101 *et seq.*

3. 17 U.S.C. § 302(a), (b).

4. "Music Modernization Act," *Copyright.gov*, October 2018, https://www.copyright.gov/legislation/2018_mma_amendments.pdf.

5. Mark Twain died in 1910. "Frequently Asked Questions," Mark Twain Museum, accessed December 7, 2019, https://www.marktwainmuseum.org/frequently-asked -questions/.

6. 17 U.S.C. § 102.

7. 17 U.S.C. § 411(a).

8. 17 U.S.C. § 412.

9. 17 U.S.C. § 106.

10. 17 U.S.C. § 107.

11. Bruce Handy, "Steven Stealberg?" *Time*, June 24, 2001, http://content.time.com/ time/magazine/article/0,9171,136923,00.html.

12. "Writer Settles Claim Against Film 'Amistad'," *Los Angeles Times*, February 10, 1998, https://www.latimes.com/archives/la-xpm-1998-feb-10-fi-17374-story.html.

13. 17 U.S.C. § 504(b).

14. 17 U.S.C. § 504(c).

15. 17 U.S.C. § 502.

16. 17 U.S.C. § 503.

CHAPTER 18
1. 37 C.F.R. § 202.1(a).

2. 15 U.S.C. § 1111.

3. *E.S.S. Entertainment 2000, Inc. v. Rockstar Videos, Inc.*, 547 F.3d 1095 (9th Cir. 2008).

4. "Domain Name Dispute Resolution," *WIPO*, accessed December 7, 2019, www .wipo.int/amc/en/domains/.

5. *Starbucks Corp. v. Lundberg*, 2005 U.S. Dist. LEXIS 32660; 2005 WL 3183858 (D. Ore. 2005).

CHAPTER 19
1. *Dyer v. Childress*, 147 Cal. App. 4th 1273, 1280, 1284 (2007).

2. *Whitaker v. A&E Television Networks*, 2009 WL 1383617 (Cal. Ct. App. May 18, 2009).

3. *Prozeralik v. Capital Cities Communs.*, 82 N.Y.2d 466, 470-471 (1993).

4. *Prozeralik*, 82 N.Y.2d at 471.

5. *Prozeralik*, 82 N.Y.2d at 471.

6. *Prozeralik*, 82 N.Y.2d at 475-476.

7. *Jane Doe 72511 v. Morgan*, 2018 ONSC 6607 [Morgan].

8. Lindsay A. Eriksson, "Lessons from the Erin Andrews Verdict: It's Not about the Money," *ABA*, March 31, 2016, https://www.americanbar.org/groups/litigation/committees/mass-torts/practice/2016/erin-andrews-verdict/.

9. Sheila Burke, "TV Host Erin Andrews Settles Nashville Marriott Case, Ends Appeals," *Insurance Journal*, April 28, 2016, https://www.insurancejournal.com/news/southeast/2016/04/28/406884.htm.

10. *Christoff v. Nestle USA*, 42 Cal. 4th 554 (2009); Kevin Underhill, "How *Did That Taster's Choice Case Turn Out?" Lowering the Bar*, March 5, 2015, https://loweringthebar.net/2015/03/how-did-that-tasters-choice-case-turn-out.html.

11. *Comedy III Productions, Inc. v. Gary Saderup, Inc.*, 25 Cal. 4th 387 (2001).

12. *Lindsay Lohan v. Take-Two Interactive Software, Inc.*, New York Courts, accessed December 7, 2019, http://www.courts.state.ny.us/reporter/3dseries/2016/2016_05942.htm.

13. See chapter 17 for a discussion of fair use of copyrights.

14. *Burnett v. Twentieth Century Fox Film Corporation*, 491 F. Supp. 2d 962 (2007).

CHAPTER 20

1. 17 U.S.C. § 101.

2. "Production Center," *SAG-AFTRA*, accessed December 7, 2019, https://www.sagaftra.org/production-center.

3. "Resources for Producers," *Actors' Equity*, accessed December 7, 2019, https://www.actorsequity.org/resources/Producers/.

CHAPTER 21

1. *Garcia v. Google, Inc.*, 786 F.3d 733 (9th Cir. 2015).

2. *16 Casa Duse, LLC v. Merkin*, 791 F.3d 247, 252 (2d Circ. 2015).

3. As of the writing of this book, the 16 Casa Duse case was still continuing, with further proceedings ongoing in both the trial and appeals court concerning the award of attorney's fees and costs.

CHAPTER 22

1. Kevin Rawlinson, "YouTube star Michelle Phan sued over copyright breach," *BBC*, July 22, 2014, https://www.bbc.com/news/technology-28418449.

2. Ina Fried, "Eminem settles with Apple over iPod commercial," *CNET*, May 10, 2005, https://www.cnet.com/news/eminem-settles-with-apple-over-ipod -commercial/.

3. Free Stock Music, accessed December 7, 2019, https://www.freestockmusic.com.

4. See the discussion of the six exclusive rights of a copyright owner in chapter 17.

5. There is another performance rights society which is quite large in Europe, but rather small in the United States, called SESAC.

6. Kevin Curtin, "ASCAP Levels Lawsuit Against Sixth Street Music Venue the Nook," *Austin Chronicle*, February 26, 2019, https://www.austinchronicle.com/daily/ music/2019-02-26/ascap-levels-lawsuit-against-the-nook/.

7. Paul Hammel, "Nebraska bar owners say music licensing firms are 'relentless.' A bill in the Legislature may provide relief," *Omaha World-Herald*, April 11, 2018, https://www.omaha.com/news/legislature/nebraska-bar-owners-say-music-licensing -firms-are-relentless-a/article_6e7ec8e8-c574-50f5-b9be-a1250ce8dba4.html.

8. Olivia Clement, "3 New Musicals Will Use BMG Catalog, Including Songs of Dolly Parton, Culture Club, and More," *Playbill*, April 3, 2019, http://www.playbill .com/article/3-new-musicals-will-use-bmg-catalog-including-songs-of-dolly-parton -culture-club-and-more.

Index

#MeToo movement, 125
16 Casa Duse, LLC, 195–196
20th Century Fox Film Corporation, 182
8 Legged Productions, LLC, 125
A&E Television Networks, 176, 179
ABC Television, 20–21
above the title, 31, 41
acceptance (of offer), 3, 4
Actors' Equity, 11, 25, 29–31, 33–34, 57, 58, 61–63, 64, 116, 131, 192
ADA, 121–122
adjusted gross receipts, 39
ADR, 38
AFTRA, 5, 25, 37, 39, 42, 43, 49–54, 57, 58, 61, 63–64, 87, 124, 126, 131, 133, 187, 191–192
Age Discrimination in Employment Act, 122–123
AGMA, 58–59, 61, 62, 64
AGVA, 57–58, 61, 64
AIDS, 176, 179
Air Jordan, 45
alter ego, 150, 152

Amblin Entertainment, 162
American Federation of Television Radio Artists. *See* AFTRA.
American Guild of Musical Artists. *See* AGMA.
American Guild of Variety Artists. *See* AGVA.
American Society of Composers, Authors, and Publishers. *See* ASCAP.
Americans with Disabilities Act. *See* ADA.
Amistad, 162
Apple, Inc., 156, 200
arbitration, 81, 94
articles of incorporation, 143–146, 150
articles of organization, 146, 150–151
ASCAP, 201, 203–204
assignment, 99, 110–113
authority of agent, 68–69, 71, 72, 77, 92; actual, 68–69; apparent, 69; implied, 68–69
automatic dialogue replacement. *See* ADR.
Avengers: Endgame, 40

Bacile, Sam, 194
Back to the Future, 7
background instrumental, 199
background vocal, 199
Bad Santa, 9
basic cable, 51
Basinger, Kim, 8, 13
Behind the Lie, 30
below the title, 31, 41
billing, 31
blanket license, 156, 202–203
Bloomsbury Publishing, 159
BMI, 201, 203–204
board of directors, 141–142, 144–146,
    149, 151
Bono, 108
Bowen, Julie, 21
Boxing Helena, 8
Broadcast Music Incorporated. *See* BMI.
Burnett, Carol, 182–183
Burrell, Ty, 21
bylaws, 144–146, 151

Capital Cities/ABC, 177–178
Carey, Drew, 121
casting couch, 124
Cathy Parker Management, 76–77
Cavill, Henry, 46
Charbanic, Joe, 12–13, 18
Chartoff-Winkler Productions, 131
Charwoman, 182
Chase-Riboud, Barbara, 162
Childress, Helen, 174–175, 179
Christoff, Russell, 181
Civil Rights Act of 1964, 117–118
Coca-Cola, 52, 165, 168
Cochran, Brandi, 120–121
competence to contract, 13–16

consideration, 11–13, 26
constructive eviction, 105–107
corporate veil, 149, 152
corporation, 132, 139–152
corporation meeting minutes, 145, 149,
    151
counteroffer, 4–5, 39
Cuoco, Kaley, 50
cure clause, 88

defamation, 90, 132, 173–178, 179, 180,
    183, 189, 190, 194
Designated Survivor, 122
DeVito, Danny, 174
DGA, 192
dilution by blurring, 170–171
dilution by tarnishment, 170–171
Dinklage, Peter, 122
Directors Guild of America. *See* DGA.
disaffirm, 15–16
dividend, 148–149
duress, 19–20, 22
Dyer, Troy, 174–176, 179

Echo of Lions, 162
EEOC, 117, 118, 124
EMCP, 62
Eminem, 200
employment at will, 115–116
Equal Employment Opportunity
    Commission. *See* EEOC.
Equity Guest Artist, 29, 33
Equity Membership Candidate Program.
    See EMCP.
errors and omissions insurance, 173,
    185
ESS Entertainment, 169
exclusivity, 45, 52, 54

fair use, 160–161, 168–169; copyright, 160–161; trademark, 168–169
Family Guy, 182
Family Ties, 8
Fenn, Sherilyn, 8
Ferguson, Jesse Tyler, 21
fictitious business name statement, 132–133
fiduciary, 67, 80, 88, 137
First Amendment, 121, 125, 140, 169, 174–176, 182–183
fixtures, 104, 108–109
Fox, Michael J., 122
Foxx, Jamie, 45
Franzoni, David, 162
fraud, 17–18, 81
Friends, 21

Galecki, Johnny, 50
Game of Thrones, 122
Garcia, Cindy Lee, 193–195
Generation X, 175
GIAA, 61–62
Google, Inc., 194, 196
Grand Theft Auto 5, 182
Grand Theft Auto: San Andreas, 169
Greco, Kathy, 121
Grey's Anatomy, 21
gross profit participation, 39
Gross, Garry, 16
Guild of Italian-American Actors. *See* GIAA.

Harrelson, Woody, 9
Harry Potter and the Cursed Child, 159
Harry Potter and the Order of the Phoenix, 40
Hathaway, Anne, 122–123
Hawke, Ethan, 174

Heads Up, 195
hiatus, 20
HIV, 176, 179
honey wagon, 44
hostile work environment, 123–125
Hudson, Rock, 176
Hudson's Bay Company, 140

IATSE, 192
IDI, 24
incorporator, 144–146
Indecent Proposal, 9
indemnity, 82
infringement, 158, 161–163, 166–171, 178, 182; copyright, 158, 161–163, 178, 182; trademark, 166–171, 182
injunction, 83, 162–163, 171, 196
injunctive relief, 82–83
Innocence of Muslims, 194
International Alliance of Theatrical Stage Employees, Moving Picture Technicians, Artists and Allied Crafts. *See* IATSE.
Intimacy Directors International. *See* IDI.

Jagged Little Pill, 204
Jersey Boys, 204

Kasem Company, 157
Krakovski, Robert, 195–196

L'Amistad, 162
landlord, 99–114
League of Resident Theatres. *See* LORT.
legality (of contracts), 17
lessee, 99–100
lessor, 99–100
libel, 174

limited liability company. *See* LLC.
Living in Oblivion, 122
LLC, 150–152
LLC veil, 152
Locklear, Heather, 120
Lohan, Lindsay, 182
LORT, 30
Los Santos, 169
Lundberg, Samantha, 170–171

Main Line Pictures, 8
malpractice insurance, 95
Mamma Mia!, 204
Man of Steel, 46
Martin, Steve, 108
Matlin, Marlee, 122
Melrose Place, 120
member (of LLC), 150
Merkin, Alex, 195–196
Middleton, Clark, 122
Mini Cooper, 45
Modern Family, 20–21, 50
Moore, Demi, 9
more remunerative employment clause.
    See MRE clause.
most favored nations, 35–36, 41, 43, 44
Motown the Musical, 204
MRE clause, 32, 36
Murray, Bill, 9, 90
mutuality (in contracts), 11–12, 16–17

Nakoula, Basseley Nakoula, 194
Nederlander, James L., 108
Nestlé Company, 181
net profit participation, 59–60
net profits, 40, 187
new media, 49, 54, 64
Nike, 45, 165
nondisclosure agreement, 53

nonunion, 5, 25, 29–31, 37, 42–43, 51,
    53–54, 57, 59, 63–64, 133, 192
nuisance, 107–108

O-1B Visa, 127
O'Neill, Ed, 21
Occupational Safety and Health Act,
    125–126
Occupational Safety and Health
    Administration. *See* OSHA.
offer, 3–10, 11
offeree, 4–5
offeror, 4–5
Oliver Morosco Photoplay Company,
    157
OSHA, 125–126
Othello, 173–174
overage, 37, 38

P Visa, 127–128
packaging, 79–80
Paramount Pictures, 157
Parsons, Jim, 50
partnership, 80, 131, 132, 135–138, 148,
    150, 151, 152
Pasquantino, David, 177, 178
pay-or-play, 39
Penguin Random House Audio
    Publishing, 159
Pepsi-Cola, 52, 165, 168
per diem, 34, 35, 37, 43
performance rights society, 201, 204
Phan, Michelle, 200
Pig Pen, 169
Pirates of the Caribbean, 126
Play Pen, 169
Pompeo, Ellen, 21
Pregnancy Discrimination Act,
    118–121

Priscilla, Queen of the Desert, 204
Pritzker, J. B., 103
profit participation, 39–40, 187
Prozeralik, John, 177–178
public domain, 156–157

quid pro quo, 123

Reagan, Ronald, 176
Reality Bites, 174–175, 179
Redford, Robert, 9
Reeves, Keanu, 12–13, 43
Renae, Jessica, 124
rent control, 99, 102–103
residuals, 50–51
respondeat superior, 134, 147
retainer agreement, 89, 91–96
right-to-work state, 59
Rinna, Lisa, 120
Ripa, Kelly, 76–77
Rock of Ages, 204
Rocky, 131
Rodis, Alicia, 124
Rowling, J. K., 159
Rudin, Scott, 108

Saderup, Gary, 182
SAG, 5, 13, 25, 37, 39, 42–43, 49–54, 57,
    58, 61, 63–64, 87, 124, 126, 131, 133,
    187, 191–192
SAG-AFTRA, 5, 13, 25, 37, 39, 42–43,
    49–54, 57, 58, 61, 63–64, 87, 124, 126,
    131, 133, 187, 191–192
Sambuck's, 170–171
scale (*aka* minimum compensation), 5,
    13, 38, 51, 52, 78
Schnakenberg, Robert, 9
Scholastic Press, 159
Screen Actors Guild; *see* SAG.

Shakespeare, 173–174
Shamberg, Michael, 174
shared card, 41–42
shareholder, 139–141, 143–150
Sher, Stacey, 174
Shields, Brooke, 16
Sina, Tonia, 124
single card, 41–42
slander, 174
Slattery, John, 40–41
sole proprietorship, 131–134, 139, 141,
    148, 151, 152
Soundexchange.com, 204
Spader, James, 12
Spelling Entertainment Group, 120
Spider-Man: Turn Off the Dark, 125,
    126
Spielberg, Steven, 108
Squier, Billy, 108
Stallone, Sylvester, 131
Starbucks Coffee Company, 170–171
statutory damages, copyright, 158,
    162–163
Stiller, Ben, 174
Stoltz, Eric, 8
Stonestreet, Eric, 21
Stora Kopparberg, 140
Studio Actors Guild-American
    Federation of Television Radio
    Artists. *See* SAG-AFTRA.
sublease, 110–113
sunset clause, 79, 87, 93
supernumerary, 63
Swift, Taylor, 156
synch license, 197–198
synchronization license, 197–198

Taft-Hartley, 63–64
Taster's Choice, 181

tenancy, 100–103; assignment, 99, 110–
113; periodic, 101; sublease, 110–113;
sufferance, 102; years, 100–101
tenant, 99, 110–114
Terminator 3, 39
The Big Bad Book of Bill Murray, 9
The Big Bang Theory, 50
The Blacklist, 122
The Carol Burnett Show, 182
The Good Wife, 122
The History of Sex, 176
The Italian Job, 45
The Lion King, 16
The Matrix, 12
The Path, 122
The Price Is Right, 120–121
The Simpsons, 21
The Three Stooges, 182
The Watcher, 12,
The West Wing, 21
Thorne, Jack, 159
Thornton, Billy Bob, 9
Tom Sawyer, 156–157
Tomei, Marisa, 12
tort, 90, 132, 169, 173–174, 177, 179,
180–181
Travolta, John, 90
Twain, Mark, 156–157
Twentieth Century Fox Television, 35
Tylo, Hunter, 120

US Customs and Immigration Service, 127
Ultra Records, 200
undercapitalizing, 149, 152
undue influence, 18–19
union, 5, 25, 29–31, 37, 42–43, 51–54,
57–64, 70, 89, 90, 124, 125, 126, 139,
185, 187, 188, 191–192

United Artists, 131
United Parcel Service. *See* UPS.
Universal City Studios, 174
Universal Pictures, 12
University of Southern California.
See USC.
upfront, 20–21
UPS, 88, 118–119
USC, 162, 174–175
Vergara, Sofia, 21

visual instrumental, 199
visual vocal, 199

Walt Disney World, 30, 126
Warner Bros., 155, 159
warranties and representations, 81–82,
187, 189–190, 200
warranty of habitability, 104–106
Weinstein, Harvey, 124
WGA, 188
Whitaker, Miles, 176, 179
White House Down, 45
WIPO, 170
work made for hire, 158, 186–187, 189,
193, 195–196, 200, 202, 204
workers' compensation insurance, 34–
35, 126, 132, 133, 173, 185
World Intellectual Property
Organization. *See* WIPO.
Writers Guild of America. *See* WGA.

Youssef, Mark Basseley, 194
YouTube, 32, 53–54, 136–137, 148, 160,
161, 165, 193–194, 200

Zwigoff, Terry, 9